ROYAL HISTORICAL SOCIETY

STUDIES IN HISTORY

New Series

GREAT BRITAIN, GERMANY AND THE SOVIET UNION

GREAT BRITAIN, GERMANY AND THE SOVIET UNION

RAPALLO AND AFTER, 1922–1934

Stephanie Salzmann

THE ROYAL HISTORICAL SOCIETY
THE BOYDELL PRESS

First published 2003

A Royal Historical Society publication
Published by The Boydell Press
an imprint of Boydell & Brewer Ltd
PO Box 9, Woodbridge, Suffolk IP12 3DF, UK
and of Boydell & Brewer Inc.
PO Box 41026, Rochester, NY 14604–4126, USA
website: www.boydell.co.uk

ISBN 0 86193 260 9

ISSN 0269–2244

A catalogue record for this book is available
from the British Library

Library of Congress Cataloging-in-Publication Data
Salzmann, Stephanie, 1966–
   Great Britain, Germany, and the Soviet Union : Rapallo and after,
1922–1934 / Stephanie Salzmann.
      p. cm. – (Royal Historical Society studies in history. New
series, ISSN 0269–2244)
Includes bibliographical references and index.
ISBN 0–86193–260–9 (hardback : alk. paper)
   1. Great Britain – Foreign relations – 1910–1936.   2. Germany
– Foreign relations – Soviet Union.   3. Soviet Union – Foreign
relations – Germany.   4. Germany – Economic policy – 1918–1933.
5. Great Britain – Politics and government – 1910–1936.   I. Title.
II. Series
DA578.S33 2003
327.41043 – dc21   2002006924

This book is printed on acid-free paper

Printed in Great Britain by
St Edmundsbury Press Ltd, Bury St Edmunds, Suffolk

Contents

Acknowledgements

This study owes much to the generous help, advice and support I received from so many people during the years of demythologising the treaty of Rapallo. My special thanks go to Dr Zara Steiner (New Hall, Cambridge), for her continuous encouragement, assistance and interest in my work, and the intellectual stimulation I received from my frequent discussions with her. Professor Jonathan Steinberg (Trinity Hall, Cambridge, now the University of Pennsylvania), and Professor Tony Nicholls (St Anthony's College, Oxford), kindly acted as examiners of the thesis and immediately supported its publication. Dr Neville Wylie (University of Nottingham), Dr Lisa Pine (South Bank University, London), Dr Brendan Simms (Peterhouse, Cambridge), Dr Keiran Sharpe (The Queen's College, Oxford), Dr Verena Salzmann (London) and Irmgard Salzmann (Meerbusch) commented on the manuscript or proofread it at various stages. I am most grateful to my parents, Irmgard and Heinrich Salzmann for their unflagging support during my years in Cambridge.

I would like also to thank the Masters and Fellows of Trinity Hall, Cambridge, for providing the stimulating environment in which this study was written as well as financial assistance. The Cambridge University Kurt Hahn Trust, the Cambridge University Stanley Baldwin Trust and the Cambridge University Prince Consort and Thirwall Fund likewise supported me at various stages. The Institut für Europäische Geschichte (Mainz, Germany) was the inspiring place from which I conducted German archival research, and I greatly benefited from the frequent exchanges of view with its academic staff, notably Professor Manfred Vogt, Dr Ralph Melville and Claus Scharf, as well as the international fellow *Stipendiaten* community.

Without the professional expertise and co-operation of the staff of a large number of archives and libraries, collecting vital material would have been so much more difficult – their contribution to this thesis cannot be over-emphasised. My thanks also go to the following who have kindly given me permission to quote from unpublished sources: Professor Peter Krüger (Marburg, Carl von Schubert papers), Birmingham University Library (Austen Chamberlain papers), Cambridge University Library (Baldwin, Crewe and Templewood papers), the British Library (Balfour papers and Cecil papers) and the British Library of Political and Economic Science (Dalton papers). Quotations from the India Office Library appear by permission of the Controller of Her Majesty's Stationery Office. Crown copyright material is reproduced with the permission of the Controller of HMSO.

Every effort has been made to trace all the copyright-holders but if any have been inadvertently overlooked the publishers will be pleased to make the necessary arrangements at the first opportunity.

This book is dedicated to my husband, Ulrich Schlie, whose contribution from its very first days is immeasurable.

Stephanie Salzmann
January 2002

Abbreviations

AA	Auswärtiges Amt
ADAP	*Akten zur deutschen auswärtigen Politik*
BA	Bundesarchiv
BA-MA	Bundesarchiv-Militärarchiv (Freiburg)
BA-Po	Bundesarchiv, Abt. Potsdam
BDFA	*British documents on foreign affairs*
BJIS	*British Journal of International Studies*
BL	British Library
BLPES	British Library of Political and Economic Science
BoT	Board of Trade
BUL	Birmingham University Library
C	Central department of the Foreign Office
CCAC	Churchill College Archives Centre, Cambridge
CEA	*Journal of Central European Affairs*
CEH	*Journal of Central European History*
CHRS	Christie Papers
CUL	Cambridge University Library
DBFP	*Documents on British foreign policy*
Dipl. Hist.	*Diplomatic History*
DOT	Department of Overseas Trade
EcHR	*Economic History Review*
ESR	*European Studies Review*
FO	Foreign Office
GWU	*Geschichte in Wissenschaft und Unterricht*
HoC	House of Commons
HJ	*Historical Journal*
HZ	*Historische Zeitschrift*
IfZ	Institut für Zeitgeschichte (Munich)
IHR	*International History Review*
IMCC	International Military Control Commission
IOL	India Office Library
JbfGO	*Jahrbücher für Geschichte Osteuropas*
JBS	*Journal of British Studies*
JCH	*Journal of Contemporary History*
JEH	*Journal of Economic History*
JMH	*Journal of Modern History*
MAE	Ministère des affaires étrangères (Paris)
MGM	*Militärgeschichtliche Mitteilungen*
N	Northern department of the Foreign Office
NSDAP	Nationalsozialistische Deutsche Arbeiterpartei
PA-AA	Politisches Archiv des Auswärtigen Amtes (Berlin)
PRO	Public Record Office (London)

RHMC	*Revue d'histoire moderne et contemporaine*
SIS	Secret Intelligence Service
VfZg	*Vierteljahrshefte für Zeitgeschichte*
VSWG	*Vierteljahresschrift für Sozial- und Wirtschaftsgeschichte*
W	Western department of the Foreign Office
WO	War Office

Introduction

The policing of the Versailles agreement was based on two general concepts which cancelled each other out. The first failed because it was too sweeping, the second, because it was too grudging. The concept of collective security was so general as to prove inapplicable to circumstances most likely to disturb the peace; the informal Franco-English co-operation which replaced it was far too tenuous and ambivalent to resist major German challenges. And before five years had elapsed, the two powers vanquished in the war came together at Rapallo. The growing co-operation between Germany and the Soviet Union was a crucial blow to the Versailles system, something the democracies were too demoralised to grasp immediately.[1]

The treaty, which Germany and Bolshevik Russia[2] concluded in the small Italian seaside resort of Rapallo in the spring of 1922 ranks among the diplomatic *coups de surprise* of the twentieth century – perhaps only comparable to the big *renversement des alliances* of the eighteenth century. Up to the present day, the 'ghost of Rapallo' has lost little of its original fascination. However, the signing of the treaty received a level of attention, and the agreement itself was attributed a degree of importance that neither the Germans nor the Soviets had intended or expected. Besides the myths and historical re-interpretations, the real historical impact of the treaty of Rapallo lies in its consequences, particularly for the two victorious powers which dominated and largely determined the European order after the First World War: Great Britain and France. But the treaty also impacted significantly on the newly created small states in east central Europe.

A great deal has been written about the treaty of Rapallo, about its origins and its subsequent history.[3] However, a close look at the literature on European

---

1   H. Kissinger, *Diplomacy*, New York 1994, 246.
2   In this study certain terms will be employed in accordance with contemporary usage. 'Russia' hence stands as a synonym for the Soviet Union, and the Polish names 'Vilna' and 'Kovno' are used for the Lithuanian cities of 'Vilnius' and 'Kaunas'.
3   The most important studies are H. Graml, 'Die Rapallo-Politik im Urteil der westdeutschen Forschung', *VfZg* xviii (1970), 366–91; P. Kluke, 'Deutschland und Rußland zwischen den Weltkriegen', *HZ* clxxi (1951), 519–52; T. Schieder, *Die Probleme des Rapallo-Vertrages*, Cologne 1956; H. Helbig, *Die Träger der Rapallo-Politik*, Göttingen 1958; K. D. Erdmann, 'Deutschland, Rapallo und der Westen', *VfZg* xi (1963), 105–65; T. Schieder, 'Die Entstehungsgeschichte des Rapallo-Vertrages', *HZ* cciv (1967), 545–609; E. Laubach, *Die Politik der Kabinette Wirth 1921/22*, Lübeck–Hamburg 1968; H.-G. Linke, *Deutsch-sowjetische Beziehungen bis Rapallo*, 2nd edn, Cologne 1972; E. Laubach, 'Maltzans Aufzeichnungen über die letzten Vorgänge vor dem Abschluß des Rapallo-Vertrages', *JbfGO* xxii (1974), 556–79; H. Pogge von Strandmann, 'Rapallo – strategy in preventive diplomacy: new sources and new interpretations', in V. Berghan and M. Kitchen (eds), *Germany in the age of total war*, London–Totowa, NJ 1981, 123–46; E. Schulin, 'Noch etwas

politics during the 1920s and early 1930s reveals a meagre harvest as far as Rapallo's place in the wider context of international relations is concerned. Also the literature on British foreign policy of the 1920s and early 1930s is somewhat thin. Although a number of studies on British foreign policy have been published in recent years, they usually concentrate on certain aspects of British policy; overviews or works covering a larger period of time are missing. The only recent exceptions are G. H. Bennett's study, *British foreign policy during the Curzon period, 1919–1924*, and R. Grayson's book, *Austen Chamberlain and the commitment to Europe* which covers the whole Locarno period (1924–9). Bennett's analysis is thoroughly researched and provides a useful overview over the five years under consideration. Grayson, by contrast, comes to incomprehensible conclusions because of erroneous interpretations of the term 'concert of Europe', or a misleading understanding of the role of the League of Nations and, furthermore, his interpretation is not plausible within the general context of British policy. Grayson's work is therefore of limited value.[4]

This book hopes to clarify a particularly important, yet surprisingly neglected aspect of the debate surrounding the Rapallo agreement. It examines the impact of the Rapallo treaty on British foreign policy between 1922 and 1934, the year which signalled the visible end of the Rapallo friendship when Germany signed a non-aggression pact with Poland.

In Britain, the period was marked by the last months of David Lloyd George's Liberal government, a government which had already steered Britain through the rough waters of the First World War and the first four years of peace. After the two interim Conservative governments of Andrew Bonar Law and Stanley Baldwin (late 1922–3), the first Labour government under Ramsay MacDonald came to power in December 1923 but lasted for barely a year. During the subsequent second Baldwin government (1924–9), decisive steps were made towards European conciliation, a policy which was continued by the second Labour government (1929–31) as well as the National government (1931–5). During this period, Europe was struggling to overcome the consequences of the First World War and gradually to ease the gap between victors and vanquished. Britain found herself at the centre of European affairs despite her almost persistent wish to withdraw and concentrate on the empire.[5]

---

zur Entstehungsgeschichte des Rapallo-Vertrages', in H. von Hentig and A. Nitschke (eds), *Was die Wirklichkeit lehrt. Golo Mann zum 70. Geburtstag*, Frankfurt-am-Main 1979, 177–202; C. Fink, *The Genoa conference*, Chapel Hill, NC 1984; P. Krüger, ' "A rainy day", April 16, 1922: the Rapallo treaty and the cloudy perspective for German foreign policy', in C. Fink, A. Frohn and J. Heideking (eds), *Genoa, Rapallo and European reconstruction in 1922*, Cambridge 1992, 49–64.
4 R. Grayson, *Austen Chamberlain and the commitment to Europe, 1924–1929*, London 1997.
5 On British policy see, among others, G. Bertram-Libal, *Aspekte der britischen Deutschlandpolitik 1919–1922*, Göppingen 1972; C. Stamm, *Lloyd George zwischen Innen- und Außenpolitik. Die britische Deutschlandpolitik 1921–22*, Cologne 1977; A. Orde, *Great Britain and international security, 1920–1926*, London 1978; M. L. Dockrill and D. Goold,

The 'myth of Rapallo' has been chosen as the central theme of this story. Ever since the conclusion of the treaty, Rapallo has been a byword for Russo-German secret and potentially dangerous collaboration. The 'ghost of Rapallo' immediately sprang to mind whenever the two countries intensified their relationship. After the Hitler–Stalin pact in August 1939 and the subsequent outbreak of the Second World War, people referred to Rapallo as the beginning of the aggressive policies of Germany and the Soviet Union. Every time in the post-1945 years, when West German relations with the Soviet Union seemed to improve even slightly, the 'ghost of Rapallo' returned again to peoples' minds. Even during the process of German re-unification between November 1989 and October 1990 fears of a revival of the 'Rapallo alliance' re-emerged in the various countries' press comments. It is therefore necessary to examine whether decision-makers at the time, between 1922 and 1934, attached the same importance to Rapallo as was the case in later years.

The myth of Rapallo has hardly been treated in the literature dealing with European relations during the 1920s and early 1930s. Apart from Renata Bournazel's in-depth study on the French reaction to Rapallo, which terminates in 1923,[6] historians have frequently referred to the inherent dangers in the Rapallo relationship in general but never verified their hypothesis that Rapallo had a significant and lasting impact on the foreign policy of other European powers.[7]

The British reaction to the Rapallo alliance has to be seen in the context

Peace without promise: Britain and the peace conferences, 1919–1923, London 1981; K. O. Morgan, *The age of Lloyd George*, London 1971, and *Consensus and disunity: the Lloyd George coalition government, 1918–1922*, Oxford 1979; J. Turner, *Lloyd George's secretariat*, Cambridge 1980; A. Sharp, 'Lloyd George and foreign policy, 1918–1922: the "and yet" factor', in J. Loades (ed.), *The life and times of David Lloyd George*, Ipswich 1991, 129–42; D. Marquand, *Ramsay MacDonald*, London 1977; R. Lyman, *The first Labour government 1924*, London 1957; M. Cowling, *The impact of Labour, 1920–1924*, London 1971; D. Carlton, *MacDonald versus Henderson: the policy of the second Labour government*, London 1970; R. H. Ullman, *Anglo-Soviet relations, 1917–1921*, Princeton, NJ 1961–72; S. White, *Britain and the Bolshevik revolution: a study in the politics of diplomacy, 1920–1924*, London 1979; G. Gorodetsky, *The precarious truce: Anglo-Soviet relations, 1924–1927*, Cambridge 1977; B. Jones, *The Russian complex: the British Labour party and the Soviet Union*, Manchester 1977; R. Debo, 'Lloyd George and the Copenhagen conference of 1919–1920: the initiation of Anglo-Soviet negotiations', *HJ* xxiv (1981), 419–41; J. Jacobson, *When the Soviet Union entered world politics*, Berkeley, CA 1994.

6   R. Bournazel, *Rapallo: naissance d'un mythe*, Paris 1974.

7   J. Jacobson, *Locarno diplomacy: Germany and the west, 1925–1929*, Princeton, NJ 1972; E. D. Keeton, *Briand's Locarno policy: French economics, politics and diplomacy, 1925–1929*, New York–London 1987; V. J. Pitts, *France and the German problem: politics and economics in the Locarno period, 1924–1929*, London–New York 1987; P. Krüger, *Die Außenpolitik der Republik von Weimar*, Darmstadt 1985; H. L. Dyck, *Weimar Germany and Soviet Russia, 1926–1933*, London 1966; M. Walsdorff, *Westorientierung und Ostpolitik. Stresemanns Ostpolitik in der Locarno-Ära*, Bremen 1971; A. Kaiser, *Lord D'Abernon und die britische Deutschlandpolitik 1920–1926*, Frankfurt-am-Main 1989; F. L. Carsten, *Britain and the Weimar Republic: the British documents*, London 1984; Grayson, *Chamberlain*, passim.

of the European political environment during the period. The pursuit of national interests is the aim of any foreign policy; even the establishment of the League of Nations after the First World War had its effect on the pursuit of that interest and was to take over all those decisions which did not involve vital British interests. This book is a description of how the British viewed the Rapallo co-operation and how they dealt with it, and an analysis of whether it is justified to speak of a 'myth of Rapallo' in British policy in the same sense as in French policy.

Various themes will be developed throughout the book in the hope of showing the evolution of attitudes among British decision-makers within the wider European policy-making process, a process of action and reaction to developments and decisions in other European capitals. The main responsibility for shaping this policy lay with the members of the British Foreign Office and their respective counterparts in other countries. Bureaucratic and organisational constraints – like the division of competencies between the Foreign Office and Whitehall, or the Foreign Office's responsibility for foreign political, but not for foreign economic affairs – determined their actions as much as their background, information, preferences and prejudices. The diplomatic impact of Rapallo was just as important as its military or economic consequences.

By analysing the course of events between 1922 and 1934, this study will shed new light on the decision-makers themselves as well as on the interplay of ideas between the Foreign Office and other Whitehall departments, the process of decision-making and the formulation of policy in general, as well as British policy towards Germany and Soviet Russia in particular. Several key questions lie behind this study:

1 How did British decision-makers view the original treaty of Rapallo? Did the government in London believe in a 'threat' arising from this alliance in the subsequent years?
2 What kind of Soviet–German co-operation was expected and how dangerous was this co-operation to Britain's national interests?
3 Was the British attitude towards Rapallo consistent between 1922 and 1934? Is a modification of attitudes visible among the changing officials responsible for the formulation of British policy?
4 Was there a British 'myth of Rapallo' which shaped her European attitudes?
5 How important was the Rapallo alliance, i.e. German–Soviet relations, within the overall framework of British foreign policy?

By looking at Britain and Rapallo, this study attempts to examine a triangular relationship, namely the policy of one country with regard to the combined policy of Germany and the Soviet Union. The difficulty of this approach is immediately apparent. The two Rapallo partners did not always speak with one voice; they pursued individual policies and united their actions only when it was opportune to do so. It is therefore necessary and inevitable to think in bilateral terms when looking at British policy towards Moscow and Berlin.

Britain was confronted with new political structures both in Germany and the Soviet Union. While Germany undertook its first tentative steps towards becoming a western-style democracy, the simultaneously emerging Bolshevik experiment in Russia presented Europe with a completely new phenomenon in international relations. This book attempts to shed some light on the way British decision-makers dealt with this new situation and its impact on British policy in the inter-war period. Of particular interest in this context is the comparison of the British approach towards the Bolshevik government on the one hand, and Hitler's rise to power in Germany on the other, as both were authoritarian regimes, political experiments, and hence an unknown challenge for British foreign policy.

While examining a particular aspect of international relations in the inter-war period, this book also throws additional light on the broader topic of relations within Europe in the 1920s and early 1930s, and the origins of Britain's policy of appeasement. By comparing the British approach to the National Socialist movement and the British attitude towards the communist experiment and to Rapallo, the question arises whether or not one could date the start of British appeasement policy to the early 1920s.

An analysis of the decision-making process inevitably involves some methodological problems. The main sources on which this study is based are governmental papers, minutes and private notes. They often represent spontaneous thoughts rather than elaborate comments or reflections. The challenge for the historian is to reconstruct this decision-making process despite all imponderables. The principal archives in Britain, Germany and France provided almost unlimited access, hence a wide range of mostly unpublished primary sources has been used. Only the Potsdam archives could not deliver important documents on Rapallo and the treaty of Berlin, as they had been transferred to Moscow by the authorities of the former GDR and have not, as yet, been returned by the Russian Federation. As far as Soviet sources are concerned, the archives are still not generally open to the public.

The first chapter of this study deals with the way in which the treaty of Rapallo was received by the British delegation at the Genoa conference, notably by the prime minister David Lloyd George, while the second chapter analyses the reaction of Foreign Office officials in London. Chapter 3 examines British policy during the Ruhr crisis regarding potentially dangerous Soviet–German political and military co-operation. The first Labour government's attitude towards Berlin and Moscow is discussed in the fourth chapter. Chapters 5 to 7 focus on the Chamberlain–Stresemann era, with chapter 5 examining the British attitude towards Soviet–German friendship during and after the negotiations leading to Locarno, chapter 6 dealing with British policy towards Germany and Soviet Russia during the Anglo-Soviet dispute and rupture of relations, and chapter 7 considering British policy towards

Germany and the Soviet Union against the background of the declining Locarno spirit. Chapter 8 looks at the British reaction to German–Soviet economic co-operation, while chapter 9 deals with German–Soviet activities during the disarmament negotiations. Chapter 10 examines the British attitude towards Soviet–German relations during and after Hitler's rise to power. The study terminates with an analysis of the British response to the German–Polish non-aggression pact, which marked the end of the Rapallo friendship.

1

'It Nearly Overthrew the Applecart':
Lloyd George and the Treaty of Rapallo

Genoa, Easter Monday, 17 April 1922. The news of the treaty of Rapallo exploded like a bombshell. The bilateral Russo-German agreement had been secretly concluded during the World Economic Conference the previous day. The surprise was immense, as was the anger among the participants of the conference. Would all efforts for an international co-operation to solve the post-war political and economic problems now be in vain? Had they assembled in Genoa for nothing?

David Lloyd George, the British prime minister, was particularly angry and bewildered about the German–Russian *coup de surprise*. Indeed, he almost regarded it as a personal defeat. Not only was this a major blow to 'his' conference, but it endangered his long-term political objectives of 'taming' Bolshevik Russia, and was a heavy set-back to the attempts to improve his personal image at home. During a dinner at the Hôtel de Gênes on 17 April he bitterly asked the German secretary of state, Hirsch, why this treaty had not been signed either three weeks before or after the conference, given that then the agreement would have been irrelevant[1] and he urged the Germans to withdraw from the agreement.[2] Nevertheless, his annoyance lasted only three days. During a press conference on 20 April he announced that the crisis was over.[3] The conference returned to normal as far as this was possible after Rapallo. Only the Germans were excluded from all further meetings of the first commission which was dealing with the Russian question.

Lloyd George's surprise upon learning about the Rapallo treaty on the afternoon of Easter Monday was genuine.[4] His confidant and adviser on Russian affairs, E. J. Wise, had not informed him about a conversation during which Ago von Maltzan, head of the Eastern desk of the Wilhelmstraße (the German Foreign Ministry) and member of the German delegation had

1 Hirsch's 'Auszug aus einer Privataufzeichnung, betr. Besprechung mit Lloyd George am 17.4.22', PA-AA, R 28206k. On the dinner see H. Graf Kessler, *Tagebücher 1918–1937*, ed. W. Pfeiffer-Belli, Frankfurt-am-Main 1996, 310.
2 Aufzeichnung über eine Unterhaltung am 19. April 1922, PA-AA, R 28207k; *DBFP*, 1st ser. xix, 78.
3 Kessler, *Tagebücher*, 316–17; unsigned telegram no. 129, German delegation to AA, 21 Apr. 1922, PA-AA, R 28206k.
4 Kessler, *Tagebücher*, 309–10; L. Stein, *Aus dem Leben eines Optimisten*, Berlin 1930, 236.

mentioned German reasons for an agreement with Moscow.[5] Yet a
German–Russian agreement as such did not come entirely out of the blue for
the British prime minister. From the available sources it cannot be determined to what extent Lloyd George was aware of the information received by
the Foreign Office about the extent of German–Russian co-operation prior to
Genoa. However, in his famous Fontainebleau memorandum during the Paris
peace conference, he had already warned that Germany might be driven into
the arms of Russia if the peace terms were too harsh. Lloyd George's anger
about the Rapallo agreement rather resulted from the fact that, with the new
treaty, his own attempts to conclude a pact with Moscow after the trade
agreement of 1921 were in vain. Since the end of the First World War he had
worked constantly for a better understanding with the Bolshevik government. At Genoa he had intended to crown these efforts with a new
Anglo-Soviet pact which would confound all his opponents back in Britain
who were against negotiations with Moscow. As Stephen White noted in his
fundamental study on Soviet–western relations:

> The Genoa conference of April–May 1922 was the largest and most represen-
> tative international gathering that had taken place since the Paris peace con-
> ference . . . It met to consider the economic reconstruction of the continent of
> Europe after the devastation of the First World War; and it was particularly
> concerned to re-establish a mutually advantageous relationship between the
> major western powers and the Soviet government in Moscow.[6]

All sides had attached the highest hopes to the smooth passing of the conference, as the problems on the agenda were immense. And as much as Lloyd
George sought to enforce his visionary ideas of a reconstruction of Europe, so
too did he need a political success domestically. His position as prime
minister, continuing the wartime coalition of Conservatives and Liberals,
had become politically tenuous. Britain faced social disorder following the
economic readjustment from wartime to peacetime economy; he had to fight
the Irish rebels, and consolidate a new *imperium* in the Middle East – all at
once. Moreover, within the cabinet, opinions differed on Lloyd George's
policy towards France and Russia:

> Many among Lloyd George's Tory partners in the Coalition took grave excep-
> tion to his quarreling with France . . . More generally, the very novelty and
> panache of his foreign policy, especially when it began to embrace the Soviet
> Union, became a conductor for nagging anxiety among Unionists . . . that one

5   Barthou to Quai d'Orsay, 19 Apr. 1922, MAE, sér. Z, Russie-URSS 1919–29, vol. 325;
Dufour to Schubert 18 Apr. 1922, Schubert papers, copies in possession of Professor Peter
Krüger, Marburg University (hereinafter cited as 'Bestand Krüger'), Privatbriefe, vol. 9 (the
volume numbers refer to Professor Krüger's classification); Krüger, ' "A rainy day" ', 55.
6   S. White, *The origins of detente: the Genoa conference and Soviet–western relations,
1921–22*, Cambridge 1985, p. vii.

day the Welshman would return to his demagogic roots and attempt to lead them up a garden path of his own choosing.[7]

Russia was one of the central pillars of Lloyd George's vision for a brighter European future, on which the Genoa conference, and the prime minister's hopes for a personal success, were based. But it was Russia, together with Germany, which destroyed both vision and hopes: at Genoa, by signing the treaty of Rapallo.

In historical writing the importance of Russia in British policy prior to the Genoa conference has been given little attention.[8] Most historians concentrate on the difficulties posed by France to Lloyd George's concept of European reconstruction. Yet it cannot be argued that the 'Russian card' was only a last resort in the prime minister's political concept.[9]

Lloyd George's personal background as well as his policy towards Russia after the Bolshevik revolution suggest his determination to pursue an active policy towards that country. The prime minister was the exception to the British cabinet's otherwise undifferentiated resentment towards the Bolshevik regime. While as little interested in the essentials of Bolshevik ideology as other British politicians, Lloyd George's understanding of the new movement was nevertheless much more favourable. A Liberal with a modest family background, he had worked since the early days of his political career to achieve a reconciliation of traditional liberal ideals with labour interests. His years in office after 1905 were to show how 'individual libertarianism and state intervention could make common cause'.[10] Lloyd George's attitude towards Bolshevism was also influenced by his own aversion to autocracy and the 'establishment'. He had welcomed the February revolution hoping that it would lead Russia to democracy.[11] His liberal mind was not unfavourable to Bolshevik ideals though he did not approve of their practices. Besides, Lloyd George firmly believed that the Bolshevik concept of a state-controlled economy was unrealistic and could not last forever. Time would gradually persuade the leaders in Moscow that they needed to re-admit private capital, trade and industry.

Above all, the prime minister was too much of a pragmatist not to realise the importance of Russia for his concept of European reconstruction. An early British penetration of the Russian market was an ideal means to counter domestic economic difficulties.[12] Furthermore, there was the desire not to

7   R. F. Holland, *The pursuit of greatness: Britain and the world role, 1900–1970*, London 1991, 95.
8   A. Orde, *British policy and European reconstruction after the First World War*, Cambridge 1990, 176.
9   Morgan, *Consensus and disunity*, 306–9.
10 Idem, *The age of Lloyd George*, 17–37 at p. 37.
11 Debo, 'Lloyd George', 420.
12 J. M. Thompson, *Russia, Bolshevism and the Versailles peace*, Princeton, NJ 1966, 346–63 at p. 349.

leave the Russian market to German domination. The Russian dependence on trade with the west was also useful to undermine Bolshevism.

Unfortunately, while these attitudes made perfect sense to Lloyd George, they were not shared by his cabinet colleagues. He had carefully concealed his efforts from the cabinet, since they would have almost certainly stirred up a storm of protest had they been known. His secret approaches to the Bolsheviks had been initiated by his personal envoy, E. J. Wise, with enquiries in Moscow for an end of British intervention in the Russian civil war and an exchange of prisoners-of-war.[13] In the run-up to the Anglo-Soviet trade agreement of 16 March 1921 Lloyd George, despite outspoken concern from the cabinet, had turned a blind eye to reports of the British Secret Intelligence Service (SIS) which illuminated the extent of Soviet subversive propaganda in Britain and the British empire.[14] Any protest in Moscow would bring the trade negotiations immediately to an end.

Lloyd George was sufficiently pragmatic to realise that Russia was too important a player in the international system to be ignored. In contrast to other British officials, he firmly believed that Britain would benefit from contacts with the new regime in Russia. Neither the concept of Bolshevik world revolution nor the existence of Comintern therefore disturbed the prime minister's endeavours for a *rapprochement* with the new Kremlin rulers.

As much as Lloyd George succeeded in hiding his real intentions from his colleagues in the British government, it was obvious to foreign observers that friendship with Russia was one of his basic principles. Carl von Schubert, head of the Western desk at the Wilhelmstraße, noted on 19 January 1922:

[During the last two years] it was his firm intention to come to an economic understanding with Russia. It has often been said that he wavered in his Russian policy. In my opinion, this view is absolutely wrong. Rather, his conduct of affairs has been driven by tactical considerations determined by certain circumstances. Symptomatic in this regard, for instance, was Lloyd George's famous Luzern declaration after Poland's counter-attack against the Russian invasion, which was successful contrary to all expectations. Lloyd George had obviously misjudged the situation and had expected the Poles to be defeated by the Russians. When the situation turned out to be the opposite, he was simply forced to keep a temporary distance to the Russians in order to take the wind out of the sails of French policy. Later on, however, he continued his policy unwaveringly; the last keystone being the invitation of the Russian government to Genoa.[15]

13 Debo, 'Lloyd George', 430–7.
14 C. Andrew, 'The British secret service and Anglo-Soviet relations in the 1920s: from the trade negotiations to the Zinoviev letter', *HJ* xx (1977), 673–706 at pp. 681–8.
15 Aufzeichnung Schubert, 19 Jan. 1922, Schubert papers, Privatbriefe, vol. 7; Krüger, *Außenpolitik*, passim, and 'Schubert, Maltzan und die Neugestaltung der auswärtigen Politik in den 20er Jahren', Vortrag anläßlich einer Gedenkfeier des Auswärtigen Amtes für die Staatssekretäre Ago Freiherr von Maltzan und Dr. Carl von Schubert, unpubl. MS, Bonn, 18 Sept. 1987.

Contrary to what Schubert thought, Lloyd George's invitation of the Soviets to Genoa was by no means the keystone in his Russian policy. The preparations for the World Economic Conference provide further evidence of Lloyd George's resolution to come 'to some *modus vivendi* with the Bolsheviks, even if this accommodation usually implied the destruction of Bolshevism through its economic transformation into liberal capitalism'.[16] Lloyd George's determination to realise this 'grand design' went as far as to try to force it upon France. He thereby sacrificed – somewhat innocently – the only political partner with whom he might have been able to execute his programme: the French prime minister, Aristide Briand.

On 6 January 1922, at Cannes, Lloyd George and his French counterpart agreed on a set of resolutions. Despite being considered as the basis for the overall conference agenda, these resolutions dealt almost exclusively with Soviet Russia. Moreover, they contained deliberate contradictions and ambiguities which served Lloyd George's wishful thinking of being able to re-introduce capitalism to Russia through the back-door. These demands, if met by the Soviets, would undermine the basic principles of Bolshevism: Moscow would reverse the nationalisation of foreign property, accept the pre-war tsarist debts and bring its legal system in line with western democracies before foreign investment would take place. Briand's objections to these terms were overruled by the Welshman. Lloyd George's intransigence and indifference towards French sensitivity to the Russian question thus contributed to Briand's fall. Yet with the latter's successor, Raymond Poincaré, the prime minister's concept was even more difficult to realise.[17]

Lloyd George's position was increasingly precarious. Imperial problems troubled him in India, whilst Ireland was in uproar and he faced a host of difficulties at home. The readjustment of British industry from wartime to peace production had led to high unemployment, social unrest, declining trade figures and large financial problems. An alternative to a political breakthrough in Russia was the solution of the German reparation question. This, however, was virtually impossible since Poincaré refused categorically to renegotiate the terms of the treaty of Versailles, well aware and afraid of the British prime minister's inclination towards concessions for Germany.

But Lloyd George had already raised German hopes for such a reconsideration. Moreover, he intended to link reparations with his 'grand design' for Russia. By the beginning of 1922 the British prime minister openly favoured the idea propounded by the German industrialists Hugo Stinnes and Walther

---

[16] T. S. Martin, 'The Urquhart concession and Anglo-Soviet relations, 1921–22', *JbfGO* xx (1972), 551–70.

[17] Dufour to Schubert, 12 Jan. 1922, Schubert papers, Privatbriefe, vol. 7; S. A. Schuker, *The end of French predominance in Europe: the financial crisis of 1924 and the adoptation of the Dawes plan*, Chapel Hill, NC 1976, 18–19; J. Bariéty, *Les Relations franco-allemandes après la première guerre mondiale: 10 Novembre 1918–10 Janvier 1925: de l'exécution à la négociation*, Paris 1977, 86–101.

Rathenau – the latter as former minister of reconstruction and now special envoy of the German government – for an international financial consortium to reconstruct and develop the large Russian market.[18] Germany's participation in the consortium was desirable not only because of her most useful pre-war experience in Russian business. The German export surplus achieved in Russia could also be used to pay reparations to the western powers. As a cabinet conclusion held:

> Germany is to us the most important country in Europe not only on account of our trade with her, but also because she is the key to the situation in Russia. By helping Germany we might under existing conditions expose ourselves to the charge of deserting France; but if France was our ally no such charge could be made.[19]

The combination of Lloyd George's eastern objective with the pressing German problems made the former more acceptable to his domestic opponents. Yet it concealed the fact that Russia remained the first priority on the prime minister's political agenda. Carole Fink's hypothesis that Lloyd George 'appears to have envisaged a complex series of steps that would subordinate the problems of reparations and French security to the larger questions of European reconstruction and *rapprochement* with Soviet Russia'[20] is further supported by his attitude towards France and Germany in the run-up to the conference, his handling of the German and Russian case at Genoa and his reaction to the Rapallo agreement.

During the first quarter of 1922 the British prime minister continued to nourish German hopes that reparations would be discussed at Genoa. To Rathenau Lloyd George appeared co-operative.[21] Extensive conversations took place between British and German officials which seemed to indicate Britain's divergence from the policies of Poincaré. At the same time secret negotiations proceeded with Moscow about Anglo-Russian trade relations and Russian participation in the consortium.[22] During these talks Lloyd George hinted to the Russians that he would force France to take a more favourable attitude towards Moscow.[23] Yet Lloyd George had underestimated Poincaré. At their meeting in Boulogne on 25 February the British prime minister had to give way on the German issue if he wanted to save the conference. No reparations were to be discussed at Genoa and the treaty of

---

[18] Stamm, *Lloyd George*, 200–10; Pogge von Strandmann, 'Rapallo', 127–30; E. Schulin, *Walther Rathenau. Repräsentant, Kritiker und Opfer seiner Zeit*, Göttingen 1979.

[19] Cabinet conclusion 1 (22), 10 Jan. 1922, PRO, CAB 23/29.

[20] Fink, *Genoa conference*, 38.

[21] Rathenau diary entry, 2 Dec. 1921, in Walther Rathenau, *Tagebuch 1907–1922*, ed. H. Pogge von Strandmann, Düsseldorf 1967, 266–70; Schubert to Sthamer 16 Jan. 1922, Schubert papers, Privatbriefe, vol. 7.

[22] Undated and unsigned despatch, AA to German embassy, London, PA-AA, Deutsche Botschaft London 1008; Orde, *British policy*, 179.

[23] ADAP, ser. A, v, doc. 256, n. 4.

Versailles was to remain unchanged. On the question of Russian recognition, however, he retained some room for manoeuvre. It was Lloyd George's last but uncertain chance to realise his grand design. Yet his political future depended upon this success.

Checked by Poincaré on the German question, Lloyd George renewed his efforts of courting the Soviet Union during the run-up to Genoa. To their great surprise, the Germans were suddenly rebuffed. At the beginning of March, Lloyd George denied Rathenau the meeting that he had promised him in December 1921 to discuss a strategy for Germany's problems at Genoa. He also refused to receive a German delegation after their arrival, although he had originally invited them to London to discuss reparations. Instead, Lloyd George intimidated Berlin with the possibility of a *rapprochement* between the Allied powers and Russia, from which the Germans would be excluded if they failed to yield to the Genoa accord. In the following weeks, Lloyd George continued to boycott Germany. Rathenau was in despair. His letter to the prime minister of 2 April, requesting an exchange of opinions at Genoa, remained unanswered.[24]

Meanwhile British officials increased their preparations for an international agreement with Moscow which had been proceeding for months. A small drafting committee in the Foreign Office had drawn up preliminary articles of agreement as the basis for a treaty.[25] This draft was in line with Lloyd George's Cannes resolutions with Briand and his illusory intention to reach a *modus vivendi* with Russia on terms which he would define. The draft provisions concerning debts, property, law and religion implied a retreat from communist ideology. Despite Russian objections to the terms of Cannes and Boulogne and no official sign that they would ever fully accept them,[26] the prime minister continued his preparations for the intended Allied–Russian *rapprochement*. When he left for Genoa on 6 April he carried with him the 'London Report' of the Allied experts of 28 March concerning Russia and European reconstruction. His policy towards Moscow was only partly backed by his cabinet. A *de jure* recognition would be granted only after Russia had accepted her pre-war debts and the Cannes resolutions, and only in accordance with the other powers at Genoa.

Lloyd George was determined to get a tangible success from the Genoa conference, whatever the costs. This attitude did not pass unnoticed by several observers of the conference.[27] It was quite apparent that the prime minister virtually strove for an agreement with the Russians. It was therefore

[24] Rathenau to Lloyd George, 2 Apr. 1922, PA-AA, R 29442.

[25] Articles of agreement to form the basis of a treaty with Russia (undated), *DBFP*, 1st ser. xix, doc. 40; Orde, *British policy*, 185–90. A draft had been leaked to the Germans: Dufour to AA, 17 Mar. 1922, PA-AA, R 29442; Krüger, ' "A rainy day" ', 53.

[26] FO memo, 'The attitude of the Soviet government towards the Genoa conference', 5 Apr. 1922, PRO, FO 371/8187/N 3236.

[27] Schulin, *Noch etwas*, 184–7; Dufour to Schubert, 7 Apr. 1922, Schubert papers, Privatbriefe, vol. 9; Noel-Baker to Cummings, 20 Apr. 1922, Noel-Baker papers, CCAC,

most welcome to him that during the first meeting of the most important political sub-commission, the Russian foreign minister Chicherin declared that his delegation was not familiar with the 'London Report' and demanded some time for consultation with Moscow. It was the British prime minister who then suggested delaying the next meeting of the sub-commission by a few days in order to leave the Russians time for consideration. In the meantime, he favoured private talks with the Russians in order to discuss Russian war debts. Lloyd George was also the one who demanded that the meetings remain secret.[28] To Louis Barthou, the French minister of justice, he said: 'One advantage of a private meeting would be that the Germans would not be there.'[29]

The Germans were much disturbed upon learning about the secret negotiations. They feared that the Allies and Russia might reach agreement on article 116 of the Versailles treaty which reserved Russian rights for reparations. This article had been introduced to the 'London Report' as 'bait' for the Russians. While members of the German delegation had been able to express their concern to various lower-ranking British officials, they had been denied access to the prime minister. Lloyd George continued to evade Rathenau's numerous requests for an interview.[30]

In the event, German nervousness was unfounded. British documents give sufficient evidence that the discussions at Lloyd George's residence, the Villa d'Albertis, only dealt with Russian debts.[31] Yet the prime minister's behaviour could only increase their alarm. Even to an outside observer

> it became increasingly obvious that Lloyd George, who wanted to get a visible success at the conference à tout prix, was in fact not so keen on a material agreement with the Russians. He worked more eagerly for a diplomatic show-piece designed to hoodwink the public. . . . On Friday and Saturday before Easter rumours increased hinting at some kind of agreement . . . with the Russians although it was said that it would be only a framework agreement.[32]

It is not the purpose of this study to provide another account of the details leading to the German–Russian agreement. Nevertheless, some aspects will be recalled which provide the framework for Lloyd George's response to the treaty. Peter Krüger's study of the events leading to Rapallo gives a clearer view of the role of Walther Rathenau, while illustrating the extent to which

---

NBKR 4/447; Churchill to Chamberlain, 19 Apr. 1922 (not sent), in *Winston S. Churchill*, ed. M. Gilbert, companion to vol. iv, London 1979, 1866–7.

[28] Notes of informal meeting on 19 Apr. 1922, *DBFP*, 1st ser. xix, doc. 71.

[29] Quoted from Schulin, *Noch etwas*, 191; Bournazel, *Rapallo*, 153.

[30] Ministerrat Protokoll, 5 Apr. 1922, in *Akten der Reichskanzlei: Die Kabinette Wirth I und II*, ed. I. Schulze-Bidlingmaier, Boppard 1973, 682; Dufour to Grigg, 13 Apr. 1922, Dufour papers, PA-AA, vol. 1; unsigned telegram, Genoa, 12 Apr. 1922, BA-Po, Präsidialkanzlei 687, vol. 1; Rathenau to Lloyd George, 18 Apr. 1922, PA-AA, R 28206k.

[31] *DBFP*, 1st ser. xix, docs 72, 73, 74.

[32] Reiner to Kessler, 29 May 1929, quoted in Schulin, *Noch etwas*, 185.

Ago von Maltzan, head of the Eastern desk in the German Foreign Ministry, was personally responsible for the German–Russian understanding.[33]

At Genoa, it appeared to the outside world as if Rathenau had been the driving force behind the secret deal. On the fateful Easter Sunday morning the German delegation, headed by the foreign minister but without *Reichskanzler* Wirth, had left for Rapallo[34] to negotiate final details with the Russians. During the talks, the *Reichskanzler* called at Rapallo to inform the delegation that he and Rathenau had just been invited to a personal meeting with the British prime minister for the same day. Rathenau felt terrible. This was the moment for which he had desperately waited. Being rather more inclined to focus on the west, the foreign minister had never been entirely convinced of the necessity of the German–Russian treaty. Still, it was too late. With the words '*Le bouchon est tiré, il faut boire*' he was said to have driven off to sign the agreement.[35]

It was not Rathenau, however, but Wirth and Maltzan who were the spiritual fathers of the German–Russian negotiations which had started in the autumn of 1921.[36] Even before Genoa, Maltzan had carried the draft of a treaty with him. Rathenau had been acquainted with the preparations for a German–Russian understanding since his time in office as minister of reconstruction, but still believed that an agreement with the western powers better served German reparation interests and the policy of fulfilment. At Genoa he walked into Maltzan's trap.

Lloyd George and the British delegation as a whole regarded Rathenau as the principal protagonist responsible for the Rapallo treaty. The prime minister repeated several times to secretary of state Hirsch that Rathenau should not have signed without informing him.[37] He continued to rebuff Rathenau's request for a *tête-à-tête*.[38] Maurice Hankey, secretary of the British delegation and close confidant of Lloyd George, described the two leading Germans as follows:

> Rathenau made the worst impression on me . . . He seemed to me to be a perverse, degenerate creature, with all the disagreeable equivocable attributes of the pre-war German diplomatist. Wirth was a decent, rather stolid '*gemütlich*' kind of German, who is obviously trying to get out of the mess into which Rathenau has dragged him.[39]

---

33 Krüger, ' "A rainy day" ', passim.
34 Dufour to Schubert, 18 Apr. 1922, Schubert papers, Privatbriefe, vol. 9.
35 Schulin, *Noch etwas*, 198.
36 Aufzeichnung Wirth 'Genua 1922', June 1942, Bundesarchiv Koblenz, NL 342 Wirth, vol. 192. The Wirth papers were at the time of use only provisionally catalogued.
37 Hirsch 'Auszug aus einer Privataufzeichnung betr. Unterredung mit Lloyd George am 17. April 1922', PA-AA, R 28206k.
38 Barthou to Poincaré, 19 Apr. 1922, MAE, sér. Z, Europe 1918–29, Russie-URSS, vol. 325.
39 Hankey to Austen Chamberlain, 20 Apr. 1922, Hankey papers, CCAC, HNKY 8/23.

Lloyd George's anger about Rapallo soon evaporated. His political existence was at stake, and this depended not on the Soviets but on returning home with a positive result from Genoa.[40] Still dreaming of bringing Bolshevik Russia to reason[41] he decided that only the Germans were to be excluded from the meetings of the political sub-commission. On 20 April, only four days after Rapallo, Lloyd George redoubled his efforts to resume negotiations with the Bolsheviks.[42] They soon reached a stalemate. The proposal of German mediation between the British and the Russians made by Albert Dufour-Féronce, counsellor at the German embassy in London, to Sir Edward Grigg, Lloyd George's personal secretary, was therefore most welcome to the British prime minister.[43] When the latter met Wirth and Rathenau on 4 May, he begged the Germans to point out to the Russians the British desire for an agreement. It would also be in the German interest to play a successful role as mediator.[44] Wirth and Rathenau in turn, stressing the hopeless situation of the German budget, demanded that Lloyd George use his influence in France on the reparations issue. The prime minister did not turn these requests down. Lloyd George was in such despair that during the two-hour long conversation with the Germans, he did not comment once on the negative aspects of the Rapallo treaty but, on the contrary, emphasised the usefulness of the German–Russian agreement.

Three days later the prime minister had another lengthy conversation, this time only with *Reichskanzler* Wirth.[45] Rathenau's presence had not been desired.[46] Again Lloyd George urged Wirth to talk to the Russians on his behalf. If the conference was to continue, it would be vital for Britain to come to an agreement on the Russian question. Lloyd George hinted to the *Reichskanzler* that if France and Belgium were to be obstructive, Britain and Italy would sign a treaty without them. Everything, however, would depend on a conciliatory Russian reply. Now Wirth began to bargain. The Reparation Commission's deadline for Germany of 31 May was looming large, and with it

[40] Dufour to Schubert, 1 May 1922, Schubert papers, Privatbriefe, vol. 10; diary entry, 26 Apr. 1922, in Kessler, *Tagebücher*, 321.
[41] *DBFP*, 1st ser. xix, docs 71, 77.
[42] Secret record of a conversation between Lloyd George, Grigg, Worthington-Evans, Wise, Chicherin, Litvinov and Krassin, 20 Apr. 1922, Curzon papers, MSS Eur F 112/227; Wirth to Ebert, 20 Apr. 1922, in *Deutsch-sowjetische Beziehungen von den Verhandlungen in Brest-Litowsk bis zum Abschluß des Rapallo-Vertrages. Dokumentensammlung*, ii, ed. Ministerium für Auswärtige Angelegenheiten der DDR and Ministerium für Auswärtige Angelegenheiten der UdSSR, Berlin (East) 1971, doc. 284.
[43] Aufzeichnung Dufour, 29 Apr. 1922, PA-AA, R 28207k.
[44] Wirth to Ebert, 4 May 1922, BA-Po, Präsidialkanzlei 687/0/1, Wirtschafts- und Finanzkonferenz Genua, vol. 2; Aufzeichnung über die Zusammenkunft zwischen Wirth, Rathenau, Lloyd George etc. am 4. Mai 1922, PA-AA, R 28207k; note of a conversation held at the Villa d'Albertis, 4 May 1922, *DBFP*, 1st ser. xix, doc. 111.
[45] Wirth to Ebert, 8 May 1922, BA-Po, Präsidialkanzlei 687/0/1, Wirtschafts- und Finanzkonferenz Genua, vol. 2.
[46] Wirth Aufzeichnung 'Ostpolitik', Aug. 1942, Wirth papers, NL Wirth 32, vol. 192.

the French threat to invade the Ruhr in the case of a German default. In view of the growing Anglo-French differences, Britain's unilateral support for Germany would have infuriated France even more than had Rapallo. Only with a firm British guarantee of support could Germany take the political initiative. The *Reichskanzler* therefore suggested that Lloyd George issue a declaration pointing out Britain's most important political objectives, viz., first, the Russian question, second, a general European peace, and third, that the German reparation question be solved without resort to force. In turn, he would then arrange a contact with the Russians. Wirth also demanded that the last aspect should be specifically stressed. Having considered the matter with Hankey and Grigg for some time, the prime minister expressed his readiness to make such a declaration, provided the Russian reply would be sufficiently conciliatory.

This was a bold statement in the face of British controversies with France. To a considerable extent, the prime minister blamed Paris for the German–Russian treaty. He was convinced that had Poincaré not been so destructive on the question of Russian pre-war debts, while at the same time refusing to discuss the German problems, there would have been no Rapallo.[47] Lloyd George's negative attitude towards France grew as Poincaré ordered his delegation to stand firm against Britain. The French *premier ministre* had further reasons for steering an uncompromising course. The Quai d'Orsay had been confidentially notified of both Anglo-German meetings, though it had no specific information about the second. 'It seems nevertheless that precisely during the course of this meeting one came to an understanding about Germany acting as intermediary between the British and the Soviets.'[48]

The Allied–Russian negotiations dragged on without visible success. After 12 May, the French and Belgian attitude towards Moscow stiffened even further. Lloyd George was furious. It was decided to continue negotiations on the Russian question at a further gathering in The Hague. The German delegation would again be excluded, formally on the grounds that they already had their agreement with Moscow. But Lloyd George had told Dufour that the Germans could usefully participate in questions of Russian reconstruction through their delegate on the executive committee of the international corporation. 'You will probably . . . be able to work equally successfully as you did here at Genoa between us and the Russians (about which the French are innocent) [sic] despite, or rather even because of the fact that you are no longer a member of the sub-commission.' When Dufour then asked him whether he now quite approved of the Rapallo agreement, Lloyd George

---

47 Hankey to his wife, 12 Apr. 1922, Hankey papers, HNKY 3/30; secret record of a conversation between Lloyd George, Grigg, Worthington-Evans, Wise, Chicherin, Krassin and Litvinov, 20 Apr. 1922, Curzon papers, MS Eur F 112/227; Aufzeichnung über Unterredung zwischen Grigg und Dufour, 29 Apr. 1922, PA-AA, R 28207k.
48 Unsigned report, 12 May 1922, MAE, sér. Z, Europe 1918–29, Russie-URSS, vol. 327.

GREAT BRITAIN, GERMANY AND THE SOVIET UNION

'smiled mischievously and said after a little while: "Well, it nearly overthrew the applecart." '[49]

Lloyd George was a master at playing off one party at the conference against another, and was ever-ready to interpret every change in the course of the conference in his favour – however negative at first glance. He twisted anybody's words if this helped his pursuit of his 'grand design'. In the report from Genoa to the *Reichspräsident* Friedrich Ebert quoted above, Dufour gave a very realistic account of the situation:

> The way and the speed of the development of the Genoa conference is largely dependent on the Russians. Lloyd George's momentous remarks illustrate how quickly political love can turn into hatred. Obviously, these expressions have to be treated extremely carefully. It currently suits Lloyd George to be friendly with Germany, as we might be useful in his great game. Yet the mood of this incorrigible opportunist can change rather too quickly. France is currently all too inconvenient for him, and he needs the support of others in order to revive the old game of balance of power on the European continent.[50]

The Hague meeting failed to solve the Russian question. Lloyd George's promises for a second German mediation did not materialise. The Russian memorandum of 11 May showed that hope for a quick success in the attempt to undermine Bolshevism was futile. Lloyd George's chosen role as missionary in Soviet Russia had failed. It was only a question of months before this failure, amongst other reasons, led to his fall as prime minister. The Genoa conference marked the end of Lloyd George's political career. It was not, however, the Rapallo treaty which set the ball rolling, but an idealistic vision turned into an unrealistic attempt of the prime minister to deal with a country without studying its mentality, and developing a realistic (i.e. implementable) strategy.

---

[49] Aufzeichnung Dufour über Unterredungen mit Lloyd George und Grigg am 14., 15. und 16. Mai 1922, BA-Po, Präsidialkanzlei 687/0/1, Wirtschafts- und Finanzkonferenz Genua, vol. 2.
[50] Ibid.

2

'The Most Important Event Since the Armistice': The Foreign Office and Rapallo

'We seem to be relapsing in the case of all the great continental powers into the deepest slime of pre-war treachery and intrigue',[1] fumed foreign secretary Curzon when learning of the Rapallo treaty.

Tempers ran high in Britain over the German–Russian agreement. The indignation among London decision-makers was unanimous. The news of the Rapallo treaty came out of the blue for the Foreign Office on 18 April 1922. It was clear from the outset that Germany was blamed as the principal culprit in the agreement. After all, the German government was at least indirectly responsible for the existence of Bolshevism in Europe, for Berlin had permitted the passage of Lenin from Zürich to Russia in 1917, after Britain and France had specifically vetoed his journey. It was, however, not so much the Rapallo treaty as such, or the contents of the agreement, which created such a stir in Whitehall. Rather, the Foreign Office slowly but surely realised that it had fallen victim to the policy initiated by Lloyd George. Moreover, it shared responsibility with the prime minister for the international disturbances caused by the German–Russian agreement because it had overlooked incoming warnings.[2]

The British prime minister's aversion to diplomatic channels was well known. Consequently, he tended to by-pass the Foreign Office in important decisions, and instead consulted his personal entourage – the Cabinet Office and his private secretariat.[3] The Foreign Office's influence, steadily declining since 1914,[4] was reduced further after the war. Lloyd George preferred 'diplomacy by conference' where he could talk matters over with his counterparts from other countries. Foreign Office advice was neither sought nor desired. In addition, there were personal animosities between the prime minister and the foreign secretary as well as rivalries with other Whitehall departments. After the end of the war, the War Office, the Treasury and the Board of Trade had curtailed Foreign Office competencies by assuming part of its functions. As

1   Curzon minute, 29 Apr. 1922, PRO, FO 371/8188/N 3869.
2   Gregory to FO, 18 Apr. 1922, PRO, FO 371/8202/N 3725/N 3869; Tyrrell to Curzon, 26 Apr. 1922, Curzon papers, MSS Eur F 112/227.
3   D'Abernon diary entry, 18 Dec. 1921, D'Abernon papers, BL, MS 48953B; Morgan, *Consensus and disunity*, passim; Turner, *Lloyd George's secretariat*, passim.
4   See Z. S. Steiner, *The Foreign Office and foreign policy, 1898–1914*, 2nd edn, Cambridge 1986.

far as military issues relating to Germany were concerned, a further body, the Inter-Allied Military Control Commission (IMCC) was in charge. Thus, structural shortcomings in Whitehall gave the impression of confusion in day-to-day political business: it seemed that nobody knew who took responsibility for what types of political events.[5]

The Foreign Office's largest and most difficult problem was their dearth of information about the prime minister's foreign policy objectives and activities. In the run-up to Genoa Lloyd George drastically reduced the role of Curzon and his staff, due to the importance of the conference to the prime minister and the scepticism at the Foreign Office about the need for an international gathering. A foreign embassy, in turn, complained that the jealousies between the Foreign Office and 10 Downing Street aggravated its (the embassy's) conduct of the negotiations.[6]

The Foreign Office had gradually acquiesced in being cast aside in foreign affairs as long as Lloyd George remained prime minister. Yet as a result, it was less attentive in observing and reacting to political events and unable to adapt quickly to changing circumstances. Not only had Lord D'Abernon, the British ambassador to Berlin, been 'caught napping'[7] by failing to transmit to London his knowledge about the German–Russian treaty, but the Foreign Office had to face the unpleasant fact that it had overlooked the many signs to Russo-German *rapprochement.*

Since the beginning of 1922 the Foreign Office had received an increasing number of reports concerning various German–Russian activities. The first had been a despatch by D'Abernon concerning Comintern delegate Karl Radek's negotiations in Berlin in January 1922.[8] However, at the time the British ambassador had been quick to reassure the Foreign Office that the Berlin government would take no steps conflicting with British interests with regard to Russia.

The possibility of a Russo-German combination also concerned the British envoy extraordinary in Warsaw, Sir William Max Muller. In connection with the Anglo-French security pact contemplated before Genoa, he wired that the French apparently suspected an imminent Russo-German alliance, probably directed against Poland. Otherwise France would not press so urgently for a British guarantee.[9] Curzon dismissed this report as a 'great deal of nonsense'. A Russo-German combination was not regarded as a sufficient justification for a firm British commitment to European security, he argued. If

---

5 A. J. Sharp, 'The Foreign Office in eclipse, 1919–1922', *History* lxi (1976), 198–218 at pp. 201–2.
6 Fink, *Genoa conference*, 12.
7 Tyrrell to Curzon, 27 Apr. 1922, Curzon papers, MSS Eur F 112/227.
8 D'Abernon to Foreign Office, 28 Jan. 1922, PRO, FO 371/8184/N 911; M.-L. Goldbach, *Karl Radek und die deutsch-sowjetischen Beziehungen 1918–1923*, Bonn–Bad Godesberg 1973, 106–12.
9 Max Muller to Curzon, 26 Jan. 1922, and minutes, PRO, FO 371/8250/N 1128.

Germany wanted to upset the treaty of Versailles she would do so in spite of any guarantees.

The telegraph wires remained hot with news of German arms sales to Russia, German officers serving in the Russian army and navy and Afghan arms purchases in Germany, which would be transported via Russia to Afghanistan.[10] Foreign Office officials noted those violations of articles 170 and 179 of the treaty of Versailles, but nothing happened. At no time did the Foreign Office visibly react to the incoming information. In reply to a parliamentary question concerning German–Russian negotiations Curzon simply evaded the issue by stating that His Majesty's Government had no *official* information about the talks.[11] Contradictory information further distorted the Foreign Office's perception of German–Russian co-operation. The War Office confirmed on 6 April that there had been rumours in the past, which were known to Curzon, regarding the existence of a secret military agreement between Berlin and Moscow. However, an SIS report of the same day stated that the Radek mission earlier in the year had been a failure. Reports on a Soviet troop concentration along the Polish border had been equally dismissed. The prevailing opinion in London was that rumours of a Russian spring offensive circulated every year. An actual Russian attack meanwhile seemed unlikely since this would wreck Moscow's chances for any kind of support from abroad.[12]

This accumulation of reports on German–Russian activities should have made an attentive observer in the Foreign Office suspicious. Yet nothing happened, not the least since there were no warnings from the British ministers in Moscow and Berlin. In fact, British ignorance of Soviet–German relations was the cumulation of a lack of interest on the part of all people in charge of the issue: officials of the respective Foreign Office desks, but just as importantly, British observers at the ambassadorial level in Germany and Soviet Russia. The consequences were the same: the unpleasant surprise of Rapallo. Their motives or reasons, however, were very different.

The Foreign Office's attitude towards Germany was ambivalent. 'Old', high-ranking civil servants like Sir Eyre Crowe, permanent under-secretary of state, or Sir William Tyrrell, assistant under-secretary of state, had shaped their views of Germany before the war and were slower in overcoming their prejudices against Germany's intentions. More pro-French, they believed that France was at least partially right to fear Germany. Although the German menace did not seem immediate, they were sufficiently sensitive to

---

[10] Barclay (Stockholm) to Curzon, 23 Jan. 1921, PRO, FO 371/6164/N 255; telegrams and despatches, 1, 8, 31 Mar., 1, 9 Apr. 1922, FO 371/8206/N 1999/N 2258/N 3111/N 3613; Grove (Moscow) to FO, 21 Mar. 1922, FO 371/8187/N 2925/N 2867.
[11] Davies, parliamentary question, 30 Mar. 1922, PRO, FO 371/8208/N 2169 (author's emphasis).
[12] WO to FO, 6 Apr. 1922, PRO, FO 371/8178/N 3304; SIS report, 6 Apr. 1922, FO 371/8208/N 3725; Max Muller to FO, 15 Mar. 1922, FO 371/8120/N 2501.

see a proof of Germany's true, negative intentions in the circumvention of articles of the peace treaty without, however, being willing or capable of drawing conclusions for German co-operation with the Soviet Union.

The views of the younger officialdom contrasted considerably with the 'old top', and they had Curzon, the foreign secretary, on their side. Officials like the assistant secretaries Victor Wellesley and John Duncan Gregory, or the clerks Miles Lampson and Harold Nicolson, who worked in the Northern, Central and Western departments, believed that the harsh peace terms had quite the opposite of the desired effect on the Berlin government. Not only did they provoke Germany to bypass their restrictions in her search for moderation, but they might also drive Berlin into Moscow's arms. The *entente* with France should be maintained to moderate French policy towards Germany rather than to put too much pressure on Berlin. Curzon, the foreign secretary, was ambivalent towards both France and Germany. Given that his primary interest, involvement and influence lay in imperial affairs, and facing an immediate crisis in the Near East with the Greek–Turkish conflict, he looked at the two countries from a wider perspective. Curzon regarded France primarily as an imperial rival, whose ambitions in the east could be curtailed by a limited revival of Germany. The French paranoia about security carried less weight for him. Britain would benefit economically from a stronger Germany, and Germany could act as a bulwark against the spread of communism. If Germany remained weak, the communist menace seemed more immediate. In the case of Germany he disagreed little with the prime minister,[13] and his thinking was more or less in line with that of the younger officials within the Foreign Office.

Despite the diverging opinions on German policy within the Foreign Office there never was an open confrontation between the two groups. The prevailing view was that, for the moment, the treaty of Versailles was the basis of European relations. Moreover, until 1922 no long-term strategy for a policy towards Germany had been formulated. This was largely due to the number of short-term crises, which came up every now and again, mainly because Germany sought to evade certain articles of the peace treaty. The implications of Germany's relationship with the Soviet Union had retreated into the background against these seemingly more important problems. The lack of attention paid to incoming reports on this issue therefore was the reason for the Foreign Office's consternation about Rapallo.

The Foreign Office's attitude towards the Soviet Union, by contrast, was unanimous – everything about the new Russia was abhorrent. To old and young officials alike, the philosophy which the Soviet leaders put forward as the justification for their internal policy and their provocative external behaviour, was simply disgusting and offensive. The Foreign Office, expecting the imminent end of the Soviet regime, believed that the best way of dealing with the Bolsheviks was to ignore them. Curzon's view on Russia was once

---

13 D. Gilmour, *Curzon*, London 1994, 528.

again more influenced by its imperial rather than by its European dimension, as the unstable situation in Central Asia following the Bolshevik seizure of power in 1917 posed a significant challenge to British interests in this region.[14]

The cumulative emotional resentment against Moscow, however, turned out to be fateful, as Sir Robert Hodgson, the British commercial counsellor and *chargé d'affaires* in Moscow, also fell victim to the general British attitude towards the communists, which manifested itself in misinterpretations of Soviet policy.

Hodgson had taken up his post as head of the British commercial mission in Moscow in August 1921, immediately after the ratification of the Anglo-Russian trade agreement.[15] This agreement, together with Moscow's new economic policy (NEP), seemed to indicate an opening to the west and a gradual retreat from Bolshevism. To British observers Soviet communism was in decline, which made detailed knowledge about its ideological basics superfluous. Hodgson had left for Moscow ill-prepared for his job. He looked at Soviet policy through pre-war glasses and was unaware of the fundamental difference between tsarist Russia and a Soviet policy based on and driven by ideology. He was neither familiar with Marxism, nor could he imagine that a country would base its policy on values other than power politics.

Hodgson's attitude towards Russia was, to some extent, typical of the British diplomatic service. Neither he nor his colleagues had detached themselves from their earlier pictures of the tsarist empire. For the Foreign Office, the Russian autocracy continued after 1917. It had merely changed its rulers, names and the capital. Russo-British antagonism, based on the British diplomats' dislike for the imperialistic, 'Asiatic' and undemocratic rival in many parts of the world, was deep-rooted. Britain had welcomed the February revolution in St Petersburg hoping that it would introduce democracy in Russia. Yet with the Bolsheviks assuming power, Russia seemed to relapse into its old dictatorial traditions. Moreover, there was the ideological impact of Bolshevism and its claims to world revolution. After the armistice British politicians were terrified by the prospect of Bolshevism infecting British society. Would the communist message – appealing to the dissatisfied, war-weary people in Europe and promising utopian salvation from social underdevelopment and injustice – not be all too tempting to the British working class which was shattered by strikes and riots?

British officials' knowledge of communism was superficial and their arguments imbalanced and irrational. Even in the run-up to the Genoa conference, the Foreign Office consistently failed to develop a strategy against Bolshevism. It was accustomed to think in terms of the political power and

14 Bennett, *British policy*, 62–5.
15 R. Hodgson, 'Memoirs of an official agent', *World Today* viii (1954), 522–8, 613–17 at p. 524. On the NEP see E. H. Carr, *The Bolshevik revolution, 1917–1923*, London 1988 (first edn 1961), iii. 272–305.

strength of a country rather than in moral or ideological dimensions.[16] It therefore underestimated the impact of ideological forces on Russian foreign policy. London believed that it was only a question of time until the Bolshevik government would be brought down to earth by political and economic realities.[17] Officials such as Lampson and Tyrrell, as well as foreign secretary Lord Curzon, were instinctively so hostile towards Moscow that they hardly examined, let alone attempted to understand, communist ideology. International isolation was considered the best means to bring Russia to its senses.

Once installed in Moscow, Hodgson failed to produce reports which adequately depicted the political situation in Russia. In early April 1922 he was still convinced that the Russian government would accept the Cannes resolutions in return for western credits and diplomatic recognition, despite repeated Russian statements, including Lenin's speech of 6 March, which stipulated that Moscow would tolerate no western demands which conflicted with Soviet principles.

In the week before Genoa the Foreign Office compiled a memorandum on the attitude of the Soviet government towards the Genoa conference and western demands, relying primarily on Hodgson's reports.[18] This memorandum clearly reveals the extent to which both Hodgson and the Foreign Office were mistaken in their perception of Soviet intentions. On the question of Russian national debts, the key question in Allied–Russian negotiations, it was 'not anticipated that the Soviet government [would] raise any serious objections to admitting in principle its obligations to pay the pre-war national [i.e. tsarist] debt'. As far as private claims of British nationals towards the Russian government were concerned, 'again no difficulty is anticipated in getting the Soviet government to admit its liability'.

Hodgson had also diverted British fears of communist propaganda in the British empire and believed that the number of German officers serving in the Red Army was too small to be dangerous.[19] Furthermore, Hodgson failed to communicate extracts from the Russian *Izvestija* newspaper of 5 April 1922, which described in detail the Soviet delegation's visit to Berlin on its way to Genoa.[20] On the whole, therefore, Sir Robert Hodgson provided a rather unrealistic account of the situation in Moscow. The Foreign Office was not merely unaware of this fact; on the contrary it had great confidence in its envoy.

---

[16] F. S. Northedge, 'The adjustment of British policy', in F. S. Northedge (ed.), *The foreign policy of the powers*, London 1974, 161–202 at pp. 176, 179.

[17] Carr, *Bolshevik revolution*, 339–41.

[18] FO memo, 5 Apr. 1922, PRO, FO 371/8187/N 3236.

[19] Hodgson to FO, 9 Apr. 1922, PRO, FO 371/8206/N 3613; M. Zeidler, *Reichswehr und Rote Armee 1920–1933. Wege und Stationen einer ungewöhnlichen Zusammenarbeit*, Munich 1993, 51–3.

[20] Letter to the editor, *Manchester Guardian*, 24 Apr. 1922, PRO, FO 371/8188/N 3985.

Hodgson's despatches were even regarded as more reliable than those of ambassador D'Abernon and were eventually decisive for the Foreign Office's restrained reaction to Rapallo. D'Abernon, for his part, gave no warning about the imminent German–Russian agreement. In retrospect this silence is even more serious than Hodgson's since D'Abernon had been aware of Russo-German negotiations since August 1921.[21]

Already in January 1922 D'Abernon had left the Foreign Office in the dark about the real importance of Comintern delegate Karl Radek's visit to Berlin. More importantly, however, he did not pass on the sensational news that Germany and Russia took an almost complete draft of the Rapallo treaty to Genoa. D'Abernon had received this information from the Swiss professor and journalist, Ludwig Stein, according to D'Abernon 'something of a bore and a good deal of a busy body'[22] who wrote for several Berlin newspapers. Stein was on good terms with many officials in Berlin and unusually well informed politically. During an interview with Chicherin for the *Vossische Zeitung* on 3 April in Berlin he seems to have found out about the German–Russian preparations for the subsequent Rapallo agreement. On the evening of the same day Stein had given a dinner party at his house where he introduced the British ambassador to the members of the Russian delegation. Here he probably informed D'Abernon confidentially about the ongoing German–Russian negotiations. However, D'Abernon did not forward this sensitive information to London but kept Stein's message to himself. He only gave Stein, who attended the Genoa conference as a correspondent for several German newspapers, a letter of introduction to Lloyd George in case of any difficulties arising at Genoa.[23]

D'Abernon's decision not to transmit his knowledge of the Russo-German agreement[24] was a serious omission and a decision with far-reaching consequences for European affairs. His motives will remain a matter of speculation. It is possible that the Germanophile ambassador did not want to exacerbate further the precarious German situation at Genoa by biasing Lloyd George against Berlin in advance, or to risk a leak to the French, which would have been the end of the conference. However, the effects of D'Abernon's silence on British foreign policy were just as important. Even before Rapallo he had been watched suspiciously by many of his colleagues since he was not a career

[21] Unpublished diary, 21 Aug. 1921, D'Abernon papers, MS 48953B. Kaiser, *D'Abernon*, neglects his views on Russo-German co-operation.

[22] Diary entry, 7 Apr. 1921, unpubl. diary, D'Abernon papers, MS 48953A.

[23] Stein–Chicherin interview, *Vossische Zeitung*, 4 Apr. 1922, sent to London with D'Abernon to FO, 6 Apr. 1922, PRO, FO 371/8187/N 3399; unsigned report 'Clauses secrètes du traité russo-allemand', Berlin, 20 Apr. 1922, to Quai d'Orsay, MAE, sér. Z, Europe 1918–29, Russie-URSS, vol. 325; Hankey to his wife, 18 Apr. 1922, Hankey papers, HNKY 3/30; F. Rosen, *Aus einem diplomatischen Wanderleben*, ed. H. Müller-Werth, iii/4, Wiesbaden 1959, 366–70; Stein, *Aus dem Leben*, 233–4.

[24] Unsigned report 'Clauses secrètes du traité russo-allemand', Berlin, 20 Apr. 1922, to Quai d'Orsay, MAE, sér. Z, Europe 1918–29, Russie-URSS, vol. 325.

diplomat but an outside financial expert and Lloyd George's choice.[25] As British ambassador, he had to work for 'native' British interests. His task was to observe and to analyse German policy, to report to London and to execute Foreign Office directives in negotiations with the German government. However, the longer D'Abernon stayed in Berlin, the more he identified himself with the German point of view on many issues, thereby losing the critical distance necessary to represent British interests. After Rapallo this tendency, which reached its peak in the run-up to Locarno, manifested itself in D'Abernon's detailed instructions to the Germans as to how best to deny publicly the existence of German–Russian military co-operation.[26] His intimate knowledge of, and close contacts with, the German political establishment were appreciated in London but equally provoked uneasy feelings.

The Foreign Office never realised how much D'Abernon had known about the preparations for Rapallo. Nevertheless, London was outraged by the ambassador's apparent inattentiveness. Curzon ordered a sharp despatch to the British embassy to enquire why Berlin had reported the failure of Russo-German negotiations in January.[27] The ambassador's excuse was feeble and left Tyrrell with the impression that he had underrated the importance of the German action. Tyrrell's view differed sharply from the ambassador's:

> The Russo-German pact strikes me as the most important event which has taken place since the Armistice, but this is not a view which our embassy at Berlin apparently take . . . The treaty seems to me to impair very considerably the power of France to give forcible effect to sanctions in Germany, as behind this treaty there is certainly a military understanding between the two powers.[28]

D'Abernon wrote a second apologetic letter to Curzon. This, too, failed to satisfy the Foreign Office. Commenting on D'Abernon's tendency to embrace the German view without adequate reflection, Tyrrell noted:

> If he continues in this state of mind he is liable to be again taken in by the Germans, who have relapsed into their pre-war shuffling methods. Moreover, his telegram denying that there are any military and naval conventions attached to the treaty, does not comfort me, as I am convinced that even in the absence of such conventions there is a perfect understanding between the two parties that the Germans will help to build the Russian army and especially the Russian navy: such a co-operation revolutionises the outlook in Europe, and makes it more than ever imperative that we should come to an

25 Kaiser, *D'Abernon*, 14–18.
26 Haniel to Rathenau, 25 Apr. 1922, *ADAP*, 1st ser. vi, doc. 71.
27 Tyrrell to Curzon, 24 Apr. 1922, Curzon papers, MSS Eur F 112/227.
28 Ibid; Saint-Aulaire to Quai d'Orsay, 19 Apr. 1922, MAE, sér. Z, Europe 1918–29, Russie-URSS, vol. 49.

understanding with France, since the situation created by the treaty is a threat to both nations alike.[29]

Tyrrell clearly articulated the dilemma confronting British policy. Where would Britain stand in the face of Rapallo? Would the Anglo-German pre-war naval rivalry flare up again through the back door with Russia assisting Germany? The potential German–Soviet military agreement was not the only British concern. Equally important was the French attitude, both because of French support of her east central European allies in the case of a Soviet attack and the Franco-German antagonism over reparations. The possibility of France invading the Ruhr area constantly loomed on the horizon. Tyrrell's attitude was not devoid of anti-German sentiments. By contrast, he had always been sympathetic to the idea of closer co-operation with France. His criticism of D'Abernon's report was therefore combined with the suggestion of closer Anglo-French co-operation to keep Paris in check.

Tyrrell was the most outspoken exponent of the pro-French and anti-German group within the Foreign Office. It was this group which best represented the overall mood in the Foreign Office: unanimous irritation and condemnation of the Soviet–German agreement. Even otherwise more German-friendly officials agreed that Rapallo's political and particularly military implications for European relations, and British policy in particular, were not yet foreseeable.

Rumours of military co-operation between Berlin and Moscow emerged throughout the 1920s. In the weeks after Rapallo these rumours grew 'like the cut-off heads of a hydra',[30] despite continuous denials from Moscow and Berlin. The international press bent over backwards to provide ever more 'proofs' of the existence of an agreement. British, French and Polish–Russian papers even printed the text of an alleged German–Russian military convention signed on 3 April 1922 in Berlin.[31] London enquired via Foreign Office, War Office and SIS channels whether there was any truth in these reports, but the replies, except one, were non-alarmist.[32] Only General Bingham, the British military attaché in Berlin, believed in the existence of a military agreement after a conversation between senior British and German officers.

29 Tyrrell to Curzon, 27 Apr. 1922, Curzon papers, MSS Eur F 112/227. On Tyrrell see Steiner, *Foreign Office*, 118–20; E. Maisel, *The Foreign Office and foreign policy, 1919–1926*, Brighton 1994, 54–6.
30 Sthamer to AA, 1 June 1922, PA-AA, R 83437.
31 *The Times*, 6 May 1922, printed in *Soviet treaties series: a collection of bilateral treaties, agreements and conventions concluded between the Soviet Union and foreign powers*, ed. L. Shapiro, Washington, DC 1950–5, 383; *L'Eclair*, 11 May 1922, PRO, FO 371/8190/N 4591; *Sa Swoboda*, 27 Apr. 1922, PA-AA, R 83436 (in German translation).
32 D'Abernon to Curzon, 23 Apr. 1922, D'Abernon papers, MS 48924B; D'Abernon to Curzon, 29 Apr. 1922 (not sent), ibid; D'Abernon to Curzon, 29 Apr. 1922, PRO, FO 371/8190/N 4374; Hodgson to Curzon, 24 Apr. 1922, FO 371/8188/N 3918; Hodgson to Curzon, 2 May 1922, FO 371/8208/N 4481.

He quoted a German Colonel Böhme as saying: 'You will see that in a short time, possibly less than ten years, Germany and Russia will make war against France now that our rear is secure.'[33]

The Foreign Office at the time did not comment on Böhme's statement. Despite continuing articles in the press, and a lasting unease in Whitehall at the prospect of a Russo-German military alliance, the immediate fear was replaced by a more composed mood. The Foreign Office no longer commented on subsequent press reports about military co-operation, and Sir Eyre Crowe, permanent under-secretary at the Foreign Office, told the German ambassador, Friedrich Sthamer, that he had a low regard for these false assumptions.[34] The issue of greater and more immediate concern to the Foreign Office was France, as French policy interfered with British interests. Was France now likely to invade the Ruhr? And how should Britain react in the event? Could Rapallo have been avoided by a different British conduct of affairs since Versailles? What were the consequences for future British foreign policy if the French committed themselves elsewhere in eastern Europe and made further British co-operation with her to enforce the reparation clauses of Versailles impossible?[35] Now that British interests – the desire to reduce commitment in Europe – were affected, officials sprang into action.

The result was a self-critical Foreign Office analysis of the strengths and weaknesses of Britain's policy since the armistice. The result was devastating. The memorandum admitted that Britain had made fateful mistakes, although France was blamed for the difficulties created by French obstinacy on issues concerning European reconstruction and what the British regarded as reckless pursuit by the French of purely national interests.[36] The long Foreign Office memorandum revealed that British methods of foreign policy had been inconsistent, lacking firmness and a clear political direction. Already the excessive reparation bill, the first grave mistake in Allied policy towards Germany, had been based on a British suggestion at Paris in 1919. British officials admitted that they could have met French demands for security, at least to some extent, by maintaining the abortive Anglo–French–American Guarantee Agreement unilaterally after the American failure to ratify the peace treaties. In addition, British officials realised their failure to make the best use of the mechanism provided by the Reparation Commission and the League of Nations to establish a lasting peace.

Unlike the French, the Foreign Office concluded, British politicians had not pursued their national interests in a straightforward manner. While the French had systematically used the Reparation Commission – officially an independent body – as an instrument to enforce their idea of a settlement,

---

[33] WO to FO, 25 Apr. 1922, PRO, FO 371/8188/N 3881.
[34] Sthamer to AA, 1 June 1922, PA-AA, R 83437.
[35] FO memo, 'British Central European policy in its relations to Genoa', 9 May 1922, PRO, FO 371/7567/C 6875.
[36] On French policy see Bournazel, *Rapallo*, 33; Bariéty, *Relations*, pt I.

Britain had, though half-heartedly, still attempted to achieve a real solution for the reparations.

The Foreign Office memorandum also admitted that British policy had made the crucial mistake of not taking the newly established League of Nations seriously. The best way of initiating a new European policy, the Foreign Office concluded, would be to combine a real development of the League with a renewed offer of the defensive pact to France, to be extended at some later point to Belgium, Italy and, eventually, Germany. This should be coupled with an offer to reduce reparation claims against Berlin. Tyrrell mentioned an additional, also highly desirable, side-effect of a pact with Paris: 'If . . . we can conclude a satisfactory agreement with France, and thereby get control of her German policy we may be able to obtain sufficient alleviation for Germany as will restrain her from becoming too intimate with Russia.'[37]

In the summer of 1922, time was not ripe for a pact intended to meet both the victorious and defeated parties' interests in the long term. The underlying principles of French and British policy were too divergent, and at this point even the otherwise strongly pro-French members of the Foreign Office retreated. The Foreign Office, still in line with traditional British political objectives, was unwilling to assume responsibility for parts of Europe that lay outside the direct British sphere of interest, particularly the German–Polish border. Even in Whitehall no consensus about a new strategy for European affairs could be reached.[38] The offer of a security pact was dependent on a parallel change in reparation policy. This, however, was outside the Foreign Office's sphere of influence.

A change in policy was more easily made on paper than turned into reality. While the above-mentioned memorandum admitted that the League of Nations – as target of the Foreign Office's influence – had to be strengthened, British decision-makers hesitated about concrete action. After Rapallo the question of a German League membership was nevertheless soon back on the agenda. Some way or another had to be found to influence German policy and hopefully drive a wedge between Berlin and Moscow. The League should gradually integrate Berlin into the western orbit and separate her from Russia. Suddenly, however, Curzon became uncertain about the desirability of including Germany. 'If we announce our support *now* it will look as though we condone all these offences, and she may do what she likes.'[39] For the moment, however, he was overruled by the advocates of Germany's admission. The prime minister himself favoured a German entry in order to 'teach the world that she had to be treated again as an equal'.[40]

---

37 Tyrrell to Curzon, 27 Apr. 1922, Curzon papers, MSS Eur F 112/227.
38 Cabinet conclusion, 23 May 1922, CAB 23/30.
39 Curzon to A. Chamberlain, 4 May 1922, PRO, FO 371/7568/C 6656 (original emphasis).
40 D'Abernon diary entry, 12 June 1922, in E. Vincent D'Abernon, *An ambassador of peace*, ii, London 1930, 45.

Various, at times fantastic, arguments were put forward in support of German admission. Sir Eric Drummond, secretary-general of the League of Nations, especially came to London to speak in favour of Germany's entry. He argued that German admission to the League and the Council was also strongly in France's interest. The League could provide the security which Paris had failed to achieve through diplomatic means, and would make the Anglo-French security pact superfluous.[41]

On 30 June the cabinet decided that D'Abernon should sound the Germans out on whether they would join the League.[42] D'Abernon therefore talked to *Reichskanzler* Wirth, who told the ambassador that his government would find it very difficult to take up the British suggestion. The League, Wirth argued, was identified with the treaty of Versailles, which Germany would not sign for a second time. Therefore, the German preconditions for an entry into the League were that Berlin was spared another humiliating formal recognition of the peace treaty, and that she would get a seat on the Council. Moreover, Germany did not regard the League as capable of providing a solution to the reparations question. Finally, German membership would be incompatible with inter-allied military control and the occupation of the Rhineland. Until these questions were sufficiently resolved Germany would not enter the League.[43]

London, in turn, was not prepared to accept the demands as put forward by *Reichskanzler* Wirth. The Foreign Office dismissed them as excessive and misplaced – the German application had to be unconditional. After all, Lampson minuted, Germany had lost the war and was not yet in a position to bargain. Britain also had to consider French misgivings about Germany's entry into the League. If Germany came in under the patronage of Great Britain and against the will of France, it would hardly facilitate co-operation between the two Allies.[44]

Lampson's warning 'not to overdo it and not to justify the accusation of the French that *we*, the British, had been more German than the Germans in our efforts to get her in'[45] was necessary. D'Abernon, in his enthusiasm for the German case, was once again in danger of exceeding his brief. While the Foreign Office had considered it unwise to make any preliminary promises to Germany, i.e. a seat on the Council, D'Abernon had told Maltzan that Germany would naturally be admitted to the League's executive body.[46] Yet

41 Drummond to FO, 12 June 1922, PRO, FO 371/7568/C 8576; Sthamer to AA, 6 July 1922, *ADAP*, ser. A, vi, doc. 128, n. 3.
42 Cabinet conclusion, 30 June 1922, CAB 23/30.
43 Wirth to D'Abernon, 25 July 1922, *ADAP*, ser. A, vi, doc. 158.
44 Lampson minute, 26 July 1922, PRO, FO 371/7569/C 10444; Lampson minute, 27 July 1922, FO 371/7569/C 10631; Balfour memo, 1 Aug. 1922, FO 371/8793/C 13587.
45 Lampson minute, 26 July 1922, PRO, FO 371/7569/C 10444 (original emphasis).
46 Aufzeichnung Maltzan, 22 July 1922, *ADAP*, ser. A, vi, doc. 158.

the ambassador reported to London only that there was a strong prospect of Germany becoming a non-permanent member of the League Council.[47]

French objections, and a growing feeling that Germany had overstepped the mark in her demands, cooled British interest in a German application in the summer of 1922. Time was not yet ripe to meet victors' and vanquished's interests alike without committing Britain outside her sphere of influence. The brief flickering of reflections about a German League membership merely illustrated officials' temporary difficulties with traditional British political objectives. Once the storm of excitement about Rapallo had calmed down, pragmatism regained the upper hand. Even those officials who sympathised with French demands, realised that for the sake of British long-term policy, German interests had to be considered to some extent. But it was a different issue to transform this insight into the formulation of a policy vis-à-vis Germany, France and, to a lesser extent, Soviet Russia.

The German–Soviet treaty moved into the background against domestic problems, Irish riots, the Chanak crisis with Turkey and constant quarrels over reparations and other details of the treaty of Versailles, all culminating in the downfall of Lloyd George's coalition government in October 1922.[48] Still, Rapallo was not forgotten. It had poisoned Anglo-German relations. The Foreign Office now kept a close eye on reports about German–Russian co-operation. Rumours about military activities never ceased, but apart from one complaint to the conference of ambassadors,[49] the Foreign Office chose not to interfere. Not even the extension of the Rapallo treaty to the other republics of the Russian federation generated much interest. The Germans had respected D'Abernon's warnings not to stress it and create suspicion among the Allies and therefore waited until November 1922. Moreover, the Foreign Office was convinced that even when combined, Moscow and Berlin were at present too weak to be dangerous.[50] A sufficient number of reports stated that particularly the economic expectations, which had been attributed to the treaty had yet to materialise, and the Soviet economy appeared to be in a disastrous condition.[51]

D'Abernon and Hodgson both contributed to the more relaxed attitude towards potential dangers from the Rapallo friendship, although Hodgson's reports gained the reputation of being the more reliable. D'Abernon's

---

[47] D'Abernon to Balfour, 21 July 1922, PRO, FO 371/7569/C 10444.

[48] For an account of the fall of Lloyd George see, among others, Morgan, *Consensus and disunity*, 346–56. On Chanak see D. Walder, *The Chanak affair*, London 1969; Bennett, *British policy*, 76–94.

[49] British legation, Helsingfors, to Curzon, 19 May 1922 (French translation); memorandum à la conférence des ambassadeurs, 27 June 1922; note secrétariat général de la conférence des ambassadeurs, 4 July 1922, MAE, sér. Z, Europe 1918–29, Russie-URSS, vol. 328.

[50] Gregory, Crowe minutes, 1 July 1922, PRO, FO 371/8195/N 6621.

[51] Hodgson to Balfour, 13, 14 June 1922, *DBFP*, 1st ser. xx, doc. 515, 516; Hodgson to Curzon, 8 July 1922, PRO, FO 371/8214/N 6835.

standing in the Foreign Office had suffered severely from his failure to report on Rapallo. The ambassador therefore obviously felt he had to make up for this blunder. Throughout his remaining time in Berlin he furnished the Foreign Office with quarterly summaries on Russo-German relations. These regular reports gradually reduced existing concerns. In the eyes of the Foreign Office, however, Berlin had broken the western front against Soviet Russia and was responsible for the stalemate now achieved in European relations. The prospects for the German economy looked gloomy. British diplomats considered it unlikely that the Germans would recover in the purely economic field by their own efforts or with Russian assistance alone, but this seemed a matter of indifference to them. Berlin had lost her chances for co-operation with the western powers; now she should struggle alone.

The excitement over the German–Soviet agreement had given way to a more composed attitude in Britain. When weighing up the possible dangers of Rapallo, the Foreign Office came to the conclusion that neither the German nor the Russian domestic situation allowed for any foreign political adventures. The incompatibility of the two contracting parties prevented a speedy development of the new friendship. 'Our attitude towards Germany has been reasonable and even generous regarding reparation – we have resisted with considerable success the attempts at the disintegration of the Rhineland, and we have prevented the occupation of the Ruhr', wrote D'Abernon to Curzon. Once again he stressed what the Foreign Office knew – consciously or unconsciously – namely that the necessity to strengthen the 'western party' in Germany would be much easier under the new Cuno government than under Wirth, and that 'Ebert is scepticism personified as to the validity of Soviet promises.' The ambassador nevertheless warned: 'The moment the possibility of a western policy vanishes . . . [Germany] will unquestionably fall back on Russian help – disliking it, and distrusting it – but quite certain.'[52]

The Foreign Office was annoyed but not alarmed about the treaty of Rapallo. Its restrained attitude towards Russo-German co-operation set the pace for a generally calm British view of German–Soviet intimacy throughout the 1920s.

---

[52] D'Abernon to Curzon, 27 Nov. 1922, D'Abernon papers, MS 48925A.

3

Rapallo's First Test: The Ruhr Crisis

By the end of 1922 the Rapallo agreement had retreated into the background of British attention. The months that had passed since the end of the Genoa conference were dominated by a number of issues which were more important to British foreign policy than the Russo-German treaty. Lloyd George had stepped down as British prime minister in October 1922 and was replaced by the Conservative Andrew Bonar Law in the November elections. Bonar Law confirmed Curzon as foreign secretary, and the Foreign Office gradually re-emerged from its backstage role under Lloyd George without, however, regaining its pre-war influence. The issues of greatest concern to British foreign policy in the last months of 1922 were undoubtedly the Greek–Turkish conflict and, to a lesser extent, the German reparation question. Curzon and Tyrrell left for the peace conference with Turkey at Lausanne in mid-November and did not return to London before beginning of February 1923. When, in early January, the Turks became increasingly obstinate in the negotiations, Crowe, the permanent under-secretary, was also summoned to Lausanne to assist Curzon in his attempts to persuade both the Turks and the French, who were supporting Turkey, to accept reasonable peace terms. More than once the Lausanne conference was on the verge of collapse, and the Anglo-French *entente* in severe danger. These developments did not facilitate Anglo-French communication on other foreign policy problems.[1]

On 11 January 1923 French and Belgian troops invaded the Ruhr basin as a reprisal for the German failure to meet reparation payments. Britain knew of these French plans at least since Bonar Law and his French counterpart Poincaré had met in London on 9/10 December 1922. Poincaré had hoped to secure British support for an Allied occupation of the Ruhr to make Germany pay, and Bonar Law 'had been unable to tell Poincaré openly of the damage which would be done to the *entente* by a Franco-Belgian occupation of the Ruhr', 'considering the importance of avoiding giving the Turks the impression of a breach in Allied unity during the Lausanne conference'.[2]

Immediately after the invasion, the fear of Russo-German co-operation was back on the British agenda. In fact, the Ruhr occupation was the acid test

---

1   Bennett, *British policy*, 76–94.
2   Ibid. 32. See also, among others, J. Bariéty, 'Die französische Politik in der Ruhrkrise', in K. Schwabe (ed.), *Die Ruhrkrise 1923. Wendepunkt der internationalen Beziehungen nach dem Ersten Weltkrieg*, Paderborn 1985; W. A. McDougall, *France's Rhineland diplomacy, 1914–1924: the last bid for a balance of power in Europe*, Princeton, NJ 1978; Orde, *Security*, 46–55.

for Rapallo. The conduct of German and Soviet policy during the crisis would reveal whether there were indeed any secret clauses as part of the agreement, which would now come into effect. Moreover, there was the possibility of additional unrest in east central Europe if countries with revisionist ambitions like Poland, Lithuania, Germany or Russia seized the opportunity to alter their frontiers while the great powers were fully engaged in the Ruhr region.

In British eyes, the French step had nothing but disadvantages. First of all, it was illegal under the Versailles treaty. Moreover, the exploitation of the Ruhr would hardly increase reparation revenues. Rather, it would provoke strikes and solidify resistance within the German population. Germany would be plunged into economic chaos, destroying her capacity for economic recovery and destabilising international trade. Whitehall was convinced that the Ruhr adventure would be both expensive and risky for France, and placed ultimate responsibility at Paris's doorstep.[3]

As worst-case scenario for British policy, the Ruhr occupation might even be the beginning of the end of Europe's shaky peace, especially if Germany turned eastwards to her Rapallo partner for military assistance. Germany was likely to seek a revision of the treaty of Versailles at the same time. Frederic von Rosenberg, foreign minister in the new government of *Reichskanzler* Wilhelm Cuno, actually mentioned to the British ambassador the possibility of closer Russo-German co-operation in the case of a French march into the Ruhr.[4] Moreover, Ago von Maltzan, former head of the eastern department of the German Foreign Office and protagonist of the 'Rapallo policy', had just been appointed secretary of state in the Wilhelmstraße. The intense dislike for Maltzan among Foreign Office officials was manifest in several minutes on his character that were far from flattering. Maltzan's new position prompted John D. Gregory, assistant secretary in the Northern department, to enquire rather alarmedly at the German embassy in London whether this meant that Germany would now shift her political focus eastwards.[5]

Despite their unease, British diplomats remained tight-lipped in public during the first weeks of the Ruhr crisis, giving the impression that London was both helpless and embarrassed by the situation.[6] It was unfortunate that most of the leading Foreign Office members were at Lausanne, while Stanley Baldwin, the chancellor of the exchequer, tried to find a settlement for Britain's wartime American debt in Washington. The prime minister, Curzon and Baldwin basically agreed that the *entente* with France had to be maintained, and that Germany would receive no active encouragement in its

---

3 Curzon to Phipps, 27 Dec. 1922, *DBFP*, 1st ser. xx, doc. 151.
4 D'Abernon to Curzon, 6 Jan. 1923, ibid. doc. 6.
5 FO minute, 3 Jan. 1923, PRO, FO 371/8699/C 203; Dufour to Maltzan, 4 Jan. 1923, Dufour papers, PA-AA, vol. 1.
6 AA memo, 27 Jan. 1923, PA-AA, R 30589; Sthamer to AA, 8 Feb. 1923, *ADAP*, ser. A, vi, doc. 80; Scherberg to Schubert, 15 Jan. 1923, Schubert papers, Bestand Krüger, vol. 15.

passive resistance. The cabinet eventually decided on a policy of 'benevolent passivity', thus 'minimizing . . . the adverse effects upon Anglo-French relations of French . . . action and reducing to a minimum the opportunities for friction upon the several inter-Allied bodies'.[7] Backed by this decision, Sir Ronald Lindsay, assistant under-secretary and in charge of the Foreign Office during the absence of his superiors, was polite but evasive when the German ambassador, Friedrich Sthamer, came to hand over a note of protest on 23 January.

British diplomats remained cautious in their attitude towards the Ruhr occupation in general as well as in the evaluation of the danger from Rapallo during these critical months. London's wait-and-see approach was in stark contrast to both French actions and Russo-German moves. In Britain's calculation the Ruhr occupation and an economically collapsing Germany would not yield any profit for France, and therefore the Foreign Office sought to exert a restraining influence on the Paris government. Equally, London discounted the possibility of a Russo-German alliance, based upon the incoming information from SIS and the British missions abroad, which painted a blurry picture of Russo-German relations. Reports from Berlin and from Moscow indicated no clear political strategy of the Rapallo partners nor hinted at common action. Likewise, reports surveying the domestic situation in both countries emphasised that a Russo-German coup to upset the territorial *status quo* in Europe, was fairly unlikely.[8]

Moscow and Berlin both sharply criticised the occupation of the Ruhr.[9] The Soviet government, in fear of Germany losing its independence, declared that Russia would not stand by if Poland assisted France in the Ruhr or seized German territories in Silesia.[10] The thought of French co-operation with Poland and the Little Entente in the occupied territories was disconcerting to the Foreign Office because of its implications for Russo-German relations. Lampson made enquiries at the British missions in Prague and Warsaw to establish whether it was true that Paris had sounded out the two governments regarding the amount of assistance upon which she could count.[11]

The replies to his enquiry managed to dispel Lampson's concerns. Intelligence reports, the War Office and William Max Muller, British envoy extraordinary in Warsaw, as well as ambassador D'Abernon in Berlin quelled Foreign Office fears with an almost identical argument: France sought to justify her advance into the Ruhr as a measure of economic – in contrast to

---

7 Cabinet conclusion, 11 Jan. 1923, CAB 23/45 (1).
8 D. G. Williamson, 'Great Britain and the Ruhr crisis, 1923–1924', *BJIS* iii (1977), 70–91 at p. 70.
9 D'Abernon to Curzon, 24 Jan. 1923, PRO, FO 371/8707/C 1682.
10 D'Abernon to Curzon, 6 Jan. 1923, *DBFP*, 1st ser. xxi, doc. 6. See also Brockdorff-Rantzau to Rosenberg, 23 Dec. 1922, PA-AA, R 28279k; Jacobson, *Soviet Union*, 131–2.
11 Lampson to Cecil (Prague) and Max Muller (Warsaw), 9 Jan. 1923, *DBFP*, 1st ser. xxi, doc. 6, n. 3.

political – pressure authorised by the treaty of Versailles. She therefore could not instigate an attack on Germany by nations that had nothing to do with executing the treaty. Poland and Czechoslovakia, moreover, both objected to military co-operation with France in Germany since they were both afraid of Russia.[12] France seemed to have abandoned the idea of Polish assistance but surprises were possible. The Foreign Office observed with some astonishment that Poincaré had started to flirt with the Bolshevik government instead.

In the eyes of the Foreign Office, a possible Franco-Russian *rapprochement* was anything but desirable. The Russo-German *tête-à-tête* at Rapallo had been badly received, but a Franco-Soviet alliance would have been even less welcome. Britain's negative experiences with the Franco-Russian alliance of the late nineteenth century seemed to have been revived in the Greek–Turkish crisis of 1921–2. French, and also Russian assistance to the Turks clashed with Britain's support of the Greeks, and Franco-Russo-Turkish co-operation during the Lausanne conference thwarted Curzon's aim of dealing a blow to Bolshevism and made the conference close without a solution. Moreover, both a nationalist Turkey and a strong Russia were dangers to the stability of the British empire.[13] If Franco-Russian co-operation now extended to the continent, it had the potential of massively altering the balance of power in Europe. The power struggle in the Ruhr would be seriously affected, not to mention that it implied an end to Franco-Polish friendship. From the French point of view, it was not unnatural to turn towards Moscow after Britain had refused to support her Ruhr policy, since it would provide a means of destroying the much-hated Rapallo treaty. Furthermore, the detachment of Russia at this moment would be a severe moral defeat to Germany.[14] Still, the French behaviour frustrated the Foreign Office's decision to counter Moscow's anti-British attitude at Lausanne with a policy of ignoring the Soviet government.[15]

Once the British delegation had returned from Lausanne, the indecisiveness of British policy in the Ruhr diminished, although it took Curzon until mid-March to formulate a British position on the crisis. Against the advice of several Foreign Office officials who wanted to issue a sharp protest to Paris against any *rapprochement* with Moscow, Curzon decided to await further developments.[16] Poincaré appeared to be serious about a closer relationship with Moscow, for both domestic and foreign political reasons. According to

12 Finlayson (WO) to Lampson, 12 Jan. 1923, PRO, FO 371/8703/C 802; Max Muller to Curzon, 17 Jan. 1923, FO 371/8205/C 1248/C 1249; D'Abernon to Curzon, 24 Jan. 1923, FO 371/8707/C 1682.
13 Gilmour, *Curzon*, 559.
14 *Daily Telegraph*, 9 Feb. 1923, and minutes, PRO, FO 371/9343/N 1339.
15 The earl of Ronaldshay, *The life of Lord Curzon, being the authorised biography of George Nathaniel Marquess Curzon of Kedleston, K.G.*, iii, London 1928, 328; H. Nicolson, *Curzon: the last phase*, London 1934, 281–350.
16 R. A. Leeper, Gregory minutes, 12 Feb. 1923, Curzon, 14 Feb. 1923, PRO, FO 371/9343/N 1339.

Lord Crewe, British ambassador in Paris, one of Poincaré's chief arguments for his new departure had been the desire to conciliate the leader of the opposition, Herriot, and the Bloc des Gauches, who had opposed the Ruhr occupation.[17] In the summer of 1922, Herriot had negotiated personally in Moscow for a commercial and ultimately political agreement and had ever since pressed the government for warmer Franco-Russian relations.[18] Crewe reported that Poincaré intended to negotiate on commercial and political issues and even seemed prepared to grant *de jure* recognition to the Soviet government. Yet there was violent opposition to Poincaré's scheme from the president of the French Council, Alexandre Millerand, and Emmanuel de Peretti della Rocca, head of the department for political and commercial affairs at the Quai d'Orsay, who were both strongly anti-Bolshevik.[19]

As time passed and information increased, the Foreign Office began to discount the chances of success for Franco-Russian co-operation. Poincaré, facing strong opposition at home, began to wonder whether France's approach to Russia was really desirable. The discouraging Russian response to France's overtures further moved Poincaré to reconsider his strategy.[20] On 3 March, he declared that political and, for the time being, commercial negotiations with Moscow were out of the question.[21] London therefore watched calmly as a French commercial delegation arrived in Moscow on 5 June. Poincaré had reassured the British that France would grant *de jure* recognition to the Soviet government only in agreement with London.

The Rapallo alliance would have ceased to be a potentially disturbing factor in international relations if the Franco-Russian flirtation had developed into a closer relationship. As this was not the case, Britain's attention was once again drawn to the co-operation between Germany and Russia. The possibility of secret military collaboration between Moscow and Berlin continued to worry the British, as rumours of a military alliance associated with Rapallo had never died. In December 1922, the *Daily Mail* published a series of articles on an alleged ten-year programme for a 'war of revenge', thus stirring up public feelings.[22] While these articles had no factual foundation, the Foreign Office had obtained precise information on the extent of Russo-German military co-operation, especially in aviation, from other sources. From various despatches, most of which had been received since the

---

17 Crewe to Curzon, 22, 23 Feb. 1923, *DBFP*, 1st ser. xxi, docs 18, 19.
18 SIS report no. 1116, 24 Mar. 1923, PRO, FO 371/9344/N 2901; SIS summary of relations Russia–France, 22 Aug. 1922–23 Jan. 1923, 2 Mar. 1923, FO 371/9344/N 2122.
19 D'Abernon to Curzon, 12 Feb. 1923, D'Abernon papers, MS 48925A; SIS report no. 1116, 24 Mar. 1923, PRO, FO 371/9344/N 2901; Crewe to Curzon, 22, 23 Feb. 1923, *DBFP*, 1st ser. xxi, docs 18, 19.
20 Crewe to FO, 26 Feb. 1923; Tyrrell, Curzon minutes, 27 Feb. 1923, PRO, FO 371/9344/N 1823.
21 Gregory, Strang minutes, 4 May 1923, PRO, FO 371/9344/N 3841.
22 Sthamer to AA, 1 Dec. 1922, PA-AA R 28277k; Sthamer to AA, 2 Dec. 1922, PA-AA, R 77005.

beginning of the Ruhr crisis, British diplomats knew that the German aeroplane company Junkers had set up a plant in Fili, near Moscow, which had embarked on the large-scale manufacture of aircraft. The plant was equipped mainly with German machines, German management and German engineers and, in addition, would organise Russian domestic air traffic as well as that between Russia and foreign countries.[23] According to Sir Robert Hodgson, British *chargé d'affaires* in Moscow, this Russian collaboration with a German firm had been the outcome of a secret agreement between Germany and Russia made at the time of the Rapallo treaty.[24]

Soviet–German military co-operation was not confined to aviation. On 5 February, Crewe transmitted rumours of general German–Soviet collaboration in military technology.[25] On 6 March, Gregory enquired in Moscow whether there was any truth to a War Office report, according to which the Soviet General Tuchachevski had visited Germany and returned to Russia together with a German military delegation.[26] Further rumours spread of a German–Russian military alliance when Chicherin, Russian people's commissar for foreign affairs, passed through Berlin on his way back to Moscow from the Lausanne conference.[27]

The Foreign Office remained uncertain as to whether German–Soviet military co-operation took place on the basis of written or just verbal agreements. For the moment, officials did not expect any trouble from the military relationship between Moscow and Berlin. British representatives had repeatedly ruled out this possibility and too many political factors argued against closer co-operation between the two governments at present. Still, the reports on which the Foreign Office mainly based its confidence came from only one side, namely ambassador D'Abernon in Berlin, whose keen interest in glossing over German defaults on the peace treaty was well known.

'The Ruhr has provoked nothing beyond passive resistance', the British ambassador concluded in his observations concerning Russo-German relations on 3 March.[28] Berlin expected outspoken assistance from Moscow in her struggle with the French but Russian support had been confined to mild verbal protests and confidential statements that Germany would receive little

---

[23] FO memo on aviation in Russia (summarising incoming reports), 21 Apr. 1923, *DBFP*, 1st ser. xxv, doc. 48.

[24] Hodgson to Curzon, 28 June 1923, *DBFP*, 1st ser. xxv, doc. 111.

[25] Crewe to Curzon, 5 Feb. 1923, *BDFA*, II/A: *The Soviet Union*, vi, doc. 206.

[26] Gregory to Hodgson, 6 Mar. 1923, PRO, FO 371/9353/N 2020; de la Panouce (French military attaché in London) to French war minister, 1 Mar. 1923, MAE, sér. Z, Europe, Russie-URSS, vol. 330; M. Zeidler, 'Reichswehr und Rote Armee 1920–1933', in *Deutschland und das bolschewistische Rußland von Brest-Litowsk bis 1941*, ed. Göttinger Arbeitskreis, Berlin 1991, 30.

[27] Conversation between Lampson and Sthamer, 12 Feb. 1923, PRO, FO 371/8713/C 2857; D'Abernon diary entries, 9, 10 Feb. 1923, in D'Abernon, *Ambassador*, ii. 170–1; D'Abernon memo, 11 Feb. 1923, D'Abernon papers, MS 48925A.

[28] D'Abernon to Curzon, 3 Mar. 1923, PRO, FO 371/8670/C 4427.

more than moral support. The Soviet government pointed out that the timing was unfavourable for active co-operation with Germany, owing to the Soviet Union's preoccupation with internal reconstruction and with the reorganisation of its army.[29] This attitude annoyed German politicians. Thus, the reception of Chicherin in Berlin on his return from Lausanne was quite reserved.[30] D'Abernon also reported that there was a group of German politicians who were strongly against close relations with Moscow. *Reichspräsident* Friedrich Ebert was known to be hostile to the Russian connection since Genoa, and, according to D'Abernon, this was equally true of *Reichskanzler* Cuno, foreign minister Rosenberg and even *Reichswehr* minister Otto Gessler. 'The bulk of public opinion is distrustful of the communist connection.'[31] In the case of Cuno, D'Abernon's evaluation was again over-optimistic as the *Reichskanzler* knew in detail of Russo-German military relations and actively supported them. Still, his reports strengthened the Foreign Office's general impression that there was little to fear from the Rapallo treaty.

Russian policy towards Germany during the Ruhr crisis had several faces. On the one hand, the Soviet government expressed its sympathy and tried to give moral support to Germany. On the other hand, it supported the German communist party financially and ideologically with particular focus on the Ruhr.[32] Britain also knew that Comintern member Radek had been in the Ruhr area for some time during 1923 and encouraged communist activities.[33] British officials, however, gained the impression from D'Abernon's reports that Moscow-directed propaganda did not have the desired effect. 'There can be no doubt that the general unrest arising out of the occupation of the Ruhr has fanned communist feeling locally, and, to a less extent, generally.'[34]

The longer the Franco-Belgian occupation of the Ruhr basin lasted, the more unrest in the region increased. The vast inflation, passive resistance, and French countermeasures provoked unprecedented social unrest in Germany. In May 1923 strikes and riots broke out, soon spreading throughout the occupied region. On 10 May, for the first time since the conclusion of the

[29] FO memo on Soviet relations with Germany in connection with the French occupation of the Ruhr, 3 Feb. 1923, PRO, FO 371/8710/C 2287.
[30] D'Abernon diary entry, 11 Feb. 1923, in D'Abernon, *Ambassador*, ii. 171; D'Abernon to FO, 11 Feb. 1923, PRO, FO 371/8712/C 2593.
[31] D'Abernon to Curzon, 26 Feb. 1923, *DBFP*, 1st ser. xxv, doc. 23; D'Abernon to Curzon, 1 Mar. 1923, PRO, FO 371/8670/C 4160; Zeidler, *Reichswehr*, 53.
[32] D'Abernon to Curzon, 11 Feb. 1923, PRO, FO 371/8712/C 2593. See also SIS report no. 1110, 16 Mar. 1923.
[33] On Radek see W. T. Angress, *Stillborn revolution: the communist bid for power in Germany, 1921–1923*, Princeton, NJ 1963, 314–77. In *Britain and the Weimar Republic: the British documents*, London 1984, 148, F. L. Carsten questions Radek's presence in the Ruhr but bases his argument on Angress, whose study provides sufficient evidence gained from German archive material for Radek's stay in Germany.
[34] D'Abernon to Curzon, 12 Mar. 1923, PRO, FO 371/8809/C 4991.

Rapallo agreement, the otherwise composed British ambassador in Berlin voiced concern about the disturbing effects of the invasion:

> One of the principal restraining forces which has helped considerably to retard the movement towards closer co-operation with Russia has been the attitude of His Majesty's Government and the belief that England would, at a given moment, intervene and bring about a solution of the reparation and security question. If anything occurred to destroy or diminish this hope, it would unquestionably have a considerable influence in driving Germany to seek help from the east.[35]

The ambassador's warnings went unheard in London, although the number of reports concerning the growing strength of communism and communist agitation increased remarkably between mid-May and mid-June. Moreover, France seemed to give active financial and material support to the communists in the Ruhr area and the Rhineland as a means of weakening the German authorities.[36] Poincaré was reported to have characterised the disorder cynically as a *malaise allemand*, leaving the German government to decide whether or not to let things escalate to a catastrophic finale.[37]

British officials did not share Poincaré's views on the unrest in the Ruhr, nor did they approve of French support for the communists. London's attention was directed elsewhere in its relations with Russia. Since February 1923, Anglo-Soviet trade relations had become so seriously disturbed that Curzon even contemplated the cancellation of the trade agreement signed in 1921. On 2 May, the foreign secretary gained cabinet approval for a very sharply worded note giving Moscow ten days to settle a number of British grievances concerning propaganda in Asia, fishing rights and outrages on British citizens, the so-called 'Curzon ultimatum'.[38] It was unlikely that the Soviet government, while being in the midst of deep international trouble, would turn to turmoil-shattered Germany for help or would grant her assistance. Nevertheless, Gregory enquired at the German embassy in London how Berlin would react in the case of Britain breaking off diplomatic relations with Moscow.[39]

Berlin found herself in an awkward position when faced with the possibility of a diplomatic rift between Moscow and London. The Soviet

---

35 D'Abernon to Curzon, 10 May 1923, received 25 June 1923, PRO, FO 371/9357/N 5667.
36 D'Abernon to Curzon, 22 May 1923, PRO, FO 371/8809/C 9454.
37 Crewe to Curzon, 28 May 1923, quoted in 'Report of events arising out of French occupation of the Ruhr, 1 May–31 May 1923', PRO, FO 371/8733/C 11094; Crewe to Curzon, 6 July 1923, Crewe papers, CUL, box C/12; D'Abernon to Curzon, 22 May 1923, D'Abernon papers, MS 48925B. See also memo 'Die Beziehungen zwischen Kommunisten und französischen Besatzungstruppen im Ruhrgebiet', 5 June 1923, *ADAP*, ser. A, viii, doc. 6.
38 Bennett, *British policy*, 72–4; E. H. Carr, *The interregnum, 1923–1924*, London 1969, 165–74.
39 Sthamer to AA, 3 May 1923, PA-AA, R 36024.

government, aware of the seriousness of the situation, enquired unofficially in Berlin whether Germany would safeguard Russian interests in Britain in case of a rupture of relations.[40] This question deeply embarrassed the German government, which depended upon a favourable British attitude in the Ruhr crisis. At the same time, Germany was unable to refuse the Russian request outright, due to threats from its ambassador in Moscow, Brockdorff-Rantzau, to resign if the German reply were negative.[41] Thus, at the height of Anglo-Soviet tensions, Germany urged moderation on both London and Moscow, although she was eager to avoid the impression that she was keen on mediating between the two conflicting parties.[42]

British attention had turned away from Germany at a critical moment. When the Foreign Office resumed its duties after the Soviet government had indicated that it would comply with the demands set out in the British memorandum, the communist crisis in the Ruhr was almost over. The recent disturbances had died down, and Lord Kilmarnock, the British high commissioner in Koblenz, reported that there was no evidence to support the belief that the communists planned any large-scale actions. He also discounted the possibility of French support for the communists.[43] Sir Eyre Crowe therefore remained indifferent towards ambassador Sthamer's complaints that the French were responsible for the riots, since the British government considered the danger from communist outbreaks in the Ruhr to be minimal.[44]

The situation throughout Germany went on to deteriorate further. Berlin had made new suggestions on 7 June for a reparation settlement, but France and Belgium, who demanded an unconditional end to passive resistance before renegotiation, had rejected the note. The *Reichsmark* fell sharply and provoked a severe food crisis. A highly alarmed D'Abernon wired to London describing the desperate government attempts to control disturbances in several German cities, such as those in Saxony – a communist stronghold – and to suppress communist attacks. When the telegram arrived in London, the Foreign Office discounted the ambassador's appeal as being exaggerated and his attitude too pro-German. After large-scale strikes and labour riots, the Cuno government eventually resigned. The new great coalition government led by Gustav Stresemann, which assumed power in August 1923, seemed more determined to fight communism. D'Abernon reported the new *Reichskanzler*'s tone to be vigorous and decisive: 'I remember a year ago talking to him about unrest, his only reply being "There must be shooting." '[45]

---

[40] Aufzeichnung Maltzan über Gespräch mit Krestinski, 23 May 1923, ibid.
[41] Brockdorff-Rantzau telegram no. 291, 24 May 1923, ibid; Schubert to Sthamer, 24 May 1923, ibid.
[42] Rosenberg to Brockdorff-Rantzau, 13 May 1923, PA-AA, R 28219k.
[43] Kilmarnock to Curzon, 11 June 1923, PRO, FO 371/8809/C 10356.
[44] Conversation between Crowe and Sthamer, 30 May 1923, PRO, FO 371/8809/C 9577; report of events arising out of the French occupation of the Ruhr, 1–30 June 1923, FO 371/8736/C 12747.
[45] D'Abernon to Curzon, 13 Aug. 1923, D'Abernon papers, MS 48925B.

Reichskanzler Stresemann officially ended passive resistance in the Ruhr area on 27 September. The Ruhr crisis had nearly bankrupted Berlin financially, and a continuation of the struggle could no longer be justified on political grounds. Moscow-supported communist agitators organised large strikes and demonstrations to protest against Stresemann's 'treachery', but with little effect. The communist disturbances were no surprise for London. At the end of August, Tyrrell predicted that Stresemann would have to choose between surrender to the communists or to the French, and that the chancellor would choose the latter. Yet as long as Moscow refrained from intervention, the Foreign Office trusted the die-hard Stresemann to tackle the crisis. Britain received no information that Moscow would reverse its policy and move openly against the German government in order to promote revolution. Leon Trotsky, the people's commissar for war, had told US senator King in an interview that 'the Soviet government would avoid intervention in a German civil war because such intervention would involve a war with Poland, and that would rekindle a European conflagration which would destroy the remnants of European civilisation'.[46]

However, October showed that Moscow had dramatically changed its attitude towards a German communist revolution. Already in August, the Politburo had concluded that the proletarian revolution in Germany was imminent as a result of the economic disaster caused by the Ruhr occupation, and had begun with preparations to support and control this event. Hodgson wired that on 1 October the central committee in Moscow had decided to abandon its attitude of neutrality and to support a communist insurrection, a 'German October'. The communist party in Moscow, on the other hand, was again wavering as to the attitude it should adopt.[47] However, the 'hard-liners' won the strategy debate, setting in motion the construction of a secret illegal infrastructure. Russian money and advisers were channelled through the diplomatic mission in Berlin, weapons were shipped via St Petersburg to Hamburg and an intensive propaganda campaign was launched in the Ruhr.[48] Large Soviet troop concentrations were reported along the borders with Poland and the Baltic states, emphasising Moscow's request to Poland to establish a transit corridor for food transports to Germany. Moscow even went as far as to threaten military action if the Poles attempted to limit the movement of goods between Soviet Russia and Germany.[49]

The Foreign Office remained stoical. With the focus of British concerns currently far removed from eastern Europe, British diplomats did not share the alarm of the Baltic and Polish leaders who feared Russian aggression.

---

46 Extract from *The Times*, 2 Oct. 1923, PRO, FO 371/9339/N 7915; de Magérie to Poincaré, 29 Oct. 1923, MAE sér. Z, Europe, Russie-URSS, vol. 330.
47 Hodgson to FO, 15 Oct. 1923, PRO, FO 371/9357/N 8219.
48 Kilmarnock to FO, 17 Oct. 1923; French communiqué, 14 Oct. 1923, PRO, FO 371/8746/C 18004/C 18074; Jacobson, *Soviet Union*, 131–4.
49 *DBFP*, 1st ser. xxiii, docs 756–66.

Gregory dismissed the Latvian and Lithuanian ministers' reports as a 'tale' and refused to give them any political advice or to consider the Lithuanian request for arms and ammunition. The Foreign Office doubted that Germany was on the verge of 'going Red' and believed that the Russian troop concentrations on the frontiers of the border-states and Poland were little more than posturing. Through Rakovsky, the Soviet *chargé d'affaires* in London, Gregory learned that, on his return from Berlin to Moscow, Radek had told Soviet leaders that it was an illusion to believe in a German revolution and that they would make complete fools of themselves if they embarked on a military adventure to support the German communists.[50]

By the end of 1923, British concern about communist upheaval in Germany as a consequence of the Franco-Belgian occupation of the Ruhr had vanished. Equally, the Foreign Office dismissed the likelihood of Russian assistance to Germany in her struggle against the French. The Rapallo treaty, put to the test, had turned out to be less dangerous than widely assumed. This, however, had been far from obvious at the outset. Russia had protested on behalf of the German government against the invasion; there was uncertainty about whether and how Moscow would support Berlin; and there had been significant undercover co-operation. Yet Britain decided to adopt a similar attitude of 'critical passivity' to the prospect of Russo-German co-operation as towards French moves in the Ruhr.

With the benefit of hindsight this attitude was probably the only realistic approach to the crisis. At the time, however, it was not without risk. British officials, still influenced by nineteenth-century balance of power diplomacy, underestimated the driving forces behind Russia's policy, the extent of the changes introduced by the revolution of 1917 and particularly the impact of revolutionary theory on international relations.[51] As Bennett observed,

British policy towards Bolshevik Russia was not characterised by its rationality. The Soviet problem or threat was viewed with such concern because it existed in a variety of potential forms: internal subversion within Britain or the empire; a victorious advance by the Red Army across Europe; hostile action against Britain's Asian empire; the undermining of established conventions of international behaviour with the repudiation of Russia's debts and nationalisation of foreign investment; and the danger that the economic and social collapse of Russia would spread to other economies. The amorphous nature of the very real Soviet threat did not make for rational attitudes in Britain. The hatred of Bolshevism displayed by ministers such as Churchill and Curzon was immense . . . Only grudgingly did the Cabinet accept that, if Britain lacked the men and money to secure the overthrow of the Bolshevik government, then they must try and live with the new regime.[52]

---

[50] Gregory minute, 26 Oct. 1923, ibid. doc. 764 n. 2. Radek had, for tactical reasons, supported the 'German October' preparations: Jacobson, *Soviet Union*, 132.
[51] White, *Origins of detente*, 30, 204.
[52] Bennett, *British policy*, 74.

British decision-makers dealt with individual features of Bolshevism – the nationalisation of property, pre-war debts or propaganda – separately as they appeared and disturbed the established order. This approach left them ignorant of the inherent dangers in the Bolshevik long-term goal, namely the concept of an armed proletarian insurrection as promoted for the first – and only – time on a larger scale by Comintern activists in the Ruhr area. The possibility that a communist world revolution loomed, namely the danger that some of the disagreable features observed in Russia could spread into other countries and possibly threaten British interests, seems to have been of less importance. In fact, neither the fear of world revolution nor Comintern activities played a significant part in British European policy during the 1920s and early 1930s. British policy towards Russia was largely determined by the Soviet threat to British imperial interests. Also, during 1923, Anglo-Russian relations were defined overwhelmingly by the tensions caused by Soviet activities in Britain's Asian empire. The Foreign Office's demand from Moscow that the Soviets behave in a civilised manner and respect British interests, British nationals and international customs, originated in British imperial needs. Its impact on European affairs was merely a welcome side-effect.

For British European policy it was fortunate that the communist menace to the European *status quo* did not materialise. The Soviet regime, in 1923, was preoccupied with stabilising its position domestically and could not embark on politically risky activities like open support for Germany. Moreover, the British realised that Soviet policy went in two different directions. Officially, Moscow backed the German government in its struggle against the Franco-Belgian occupiers, while secretly sponsoring German communist upheaval intended to overthrow the German government. The lack of open assistance for the German cause as well as moral and financial support of the German communists, frustrated Berlin and made a common policy in the Ruhr unlikely. Most of the time British officials therefore watched the development of Russo-German relations, but refrained from public comments. During the most serious moments of communist upheaval in Germany, Britain was preoccupied with her own struggle with Moscow. Once Gustav Stresemann was in power as new *Reichskanzler*, he was determined to fight communism, thus reducing the danger of Germany 'turning Red'. Under Stresemann, Berlin looked westwards for a solution to her reparation problem and a withdrawal of French troops. By the end of 1923, the interests of the two Rapallo partners appeared to be too different to pose a threat to European peace and stability.

4

The Policy of Conciliation: Rapallo and the First Labour Government

'The sun of England seems menaced by final eclipse', wrote the *English Review* after – to everyone's surprise – the Conservative Party had been defeated in the general elections of 6 December 1923. For the first time in British history Labour, in the eyes of many British 'the party of revolution . . . with the design of destroying the very bases of civilised life',[1] was to form a government. British public opinion was divided between scepticism and the desire to give Labour a chance. The question of how British socialism would distinguish itself from its Russian counterpart was particularly important in this context. This issue became even more pressing when the cabinet of Ramsay MacDonald (both prime minister and foreign secretary) established diplomatic relations with the Soviet Union as one of its first political actions.

De jure recognition of Russia, a stabilisation of the European situation, the settlement of the reparation question and the strengthening of the League of Nations had been at the core of the Labour Party manifesto during the 1923 elections. The League was particularly important as a replacement for regional alliances and as a means to establish a system of collective security. Such a framework was regarded as suitable to prevent a close Russo-German alliance against the rest of Europe in the future. This, however, did not mean that the Labour Party regarded Rapallo at any time as a serious threat. Labour considered the German–Russian alliance to be merely an economic agreement, which the Allies themselves had caused by a hostile policy. The Allied powers had simply driven Germany and Russia into each other's arms.

Labour's policy was pragmatic. European stability could not be achieved without both German and Soviet involvement. The danger was that Germany might turn eastwards if no reparation settlement was found and dissatisfaction in the country persisted. On the other hand, improving relations with Russia was considered vital for domestic reasons. Britain still faced high unemployment, and a boost in foreign trade was urgently needed. Under the Lloyd George and subsequent Conservative governments Anglo-Soviet relations had reached a deadlock, with the Foreign Office's open hostility towards Moscow blocking any initiative from business circles for a gradual approach.[2] In Labour's eyes this attitude could not be sustained

---

1 Quoted from White, *Bolshevik revolution*, 205.
2 Ibid. 175–203, 205.

without further harm to the British economy. It was therefore worth exploring whether relations could be revived. A closer co-operation between Russia and other countries would equally minimise a potential threat, both politically and economically, resulting from the treaty of Rapallo.

Labour abstained from criticising the German–Russian friendship, as it did not perceive it as a threat. The party's attitude towards Rapallo can be interpreted as one neither of sympathy, nor of hidden jealousy that Germany had achieved something – namely close relations with Moscow – which Labour itself desired. Labour leaders, despite representing workers' interests, had never been keen on greater intimacy with Soviet Russia. Their general attitude towards Moscow reflected their distance from the inhuman and undemocratic practice of Bolshevism rather than an anti-Bolshevik mentality. Patience, the search for common values and hope for a gradual change of the Soviet system characterised Labour's Russian policy which was largely formulated by its former Liberal members who had joined the Labour Party during or immediately after the First World War. This concept also flowed from Lloyd George's idea of using the civilising effect of trade and 'killing Bolshevism with kindness'.[3] The Liberal converts – among them Arthur Ponsonby, parliamentary under-secretary in the Foreign Office under MacDonald – saw a connection between the reduction of unemployment and the revival of foreign trade. They forced the party to adopt a resolution for the immediate *de jure* recognition of the Soviet government against the opposition of MacDonald who favoured a more cautious approach.

The Labour government officially established relations with Soviet Russia on 1 February 1924 without, however, appointing an ambassador.[4] The sole purpose of this declaration was to 'tame' Moscow's rulers and to integrate them into the community of nations. MacDonald's invitation to Russia and Germany to join the League of Nations was based on the same concept. But even a Labour government was not prepared to work for integration at all cost. As Lloyd George's example had shown, it was too easy for a government to fall as a result of its Russian policy. MacDonald had no intention of following suit. Hence, he was less willing to consider concessions to Moscow than to Berlin.

As far as Germany was concerned, Labour's attitude was more conciliatory than that of the Conservatives. From the outset several members sharply criticised the Versailles treaty,[5] but there had never been an official and unanimous condemnation of its provisions from the party. Labour also did not

3 See chapter 1 above. See also White, *Bolshevik revolution*, 53–4, 228–9.
4 Gorodetsky, *Truce*, 31.
5 This was not only because the final treaty was not in line with Wilson's fourteen points but also because Lloyd George had refrained from including Labour in the British delegation at the peace conference: W. Krieger, *Labour Party und Weimarer Republik. Ein Beitrag zur Außenpolitik der britischen Arbeiterbewegung zwischen Programmatik und Parteitaktik 1918–1924*, Bonn 1978, 124–8.

approve the French policy of 'productive pledges' in the Ruhr.[6] The invasion had been publicly condemned because Labour feared that it would further reduce the chances of European conciliation. Stability could only be achieved by a joint effort to come to terms by both Paris and Berlin. MacDonald faced a balancing act in his attitude towards Paris. If he made too few concessions to the French, no progress in negotiations would be made. If, however, he gave in to Poincaré's demands, he would be equally criticised. It was only clear that a Labour government would neither grant France the security guarantee that she was longing for, nor risk a rupture of the *entente* by speaking too fervently in Germany's favour.[7]

Labour was nevertheless determined to improve Germany's international situation. Once German finances were restored the country would be an important trading partner for Britain. At the London conference of July/August 1924, where final details of the Dawes plan were discussed, MacDonald urged finalising the reparation sum. The German financial situation – and with it European stability – had little chance of improving until this question, still outstanding from the treaty of Versailles, was solved. The importance which Labour attached to this question was underlined by the fact that the prime minister himself conducted the negotiations for the British side, while he left parallel Anglo-Russian talks in the hands of his parliamentary under-secretary. With the London conference, Germany re-entered European politics as a formally equal negotiation partner.

Labour and the Conservatives did not diverge in all political questions. Like any other British government, Labour would not commit Britain to a far-reaching involvement in European affairs. The party did, however, believe that world peace could only be secured by means of collective security, not through balance of power, arms races and other devices of traditional diplomacy.[8] Firmly refusing to allow Britain to act as the 'world's policeman', Labour was determined to make the League of Nations take over this task.[9]

MacDonald lost no time. In interviews and in the House of Commons he canvassed for his policy of conciliation. On 12 February 1924, he announced on the floor of the House:

I am going to use all the energy I have got to increase the representative character and the authority of the League . . . Germany must come in. I hope Russia will come in, too . . . If we wind up this week, if misfortune befalls us before the week comes to an end, we shall have made our mark on the history

6 Cowling, *Impact of Labour*, 364.
7 Sthamer to AA, 24 Jan. 1924, PA-AA, Deutsche Botschaft London, vol. 1009; Marquand, *Ramsay MacDonald*, 331–3.
8 F. S. Northedge, *The League of Nations: its life and times, 1920–1946*, 2nd edn, Leicester 1988, 91.
9 Ibid. 1. See also Müller (Bern) to AA, 12 Feb. 1924, *ADAP*, ser. A. ix, doc. 150.

of these islands, and we shall have done something in the recognition of Russia, towards the beginning of a new European policy.[10]

As a first sign of Labour's shift in its League policy, the pacifist Germanophile Lord Parmoor replaced Sir Robert Cecil who had been in charge of League affairs under the previous government. When news reached the Foreign Office that a Soviet 'freelance diplomat', M. du Chayla, had visited Sir Eric Drummond, the [British] secretary-general of the League of Nations, in order to gain information on the League in general, it was welcomed by officials as a first step towards Russian 'civilisation'.[11]

MacDonald's invitation to both Germany and Russia to join the League of Nations was a novelty in British policy. His simultaneous invitation to both countries underlined that Labour was not intimidated by a Soviet–German front. Unfortunately, MacDonald's League initiative failed to take proper consideration of the Soviet Union and Germany. While, from the German point of view, it would strengthen the League, and put heavier pressure on Poincaré to terminate his destructive policy and co-operate on the reparations question, MacDonald's initiative had the snag of not including a German or Russian seat on the council – the executive part of the League – an issue, which both countries regarded as *sine qua non*.[12] Berlin had refused all previous offers regarding League membership on these grounds[13] and thus remained sceptical of MacDonald's proposals. It was also far from certain that Russia would overcome its hostile attitude towards the League and respond favourably to MacDonald's initiative. A delegation from Geneva to Moscow suggested that the Soviet government appoint a permanent observer to Geneva similar to the American delegate at the reparations commission, but the Russian response was lukewarm.[14] MacDonald assumed that, since he bore chocolates and flowers, seduction was assured. Sadly, he failed to notice that his partners were allergic to both.

Even after the British invitation had been publicly issued, German reservations about an entry into the League without Russia were not taken seriously in Britain.[15] During a visit to London, Bernhard von Bülow, in charge of League issues at the Wilhelmstraße, expressed concern about severe

10 Parliamentary debates, HoC, 5th ser. clxxxxvi, cols 772–3, 12 Feb. 1924; MacDonald interview in *Le Quotidien*, 27 Jan. 1924, PRO, FO 371/9812/C 1538; Sthamer to AA, 24 Jan. 1924, *ADAP*, ser. A, ix, doc. 110.

11 Drummond to Cadogan, 18 Feb. 1924, PRO, FO 371/10493/N 1570. The importance of this despatch is evidenced by the fact that the minute was initialled by the leading Foreign Office members as well as by PUS Parmoor and MacDonald.

12 Müller (Bern) to AA, 12 Feb. 1924, *ADAP*, ser. A, ix, doc. 150. See also Maltzan to Sthamer, 4 Apr. 1924, PA-AA, Deutsche Botschaft London, vol. 1258.

13 See Wirth's arguments at Genoa and D'Abernon's despatches to London on this issue, the latest on 6 Feb. 1924 to MacDonald: PRO, FO 371/9820/C 2236.

14 Maltzan to Sthamer, 4 Apr. 1924, PA-AA, Deutsche Botschaft London, vol. 1258.

15 Aufzeichnung Bülow, 1 Mar. 1924, *ADAP*, ser. A, xi, doc. 176.

damage to German interests in case of a conflict, if Germany had entered the League without Russia.

Bülow's reference to the Rapallo friendship was obvious. Previous British governments had watched suspiciously any kind of German–Russian talks and had been sensitive to a revocation of the Rapallo spirit. Still, the MacDonald administration took no notice of Bülow's remarks until 3 April when the *Daily Herald* referred to Soviet–German consultations over League matters.[16] The Foreign Office now instructed D'Abernon to make enquiries, because suddenly the whole League project seemed threatened by Moscow's influence in Berlin. The hope of the Labour government rested upon Germany for political success, since Russian hostility to the League continued unabated. Accordingly, in his speech in parliament on 27 March, MacDonald referred only to German membership. Russian membership had been dropped.[17]

There was another reason for the delayed reaction of the British to Bülow's concern. Since mid-February, German diplomats had been commenting that MacDonald and Ponsonby, his parliamentary under-secretary, were over-stretched. MacDonald had obviously overestimated his capacities in taking over the posts of both prime minister and foreign secretary. Consequently, Ponsonby was overburdened with work. During a conversation with Dufour, on 23 February, Ponsonby could hardly keep his eyes open. He was also ill-informed about important political questions such as military control or reparations, and gave the impression of being lost in details and quarrels between the government and the Labour Party organisation.[18] Ambassador Sthamer reported that MacDonald's speech at the Commons on 27 March seemed unclear on many issues due to a severe lack of preparation, and complained that both MacDonald himself and the Foreign Office greeted requests for appointments with irritation.[19] It is therefore possible that the news of Russo-German consultations had been overlooked because of structural problems within the government. The burden of parallel negotiations for the new Anglo-Soviet trade agreement and for the Dawes plan reparation settlement, as well as the lack of communication between leading Foreign Office officials contributed to the weakness of British policy during 1924.

However, once Foreign Office attention was drawn to Russo-German co-operation in League matters it closely followed further developments. Maltzan and Schubert, the secretary and deputy-secretary of state at the Wilhelmstraße, had both confirmed that some arrangement, although not

---

16 *Daily Herald*, 3 Apr. 1924, PRO, FO 371/10493/N 3006.
17 D'Abernon to MacDonald, 25 Apr. 1924, D'Abernon papers, MS 48926A; Chicherin to League of Nations, 12 Mar. 1924, printed in J. Degas, *Soviet documents on foreign policy*, i, Oxford 1951, 430–4; Parliamentary debates, HoC, 5th ser. clxxi, col. 1604, 27 Mar. 1924.
18 Dufour to AA, 23 Feb. 1924, PA-AA, R 30591k (I).
19 Sthamer to AA, 1, 4 Apr. 1924, PA-AA, R 76978; Schubert to Dufour, 28 May 1924, Schubert papers, Bestand Krüger, vol. 22, pt ii; Dufour to Schubert, 3 July 1924, ibid. vol. 23.

formal, was being made between Moscow and Berlin on the basis of article 5 of the treaty of Rapallo.[20]

For the moment, MacDonald nevertheless had to give priority to political issues other than the development of the League. The negotiations for the Dawes plan, which was supposed to combine provisions for a reparation settlement with an attempt to satisfy the French demand for security, had entered into their final stage.[21] The evacuation of the Ruhr area by French troops, a reduction of French pressure on the Rhineland as well as the ever-pressing reparations problem were at the centre of German policy during these negotiations.

The negotiations were tiresome, and MacDonald did his utmost to keep the divergent interests of the powers together. Germany and France both faced imminent general elections, the outcome of which could be decisive for the continuation of talks. MacDonald therefore implored his Belgian counterparts, prime minister Theunis and foreign minister Hymans, whom he received at Chequers on 2 and 3 May, to influence France to accept the experts' provisions for the Dawes plan:

> It would be disastrous if, owing to Poincaré's unreasonable attitude, the plan were not put into operation and the last hope for a favourable and definite settlement of the reparations issue disappeared. French obstinacy, moreover, would also increase enormously the danger of Russo-German intimacy. The French felt threatened, perhaps rightly, by a thoroughly recovered and strengthened Germany with a population twice the size of the French. This danger no doubt existed. With the help of Russian manpower, resources, and other forms of assistance, Germany could become so powerful that whatever precautions France might take, there was the risk of a great catastrophe. It was, therefore, clearly in the best interest of the Allies at present not to lose the chance of settlement offered.[22]

MacDonald had never taken a Russo-German threat seriously. The fact that he played this trump card in order to put pressure on Belgium and France merely underlines the precariousness of the situation. It remained the only reference to Rapallo during the negotiations for the Dawes plan, and indeed it had the desired effect. The Belgians had no way of countering this argument and were subsequently more conciliatory. Moreover, Anglo-French relations markedly improved after the French elections, which had replaced Poincaré by the Leftist Edouard Herriot.

Despite the change of leadership, French anxiety about security continued. Britain tried in vain to convince Paris that guarantees in the case of

---

[20] D'Abernon to MacDonald, 25, 29 Apr. 1924, D'Abernon papers, MS 48926A.
[21] On the Dawes plan see W. Link, *Die amerikanische Stabilisierungspolitik in Deutschland 1921–1932*, Düsseldorf 1970; Schuker, *French predominance*, pt ii; Krüger, *Außenpolitik*, 229–47.
[22] Notes on conversation held at Chequers on 2 and 3 May 1924, PRO, FO 371/9443/C 7427.

German default were adequately covered by the treaty of Versailles and the Dawes plan. Some British officials contemplated combining the machinery of the League with the application of the experts' scheme for the Dawes plan to give it a broader authority than an Allied agreement could yield. This, they hoped, would further calm French fears. Crowe and Lampson, however, argued strongly for a separation of reparations and League issues. British policy, they suggested, should concentrate upon the introduction of the Dawes scheme, leaving other problems like inter-allied debts, security, or German League membership until later. They feared that Germany's wavering attitude towards the League, and the French demand for a security pact could only delay the application of the Dawes plan. MacDonald, finally convinced of Crowe's and Lampson's argument, gave the green light for the adoption of this strategy: 'Go steadily; the initiative must come from Germany. She must approach us before we go further.'[23]

British scepticism about German League policy was justified, as the Wilhelmstraße's attitude towards the League was ambiguous. When talking to D'Abernon and Sir Eric Drummond, Maltzan repeated Germany's principal objections to an entry into the League. Yet he also told the astonished Britons that Germany was quite prepared to enter the League without the Soviet Union joining at the same time. When Drummond pressed Maltzan on this point, the latter repeated his statement.[24] A few days later, however, D'Abernon reported that Stresemann confirmed the Soviet–German agreement to keep each other informed on League matters.[25]

Maltzan's comments nevertheless marked a change of course in Russo-German relations and Germany's attitude towards the League. While Berlin remained firm with her demands for a seat on the council and modification of the Versailles treaty, Russian approval of German membership was for the first time no longer a prerequisite. It was clear that the Rapallo 'friends' were not as close as they would have liked others to believe.[26] German–Soviet relations were in crisis. German police had searched the Soviet trade mission in Berlin for a convicted communist who had been employed by the Soviets.[27] Yet Moscow had declared unilaterally that the

---

[23] MacDonald minute, 16 June 1924, ibid. Krüger's interpretation of British policy (*Außenpolitik*, 261–3) regarding German League membership is too simplistic. Britain did not force the issue at the London conference because Foreign Office officials were convinced beforehand that the question of Germany's admission was too complicated to link to international questions, nor because Germany had managed to isolate the reparations settlement. MacDonald had made up his mind before he met Herriot at Chequers on 21–22 June 1924. He, therefore, would not consider French demands for a security pact.
[24] Wauchaupe to Lampson, 16 May 1924, PRO, FO 371/9803/C 9590.
[25] D'Abernon to FO, 21 June 1924, PRO, FO 371/9820/C 9894.
[26] This development had been noted already in Britain for some time. D'Abernon's reports since the autumn of 1922 pointed in this direction. See Preslin to Hodgson, 28 Mar. 1924, and Kiemens (Warsaw) to Gregory, 23 June 1924, PRO, FO 371/10484/N 5752; D'Abernon to A. Chamberlain, 8 Nov. 1924, D'Abernon papers, MS 48926A.
[27] Krüger, *Außenpolitik*, 267.

mission was extra-territorial. This incident, attentively observed by the British embassy in Berlin and the British press, poisoned Russo-German relations for months. Moscow tried to exploit the affair at German expense, but Britain managed to capitalise on it as well during Anglo-Russian negotiations for the trade agreement. In conversations with the Kremlin rulers, the British used the incident to express consternation about Moscow's definition of friendship, pointing out that if the Soviets treated friends in such a hostile manner what should countries with less intimate relations with the Soviet government expect? The result was a more conciliatory Russian approach to negotiations with London.[28]

Anglo-Soviet negotiations for the trade agreement proceeded slowly. The most difficult issue on the agenda was the Russian request for British credits, which London had made dependent on Moscow's acceptance of pre-war debts, and compensation for collectivised property. British financial circles would not consider the Soviets' credit demands as long as Moscow did not accept old obligations. The Soviets also demanded extra-territoriality for the Soviet trade mission in London. Britain was reluctant to meet this demand in the light of the scarcely settled dispute over the mission in Berlin, but decided to enquire in Berlin regarding the German solution to this issue.[29]

The Anglo-Soviet trade agreement was signed on 8 August 1924 without further German participation. It was sharply criticised in London by the Conservative opposition and in the city for its general character, leaving details concerning compensation of British nationals and for Russian debts open for future negotiations.[30] MacDonald's second success came one week later. On 16 August 1924, the final protocol for the Dawes plan was signed. However, two further threads remained to be tied: security and disarmament. At the League of Nations assembly in Geneva in September, Anglo-French negotiations led to what was known as the 'Geneva protocol', calling for disarmament and arbitration in the settlement of disputes.[31] Renewed efforts were made to include the Soviet Union and Germany in the system of collective security. Ponsonby questioned Rakovsky, the Soviet *chargé d'affaires* in London, over whether Moscow would now send an observer to Geneva as a first step to entering the League.[32] As far as Germany was concerned, the

---

[28] Maltzan to German embassies (Moscow, London), 11 May 1924, PA-AA, R 28281k. Only on 30 July 1924 did D'Abernon report the embassy incident to be closed: PRO, FO 371/9842/C 12199.

[29] Sthamer to AA, 9 July 1924, and reply of Maltzan to German embassy, 10 July 1924, PA-AA, R 28282k. On extra-territoriality see Maxse minute, 7 May 1924, PRO, FO 371/9842/C 7509.

[30] Sthamer to AA, 28 Aug. 1924, PA-AA, Deutsche Botschaft London, vol. 772.

[31] Marquand, *MacDonald*, 351–6; Orde, *Security*, 64–70.

[32] Runderlaß Rauscher, 4 Sept. 1924, PA-AA, Deutsche Botschaft London, vol. 772; A. E. Senn, 'The Soviet Union's road to Geneva, 1924–1927', *JbfGO* xxvii (1979), 69–84 at p. 70.

Foreign Office decided that, as long as Berlin's ambiguous attitude towards the League remained, it would continue its strategy of not pressing for a membership and await Berlin's formal application.[33] The British noted with satisfaction that Maltzan's contemplation of a German approach to the League without Russian consent indicated that the German ship had set a new course, despite a vigorous Russian press campaign intended to prevent Germany from unilateral action.[34] On the other hand, Germany continued to tie conditions to its League membership that were unacceptable to the Allies.

The Labour government did not succeed in bringing Germany or Russia into the League. It stumbled over the so-called 'Zinoviev letter' affair (the alleged Comintern letter – for it has never been proved whether it was a forgery or not – with instructions for the conduct of subversive work in Britain), and was defeated in the general election of 29 October 1924.[35] Even Labour, however, was now convinced of the need to bring Germany into the League and prevent a Soviet–German bloc.[36] This judgement had developed only gradually after visible Russian manoeuvres towards Germany.

Labour had become increasingly disillusioned with Russia. Despite a persistent lack of enthusiasm about the Soviet government and profound scepticism about communist ideology, MacDonald had hoped to 'kill Bolshevism with kindness'. To this end he had conducted tiresome negotiations with the Kremlin rulers – a strategy which proved a failure. The Bolshevik government had no intention of changing its policy. Relations with Germany, however, looked more promising. The Dawes plan was the first step towards European reconciliation. European conciliation depended on many factors, not least improving Franco-German relations. Here, the question of security stood at the centre of all countries' attention. Could the French and German definitions of security be reconciled? Would it be possible to convince Germany that the League of Nations was not related to the treaty of Versailles? Would the French ever accept that the best way of appeasing Germany was to tie her firmly to the western powers? For Britain, the alliance with France came first, beyond all doubt. But Britain's national interests needed stability in Europe. Franco-German reconciliation and a German League membership would almost certainly reduce German–Soviet intimacy, and were therefore desirable and had to be made understood in France. The major obstacle to these objectives was the treaty of Rapallo. Yet

---

[33] Lampson, Crowe and Ponsonby minutes, 13 Aug. 1924, PRO, FO 371/9820/C 13634.
[34] D'Abernon to FO, 22 Sept. 1924, PRO, FO 371/9821/C 14893; Fortlaufender Wochenbericht des AA, Berlin, 28 Sept. 1924, BA-Po, Präsidialkabinette 706; Dufour to MacDonald, 29 Sept. 1924, PRO, FO 371/9821/C 1527; Addison to MacDonald, 30 Sept. 1924, FO 371/9803/C 15354.
[35] For the Zinoviev letter affair see Gorodetsky, Truce, 35–53.
[36] FO memo, 7 Nov. 1924, PRO, FO 371/9821/C 17141.

Britain increasingly realised that the Rapallo 'friendship' was words rather than deeds. A careful and gradual policy of conciliation, British decision-makers believed, was a means of destroying Rapallo. It was left to the second Baldwin cabinet to continue on the path that Labour had paved.

5

The Battle for the German Soul: Locarno and the Treaty of Berlin

Following from secretary of state for Sir W. Tyrrell. Cock-a-doodle-do![1]

The joy was overwhelming. Months of tiresome negotiations lay behind Austen Chamberlain and his colleagues back in London, months during which the foreign secretary more than once was about to despair, either about the French, or more often about the German attitude. But patience and skilful negotiations eventually won the day. With the Locarno treaty now signed, the issue of security, the touchstone of European relations since 1919, had leaped forward a great deal. It was the breakthrough towards more amicable relations between the victors and the vanquished of the First World War, and shifted Germany's eastern orientation to a more western outlook.

By signing the treaty of Locarno, the European powers admitted that as long as they had not agreed on a set of mutually accepted principles to define 'security' a lasting peace was impossible. Given the significantly diverging national interests of the key countries, France, Germany and Great Britain, this task had not been easy. Britain often found herself sitting between all chairs because she categorically declined to give security guarantees to any single power, as this exposed her to the danger of being dragged into yet another European quarrel.

Security was the most debated issue in the mid-1920s. When the second Baldwin government took over from Labour in November 1924, it inherited from its predecessors a renewed debate on security. Ramsey MacDonald, the outgoing prime minister, and his French counterpart, Edouard Herriot, had recognised that European pacification remained illusory as long as Franco-German antagonism prevailed. The fruit of their deliberations was the Geneva 'Protocol for the pacific settlement of international disputes' of 2 October 1924, which intended to turn the League of Nations into an effective instrument for the preservation of peace. The reparation settlement under the Dawes plan, and negotiations for the Franco-Belgian withdrawal from the Ruhr area in the summer of 1924 had marked the first steps towards removing sources of friction, in this instance by forcing Paris rather than

---

1   Telegram from Locarno, 15 Oct. 1925, quoted from D. Dutton, *Austen Chamberlain: gentleman in politics*, Bolton 1985, photograph xiii.

Berlin into retreat. The Geneva protocol was therefore the tacit British acknowledgement that to some extent French demands now had to be met.[2]

The British security debate during the winter of 1924 and 1925 centred on western Europe. In contrast to Curzon, the previous Conservative foreign secretary, Austen Chamberlain was more European than empire-minded. The central purpose of his foreign policy became the formulation of a new 'concert of powers'[3] which sought to reconcile France and Germany and in which Britain would have a semi-detached, mediating role. Although Britain never lost sight of the implications for the empire as a whole in the European security debate, Chamberlain did not allow his European policy to be restricted by the dominions. As far as imperial security was concerned, the War Office concluded in early 1925 that the Soviet Union posed the greatest threat to the empire, particularly along the frontiers of Persia, Afghanistan and China. Soviet influence in western Europe, by contrast, was not seen as a potential danger to Chamberlain's western objectives.[4]

Thus, the possibility of Russian co-operation with Germany, which could have endangered European peace, played a subordinate role. Although Chamberlain's principal argument for a British commitment to France was that 'we cannot afford to see France crushed, to have Germany or an eventual Russo-German combination supreme on the continent',[5] the foreign secretary's remark must be seen more as an argument in favour of the Anglo-French alliance rather than an honest expression of concern.

---

2   On the security question related to the origins of the Geneva protocol see Orde, *Security*, 64–70; Z. S. Steiner, 'The League of Nations and the quest for security', in R. Ahmann, A. M. Birke and M. Howard (eds), *The quest for stability: problems of west European security, 1918–1957*, Oxford 1993, 35–70 at pp. 46–8.
3   Jacobson, *Soviet Union*, 167. For the following reasons I fundamentally disagree with R. Grayson's portrayal of Austen Chamberlain as trying to form a 'concert of Europe': (1) The term alludes to the nineteenth-century concert of Europe and is misleading as the political circumstances post-1919 were fundamentally different from those of the nineteenth century. Some of the states of the nineteenth-century concert were no longer in existence after 1919 (for example, Austria–Hungary). Moreover, Grayson mixes the nineteenth- century balance-of-power approach with the modern European vision of federalist, democratic and self-determining states. His approach to Chamberlain's policy suggests that Chamberlain adhered to the latter, but British foreign policy and Chamberlain's policy confirm the opposite. (2) Grayson exaggerates the role which Britain wanted to play in Europe. The Europe of the 1920s was largely designed by Britain – one of the powers responsible for the Paris peace settlements. Europe was divided into victors and vanquished, satisfied and dissatisfied powers, powers with an actual or former great power status. European security depended on the mediating British role, which London only reluctantly assumed and continually sought to reduce to the minimum possible. (3) Grayson contradicts himself repeatedly in his endeavours to attribute to the League of Nations the role of concert of Europe (for example at pp. 94–5). Primary sources give sufficient evidence that Britain sought to position the League whenever she did not want to get involved herself. The important political decisions, i.e. those vital to British interests, remained, however, outside the League's scope of action. See Grayson, *Chamberlain*, passim.
4   Jacobson, *Soviet Union*, 167.
5   Chamberlain minute, 4 Jan. 1925, *DBFP*, 1st ser. xxvii, doc. 180.

Chamberlain's undeniable preference while working on a speedy resolution of the security issue, was a British guarantee to France. A strong Francophile, with far less sympathy for Germany, he suggested an Anglo-French, or Anglo-Belgian-French security pact as an alternative to the Geneva protocol. Russia, by contrast, remained a potential trouble-spot, but, in the words of Central department official Harold Nicolson's famous memorandum of 20 February 1925:

> The Russian problem, that incessant, though shapeless menace, can be stated only as a problem; it is impossible as yet to forecast what effect the development of Russia will have on the future stability of Europe . . . The Russian problem is for the moment Asiatic rather than European; tomorrow Russia may again figure decisively in the balance of continental power; but today she hangs as a storm-cloud upon the eastern horizon of Europe – impending, imponderable, but, for the present, detached. Russia is . . . indeed the most menacing of all our uncertainties; and it must thus be in spite of Russia, perhaps even because of Russia, that a policy of security must be framed.[6]

Britain's lack of interest in eastern Europe had a longstanding tradition. Neither the Russian 'storm-cloud upon the eastern horizon of Europe' nor the knowledge that German revisionism and the treaty of Rapallo were both primarily directed against Poland, nor even Nicolson's observations that 'while . . . our minor ex-enemies [in eastern Europe] are not strong enough to create a disturbance by themselves . . . they are ready to foment the causes of insecurity and to profit by any disturbances which may elsewhere ensue', induced Britain to take a greater interest in the area. The 'natural reluctance'[7] of public opinion to recognise the newly independent Baltic states served as one explanation for the lack of interest, as well as Russia being 'much more spectacular'. More importantly, the 'rivalry and divergence of aims between ourselves and the French', and the continued instability of Polish governments, were further pretexts for British abstention. Yet this latter argument does not ring true as Anglo-French divergences were a consequence of British non-commitment, not a reason for it. Although public opinion and the differing Anglo-French policies played a role, Britain principally did not want to commit herself in Poland and the Baltic states.

French involvement in Poland was nevertheless a factor of serious concern in the British security debate during the winter of 1924/25, as Britain regarded the Polish Corridor as the only serious trouble-spot in Europe apart from Franco-German antagonism. When discussing the possibilities of a security pact with France, the Foreign Office feared that Paris would extend any guarantee automatically to Poland. From the British perspective this was impossible, since, as Austen Chamberlain paraphrased Bismarck's famous metaphor, 'no British government ever will or ever can risk the bones of a

6   Nicolson memo, 20 Feb. 1925, PRO, FO 371/10727/C 2201.
7   Gregory minute, 20 Feb. 1925, PRO, FO 371/10977/N 675.

British grenadier' in defence of the Polish Corridor.[8] If Germany one day embarked on active revisionism against Poland with Russian assistance this could turn into a new European conflict.[9] A British guarantee under these premises was out of the question, despite French urgings.

Berlin's initiative for a Rhineland security pact confirming the *status quo* on Germany's western frontiers provided an excellent way out of Britain's dilemma. The British ambassador, D'Abernon, transmitted the German proposal on 20 January 1925.[10] The German move, in fact initiated by D'Abernon,[11] was determined by a number of motives: fear that failure to satisfy the French need for security would result in the perpetual occupation of the Rhineland; concern that conciliation with the Allies would reach a dead end in the form of an Anglo-French guarantee pact; suspicion that this constellation would wreck the tentative German steps for regaining freedom of action, thus destroying Stresemann's concept of working for a peaceful return of Germany to great power status, and turn Germany again into an object of other countries' policy.[12]

The Foreign Office was initially unenthusiastic about the security pact because officials still hoped to come to a bilateral agreement with France.[13] When, after heated debates on 2 and 4 March, a cabinet majority outvoted Austen Chamberlain and rejected the Geneva protocol and a bilateral Anglo-French guarantee, the German offer seemed to provide a useful compromise for both French security and the British desire for limited commitment in Europe.

In the cabinet meeting of 4 March, Chamberlain was instructed how to explain the British withdrawal from the Geneva protocol and the support for the German proposals to the French. One of the arguments should be that 'to turn it [the German proposal] down would be to thrust Germany into the hands of Russia'.[14] Chamberlain, on his way to Geneva for the twenty-third League council meeting, stopped in Paris for talks with the French prime minister.[15] Neither he, nor Herriot, seems to have mentioned the possibility of Russia and Germany being driven into each other's arms, or a German–Russian combination against Poland if France rejected the German offer, although Franco-Polish security and the question of the Polish border were

---

8 Chamberlain to Crewe, 16 Feb. 1925, *DBFP*, 1st ser. xxvii, doc. 200.
9 D'Abernon to Chamberlain, 23 Jan. 1925, D'Abernon papers, MS 48296A.
10 D'Abernon to Chamberlain, 20 Jan. 1925 and enclosed German memorandum; D'Abernon to Chamberlain, 23 Jan. 1925, *DBFP*, 1st ser. xxvii, docs 189, 190; Jacobson, *Locarno diplomacy*, 14–21; Orde, *Security*, 83–9; Pitts, *France and the German problem*, 18–27.
11 F. G. Stambrook, ' "Das Kind" – Lord D'Abernon and the origins of the Locarno Pact', *CEH* i (1968), 233–63; Jacobson, *Locarno diplomacy*, 10–14.
12 Krüger, *Außenpolitik*, 269–70.
13 D'Abernon diary entry, 3 Feb. 1925, in D'Abernon, *Ambassador*, iii. 136–7; Jacobson, *Locarno diplomacy*, 17.
14 Cabinet conclusion 14 (25), 4 Mar. 1925, CAB 23/49.
15 Chamberlain to Crowe, 7, 8 Mar. 1925, *DBFP*, 1st ser. xxvii, docs 224, 225, 227.

discussed. The issue did not come up during the Geneva League session either, even when Chamberlain and the Polish minister for foreign affairs, Skrzynski, discussed Polish security.[16]

In its resolution of 4 March, the British cabinet obviously acknowledged the Rapallo relationship without, however, taking its threat seriously. A reference to Rapallo never failed to impress France, so ministers regarded it as a useful means of overcoming possible French resistance to the German security proposal. Hence, no action was taken.

Long and protracted negotiations followed between March and October, before the Locarno pact was eventually signed. The British had to mobilise all their skills of persuasion to convince both the French and the Germans to make certain concessions regarding Germany's entry into the League and the guarantee of Germany's borders. And, as the course of events showed, the Rapallo alliance was of greater significance than Britain and France liked. The most enthusiastic – and therefore sometimes too uncritical – interpreter of the German cause was once again the British ambassador in Berlin. Contrary to his well-meaning intentions his activities did not always facilitate the negotiation process. D'Abernon felt he had a personal 'mission' to bring about reconciliation between Germany and the west and was opposed to an Anglo-French understanding. His reports often lacked the critical distance of an outside observer, as the ambassador even actively advised the German government on how to present its policy, bearing in mind its reception in Britain.[17] D'Abernon's reports left the impression that German policy had become more conciliatory and 'reasonable', i.e. that Berlin complied with British wishes, understood that too much pressure for revision was futile, and respected the French domestic situation as well as its own. When the Foreign Office's expectations of a changing German policy did not materialise, Austen Chamberlain did not hide his annoyance and became increasingly impatient.

One of D'Abernon's most significant misjudgements was his evaluation of German–Russian relations in the run-up to Locarno. To the old Rapallo alliance suddenly a new – domestic – dimension had to be added. However, the ambassador and thus also the Foreign Office failed to appreciate this. In the German domestic debate about the pros and cons of an agreement with the western powers, the strongest opponents of Gustav Stresemann's political course were the right-wing parties.[18] They argued that a security pact with the west would automatically weaken the Rapallo friendship since it would involve an entry into the League of Nations – regarded as a hostile action in

---

[16] Chamberlain to Crowe, 14 Mar. 1925, ibid. doc. 247. See also docs 228, 232, 240, 249, 251.

[17] See, for instance, D'Abernon's negotiation tactics towards both Berlin and London during the initial stages of the security pact: Kaiser, *D'Abernon*, 373–5.

[18] R. P. Grathwol, *Stresemann and the DNVP: reconciliation or revenge in German foreign policy, 1924–1928*, Lawrence, KS 1980, 76–84; Krüger, *Außenpolitik*, 285.

Moscow – and diminish the chances of a peaceful revision of the German–Polish border. At first glance, this pro-Moscow attitude of the German Right seems implausible, and it had its share in confusing the British. Yet although ideologically fundamentally opposed to communism, the right-wing parties were first and foremost revisionist. A modification of the peace treaty could only be brought about by pressure on the victorious powers. This, again, could be best achieved by co-operation with the Soviet Union. In January 1925, however, D'Abernon repeated his conviction that 'the advent to power in Germany of a ministry with a strong bias to the Right tends rather to increase the difficulty of co-operation with the communist government in Russia.'[19] He argued that military co-operation between Germany and Russia was unlikely because the Prussian military class would not co-operate with the communists.

Yet the ambassador's assessment of Russo-German military relations was misleading. The IMCC and the War Office had numerous indications about Russo-German military co-operation and had bowed to French pressure not to evacuate the British-occupied Cologne zone because of German violations of the disarmament provisions of Versailles.[20] This, however, did not seem to have affected D'Abernon's views.[21] It is impossible to determine, though, whether he knew of the real facts and decided to gloss them over, or whether he believed in Germany's good faith.

The Foreign Office was increasingly compelled to take the Rapallo alliance into account in its considerations of the security pact.[22] Once Moscow learnt of the German initiative, Berlin came under heavy pressure not to sign a pact and to stay outside the League. D'Abernon reported strong Soviet objections for the first time on 25 February 1925.[23] A whole series of reports on this issue was to follow. Since December 1924, Moscow indeed had made desperate efforts to torpedo Berlin's *rapprochement* with the west. The Soviet offer of 24 February 1925 even included a proposal for an alliance treaty and the revision of the post-war borders according to 'ethnographic principles', later defined more precisely as joint German–Russian pressure on Poland.[24]

19 D'Abernon to Chamberlain, 23 Jan. 1925, D'Abernon papers, MS 48296A.
20 Chamberlain to D'Abernon, 12 Jan. 1925, Austen Chamberlain papers, PRO, FO 800/257, 78–81; Pitts, *France and the German problem*, 7.
21 Chamberlain to D'Abernon, 9, 12 Jan. 1925, Austen Chamberlain papers, PRO, FO 800/257, 61–2, 78–81; D'Abernon's reaction, 16 Jan. 1925, ibid. 120–2.
22 Brockdorff-Rantzau to Stresemann, 11 Mar. 1925, PA-AA, R 28222k; D'Abernon to Crowe, 11 Mar. 1925, *DBFP*, 1st ser. xxvii, doc. 234; summary of a speech by Chicherin in Hodgson to Chamberlain, 13 Mar. 1925, PRO, FO 371/11023/N 1609; FO 'Memorandum on Soviet influence on Germany in connection with the question of Germany's entry into the League and of a western security pact', 6 Apr. 1925, *DBFP*, 1st ser. xxvii, doc. 290. For the German attitude as regards article 16 in April 1925 see note of Stresemann's conversation with Krestinski, 25 Apr. 1925, PA-AA, Stresemann papers, vol. 276.
23 D'Abernon to Chamberlain, 25 Feb. 1925, *DBFP*, 1st ser. xxvii, doc. 211.
24 Aufzeichnung Brockdorff-Rantzau über Unterredung mit Rykov am 24. Feb. 1925, printed in Walsdorff, *Westorientierung*, 223–4. See also ibid. 73–5.

The reasons for Moscow's alarm, and her ceaseless endeavours to prevent Germany from fully joining the western camp, were that this called into question the fundamental precepts of post-Leninist foreign relations and challenged the Soviet security definition as formulated by Narkomindel, the Soviet Foreign Office. From Moscow's ideological perspective, the German post-Versailles problem was insoluble, and hence a conflict between the capitalist states inevitable. Such a conflict would bring about proletarian insurrection, and inter-capitalist divergencies would prevent the formation of a united anti-Soviet coalition which endangered Soviet security. According to this interpretation, the Dawes plan was the first dangerous step towards a capitalist front. Any further German *rapprochement* with the western powers, particularly if Germany joined the League of Nations and accepted article 16, would undermine the special Rapallo relationship and further threaten Soviet security, unless Moscow received sufficient guarantees from Berlin.[25]

As the Foreign Office learnt from D'Abernon, the German government did not respond to the Soviet offer for an alliance treaty. Berlin was awaiting British and French replies to the security initiative and was careful not to alienate them, no matter how strong the Russian pressure was. The Wilhelmstraße had already decided on its political priorities. Instead of looking to Moscow, it had sent a note to Geneva stressing the German willingness to join the League in principle, but expressing reservations with regard to article 16 of the covenant of the League. The note, when published, provoked great resentment in Soviet circles and prompted Chicherin, the Russian people's commissar for foreign affairs, to ask whether the German government still expected active support regarding the Polish border question if it so patently subscribed to neutrality towards Russia by entering the League.[26]

German unconditional entry into the League, with full acceptance of the covenant, was indeed the cornerstone of the negotiations for the security pact. Yet the conflict between article 16, which required unconditional German support for sanctions against an aggressor,[27] and Germany's Rapallo connection – at heart a question of whether Germany retained her eastern ties or adapted the security pact – proved a much greater stumbling block than the discussions about the German–Polish frontier and made the agreement's signing uncertain until the very end.

German entry into the League was a *conditio sine qua non* if the security scheme was to be acceptable to Britain and France. Germany had originally intended to keep the issues of the security pact and League membership apart but had to bow to the Allies' views. However, the German government argued that article 16 was incompatible with its obligations towards Russia under the treaty of Rapallo and demanded an exemption from its provisions.

[25] Jacobson, *Soviet Union*, 145–51.
[26] Walsdorf, *Westorientierung*, 68.
[27] C. M. Kimmich, *Germany and the League of Nations*, Chicago 1976, 65–7.

This request was strongly resisted by both Britain and France and provoked protracted discussions until a compromise acceptable to all parties was found.

The second controversial issue between Germany and the western powers during the negotiations for the security pact was the German–Polish border. Germany refused to sign anything that excluded the possibility of revising this border by peaceful means at a later date. The Rapallo friendship was manifest also in this matter, as the Soviets had repeatedly and publicly supported Germany in her demand. Under certain circumstances, Chamberlain was prepared to be more sympathetic to the German request that the German–Polish frontier should not be guaranteed:

> If she [Germany] comes into the League and plays her part there in a friendly and conciliatory spirit, I myself believe that within a reasonable number of years she will find herself in a position where her economic and commercial support is so necessary and her political friendship so desirable to Poland that, without having recourse to the League machinery, she will be able to make a friendly arrangement on her own account directly with the Poles.[28]

Chamberlain's attitude was in line with the Foreign Office, which did not have the slightest intention of committing itself in eastern Europe despite countless Polish requests for a British guarantee of their borders. Chamberlain told Skrzynski, the Polish foreign minister, that he had frankly 'no idea of signing any pact which included a reference to the eastern frontiers of Germany'.[29] Britain saw even less need for doing so since the German government confirmed that it intended to work under article 19 for peaceful revision, that it had no ambitions at present, and certainly none using force.[30] With growing pressure from Warsaw the Foreign Office's patience diminished rapidly. 'I do not see that the Poles have any first cause of complaint – indeed, rather the contrary, for we have extracted from the German government a disavowal of any intention to use force towards the eastern frontier', minuted Miles Lampson, now the head of the Central department. Chamberlain added that 'nothing would have been said about the Polish frontier if it had not been certain that silence on that point would have been met with a cry'.[31]

The eastern frontier question remained an issue of secondary importance as long as the proposed arbitration treaties with Poland and Czechoslovakia were signed. Chamberlain intended to advance quickly with the negotiations for the other aspects of the security pact, hoping 'that the German reply will make it clear beyond a shadow of doubt or contention that . . . Germany will

---

28 Chamberlain to D'Abernon, 1 Mar. 1925, *DBFP*, 1st ser. xxvii, doc. 255.
29 Chamberlain to Crowe, 14 Mar. 1925; Chamberlain to D'Abernon, 18 Mar. 1925, ibid. docs 247, 255.
30 D'Abernon to Crowe, 13 Mar. 1925; D'Abernon to Chamberlain, 17 Mar. 1925; Chamberlain to D'Abernon, 25 Mar. 1925, ibid. docs 242, 254, 269. See also the German report on the HoC debate in Sthamer to AA, 30 Mar. 1925, PA-AA, R 76978.
31 Lampson, Chamberlain minutes, 6 May 1925, PRO, FO 371/10731/C 6093.

seek admittance to the League without any other condition'.[32] Chamberlain's expectations were disappointed precisely because Germany was not prepared to enter the League if she had to accept article 16 as it stood. Moreover, Russian pressure further increased.[33]

Russian influence, together with German right-wing opposition to the security pact, had forced *Reichskanzler* Luther and foreign minister Stresemann to enter into economic negotiations with the Soviet government, and to extend them into secret talks for a political preamble which was at the edge of incompatibility with article 16.[34] When the British learnt of these talks they were indignant. They failed to understand why Germany embarked on commercial negotiations with Moscow parallel to the talks with the western powers. Yet Stresemann, like all German politicians before and after him, always had to conduct his foreign policy with an eye to its domestic reception and, in the run-up to Locarno, particularly with an eye to the right-wing groups in the *Reichstag*. This forced him to make both verbal and material concessions to his political opponents and sometimes made him appear dissatisfied, intransigent and unpredictable in his demands.[35] There is no doubt that Stresemann worked first and foremost for national interests, i.e. for the revision of the peace treaties. Yet he was a moderate, aiming at revision only within the limits of political feasibility and reality. International revision could be brought about only by means of reconciliation and peaceful change. For Stresemann, resorting to force was out of the question.[36]

Chamberlain, unaware of the complicated German domestic situation, was often annoyed with what he regarded as Germany's political ingratitude. From his perspective, Germany had to acknowledge that the Allies negotiated with her increasingly on an equal footing, and he expected Berlin to reward this:

> I regard it as the first task of statesmanship to set to work to make the new position of Germany tolerable to the German people in the hope that as they regain prosperity under it they may in time become reconciled to it and be unwilling to put their fortunes again to the desperate hazard of war. I am working not for today or tomorrow but for some date like 1960 or 1970 when German strength will have returned and when the prospect of war will again cloud the horizon unless the risks are still too great to be rashly incurred and the actual conditions too tolerable to be jeopardised on a gambler's throw . . . I

32 Chamberlain to Max Muller, 3 Apr. 1925, *DBFP*, 1st ser. xxvii, doc. 287.
33 Addison to Chamberlain, 25 Apr. 1925; D'Abernon to Chamberlain, 3 May 1925, ibid. docs 296, 305.
34 Walsdorff, *Westorientierung*, 108–23; Krüger, *Außenpolitik*, 294.
35 D'Abernon to Chamberlain, 29 Mar. 1925, Austen Chamberlain papers, PRO, FO 800/257, 462–3; Sthamer to Schubert, 28 Apr. 1925, PA-AA, R 28378k.
36 On the Stresemann controversy see W. Michalka and M. Lee (eds), *Gustav Stresemann*, Darmstadt 1982; Krüger, *Außenpolitik*, 284–6; M. O. Maxelon, *Stresemann und Frankreich 1914–1929. Deutsche Politik in der Ost-West-Balance*, Düsseldorf 1972, 88–9; C. Baechler, *Gustave Stresemann: de l'impérialisme à la sécurité collective*, Strasbourg 1996.

believe the key to the solution is to be found in allaying French fears, and that unless we find means to do this we may be confronted with complete breakdown of our friendly relations with France and an exacerbation of her attitude towards Germany.[37]

Chamberlain's frustration is understandable and not surprising. His position was also difficult. He had to reconcile the different German and French views whilst at the same time guarding British interests. France gave consideration to the German security proposals only because she knew that Britain would not commit herself to anything other than a security pact which included Berlin. Yet German remarks in March 1925 seemed to confirm French fears about German aggressiveness, and hence their need for security.[38] While believing that Paris's demand for security was exaggerated, Chamberlain nevertheless had to convince the Germans that Berlin had to make some allowances as *quid pro quo* for Allied concessions. In March 1925, Chamberlain made himself the advocate of German interests by pressing France to move on the question of evacuating the Cologne zone, and demanded a seat for Germany on the League council.

A set of unfortunate circumstances prevented a reward for Chamberlain's endeavours. In May 1925, the Wilhelmstraße was still waiting for a reaction from Paris on the security scheme. This reply had been delayed because the Herriot government faced severe domestic opposition to the scheme and fell from power in April 1925. The new government, with Briand as foreign secretary, disapproved of Herriot's draft reply, formulated its own note and found it necessary to discuss the draft for four weeks with the British before it was finally transmitted to Berlin. At the same time, Stresemann came under heavy Nationalist pressure to abandon the western negotiations for closer co-operation with Moscow. The German attitude, especially towards article 16, stiffened the longer France remained silent and uncertainty about her reasons increased. Chamberlain was indignant:

> Just at this moment when things really look promising and when the French attitude is better than I should have hoped, I am terribly afraid lest the Germans should commit some fault. If you show the least inclination to give a German an inch he always thinks that his proper policy is to take an ell and this is fatal to success.[39]

In September 1925, he complained to D'Abernon:

> Your Germans – I use the possessive pronoun as one says to one's wife: *your* housemaid – are very nearly intolerable. From first to last very nearly every obstacle to the Pact negotiations has come from them. Briand has almost

---

37 Chamberlain to Stamfordham, 9 Feb. 1925, Austen Chamberlain papers, PRO, FO 800/257.
38 Pitts, *France and the German problem*, 42.
39 Chamberlain to Cecil, 5 June 1925, Cecil papers, BL, MS 51078.

taken my breath away by his liberality, his conciliatoriness, his strong and manifest desire to promote peace. The German attitude has been just the contrary – niggling, provocative, crooked . . . At every stage the Germans sow distrust in my mind. At every stage Briand disproves the common assertion that the difficulty is now with France.[40]

Chamberlain's attitude towards Germany and France had changed since the genesis of the security initiative. The foreign secretary saw himself as the 'honest broker', 'perhaps even a little more honest . . . than the author of that famous phrase'[41] but overestimated what was politically feasible and both London's and his personal influence in France and Germany. For Chamberlain there was no doubt that France could only make concessions on the security question if Germany likewise reduced her revisionist demands. He was usually willing to take account of French domestic pressures on foreign policy. Chamberlain accepted that the French delayed their answer to the German security pact for four months, four weeks of which he spent discussing it in detail with Briand. Briand would do almost everything to secure some form of *entente* with Britain and largely followed Chamberlain's lead in the negotiation process.

In contrast, Stresemann was not prepared to abandon German revisionist demands for some *rapprochement* with the western powers and therefore complied less readily with British wishes. Chamberlain, unable to assess the domestic pressures on Stresemann correctly – partly due to D'Abernon's inaccurate reporting – became impatient and felt confirmed in his longstanding prejudices.

June was a critical month for the security scheme. The French reply to the German offer, the tenor of which the Foreign Office had influenced considerably, was due. Progress in the negotiations now depended on its reception in Germany. Annoyed about the French and under Russian pressure, Berlin was less ready to compromise during the forthcoming negotiations. Stresemann told D'Abernon on 10 June that 'We cannot forego the Russian connection, such as it is, without having something positive on the other side . . . I have a stiff fight in front of me.'[42] Generally, however, Stresemann resisted the temptation of playing the Rapallo card, preferring instead to concentrate on the critical issue of article 16, although it contained an important Soviet dimension.[43] However, Chamberlain's concern grew that this might endanger both

---

[40] Chamberlain to D'Abernon, 10 Sept. 1925, Austen Chamberlain papers, PRO, FO 800/258, 556–7.

[41] Chamberlain to Crewe, 2 Apr. 1925, Austen Chamberlain papers, BUL, AC 52/200.

[42] D'Abernon diary entry, 11 June 1925, in D'Abernon, *Ambassador*, iii. 3, 169.

[43] Walsdorff, *Westorientierung*, 114. Article 16 implied the participation in sanctions under the League covenant. Germany was unwilling to accept these provisions due to her geographical position, which she saw could lead to her becoming a military battleground, and because she would have to give up her neutrality in case of sanctions being applied to the Soviet Union.

the security pact and the German entry into the League. Traditional British interests clashed with traditional German ties. Exasperated, Chamberlain wrote to Amery that

> if we turn down the German proposals, Germany will not enter the League of Nations – if she enters it at all – because we insist upon this as a condition of the mutual guarantee. Russia is putting the strongest pressure on Germany to prevent her from coming to an agreement with France or Britain, and no less to prevent her from entering the League of Nations, and fear of Russia plays a great part in German policy. It was an essential factor of the Bismarckian policy that Germany should keep always on good terms with Russia, and the Germans, looking back on the rupture with Russia that followed upon Bismarck's fall and upon the events of 1914, are inclined to attribute all subsequent disasters to the breach of these friendly relations with Russia. This view . . . was confirmed . . . out of the mouth of the German Consul-General at Geneva. At the present time it is a case of 'pull devil, pull baker'. It will take all our influence and all our co-operation to secure the triumph of the peaceful baker over the Soviet devil.[44]

The negotiations went ahead slowly but steadily. The German reply to the French note of 16 June, initially much criticised by Chamberlain[45] because of its uncompromising attitude on the issues of arbitration and article 16, provided a useful basis for further negotiations. Chamberlain was relieved that 'the points raised on the German side . . . are juristic rather than substantial and ought in themselves to cause no great difficulty'.[46] The legal experts' meeting in London brought a *rapprochement* of the different positions on all but the issues of a French guarantee for the Polish arbitration treaty, and article 16. Russo-German relations cooled during July 1925. Negotiations with Russia for the commercial treaty and a political preamble nonetheless continued; the German cabinet approved the draft at the end of September.[47]

The Foreign Office paid little attention to Russian pressure on Germany over the summer. It was absorbed by upheaval in China, for which several

---

[44] Chamberlain to Amery, 19 June 1925, Austen Chamberlain papers, BUL, AC 52/38.

[45] See, for instance, Chamberlain to D'Abernon, 29 July 1925, Austen Chamberlain papers, PRO, FO 800/258, 369–72; Chamberlain to D'Abernon, 30 July 1925, *DBFP*, 1st ser. xxvii, doc. 431.

[46] Chamberlain to D'Abernon, 17 July 1925, *DBFP*, 1st ser. xxvii, doc. 416; Kimmich, *Germany*, 71–2. Germany had advanced on article 16 by dropping the condition of absolute neutrality and accepting a formula of interpretation which would release her *de facto* from the provisions. It is difficult to agree with Kimmich that the objections to article 16 were only maintained in order to placate the right and the Russians. Although the Luther–Stresemann government was in principle western-orientated, Russia was always a useful bargaining card against the west as long as the revision of the Versailles treaty had not been completed. It was in the German government's own interest to keep the Russian link, and the pressure of the right and the Russians, though inconvenient at times, served as a useful cover.

[47] Walsdorff, *Westorientierung*, 118–23, 127–32.

die-hard anti-Bolshevik cabinet members held Moscow responsible.[48] Although there was actually little evidence for Moscow's engagement in China, Chamberlain was hard pressed to break off diplomatic relations. Since coming to power the Conservatives had paid little attention to Anglo-Soviet relations. After the Zinoviev letter affair the Foreign Office believed that diplomatic isolation would bring Russia to reason, and conducted a 'policy of doing nothing', ignoring Moscow as far as possible. Chamberlain was against a breach with the Soviets because he feared the consequences for European and imperial affairs, particularly its effect on Germany at the present moment.[49] Eventually, surrendering to Home Office pressure, he adopted a stiffer line towards Russia.

Unrest in the Far East continued to absorb most of the foreign secretary's attention during the summer of 1925. He therefore paid less attention to Russian interventions in Germany against the security pact than he would perhaps have wished.

Chicherin launched a last coup in his attempt to prevent Germany from signing the security pact. From 27 to 29 September he paid a visit to Warsaw, complaining that Britain was organising an anti-Soviet front and proposing a Russian–Polish non-aggression pact.[50] Next he travelled to Berlin where he saw Stresemann on 1 October at the unusual hour of 10.30 p.m. Political arm-wrestling went on until 1.30 a.m., but Chicherin's attempt to blackmail Stresemann by renewing his December proposal for a fourth division of Poland proved futile. He succeeded, however, in getting the foreign minister's firm promise that Germany would neither voluntarily recognise the Polish border, nor strain Russo-German relations even if Germany's reservations against article 16 were not accepted.[51]

With these promises Stresemann went to Locarno to negotiate the final details of the security pact. The conference went ahead in the most amicable spirit. Lampson was carried away with enthusiasm when he wrote to Tyrrell:

> I admit having been thrilled to the bone once or twice by the eloquence and obvious sincerity of both Briand and Stresemann. Yesterday, over the question of Germany's entry into the League, they were both at their best and I have never before had the good fortune to hear a discussion conducted at so high a plane. It was really wonderful.[52]

In this friendly atmosphere the outstanding problems, especially Germany's entry into the League, were solved. Stresemann and Luther again argued at great length that Germany could not accept article 16 as it stood, for fear that

---

[48] Crewe to Phipps, 16 July 1925, Phipps papers, CCAC, PHPP 2/2; Gorodetsky, *Truce*, 67–73; Jacobson, *Soviet Union*, 168–9.
[49] Chamberlain to Baldwin, 24 July 1925, Austen Chamberlain papers, BUL, AC 52/81.
[50] Max Muller to Chamberlain, 23, 29 Sept. 1925, *DBFP*, 1st ser. xxv, docs 490, 492, 493.
[51] Walsdorff, *Westorientierung*, 132–8.
[52] Lampson to Tyrrell, 9 Oct. 1925, *DBFP*, 1st ser. xxvii, doc. 529.

if she had to support sanctions she would be dragged into a war with Moscow for which she was militarily too weak.[53] Before mentioning the USSR, they had, however, reassured the other delegations that there was no German–Russian alliance, and that Chicherin's visit to Berlin had nothing to do with this demand. During a private visit on 8 October, Stresemann gave Chamberlain a detailed account of the talks with Chicherin, omitting, however, any reference to their discussion over Poland. Chamberlain was also, for the first time, acquainted with the reasons for the strong pro-Russian sentiments among the German Nationalists, although it is doubtful whether he really understood the importance of this fact for the German domestic situation. Chamberlain was 'perfectly satisfied' with Stresemann's explanations and told him that while he had never intended to detach Germany from Russia, he had a very real desire not to throw Germany into Soviet arms by denying her opportunities of friendship or even normal relations.[54]

The Locarno treaty was initialled on 16 October; the arbitration treaty with Poland signed on the German line. Russia succeeded in preventing a German guarantee of the Polish frontier, but had to acquiesce to Germany joining the League. D'Abernon reported from Berlin that Chicherin, recognising the futility of further efforts to influence the German government, was now considering Russia's membership of the League.[55] Chamberlain was highly satisfied. To Briand he said that the effect of their work at Locarno was already becoming apparent.[56]

Nothing could disturb the joy of Locarno, not even the news of the Russo-German commercial treaty signed in Moscow on 12 October. Little information was available, but counsellor Peters in Moscow was sceptical as to its effectiveness.[57] The 'Locarno spirit' was the new magic formula, which would hopefully solve future problems between the powers. On their return from Locarno, the British delegation was given a triumphant reception in London. Honorary dinners were held to celebrate Chamberlain's success, and parliament overwhelmingly approved the treaties on 18 November 1925.[58]

Even Anglo-Soviet relations seemed to benefit from Locarno. The Foreign Office was pleased that Russian policy had been shaken severely by the agree-

[53] Chamberlain to Tyrrell, 8 Oct. 1925, ibid. doc. 522.
[54] Chamberlain to Tyrrell, 8 Oct. 1925, ibid. doc. 521. See also undated and unsigned Aufzeichnung über Unterredung mit A. Chamberlain, PA-AA, R 28222k.
[55] D'Abernon to FO, 13 Oct. 1925, PRO, FO 371/11027/N 5793.
[56] Ibid; D'Abernon to FO, 15 Oct. 1925, PRO, FO 371/11027/N 5793; D'Abernon to Chamberlain, 14 Oct. 1925, Austen Chamberlain papers, BUL AC 38/1/1; Chamberlain memo, 16 Oct. 1925, DBFP, 1st ser. xxv, doc. 332.
[57] Peters to Chamberlain, 9 Oct. 1925, DBFP, 1st ser. xxv, doc. 331; D'Abernon to Chamberlain, 29 Oct. 1925, Austen Chamberlain papers, BUL, AC 38/1/1. See also Stresemann's undated 'Aufzeichnung zu den deutsch-russischen Wirtschaftsverhandlungen', stamped 30 Sept. 1925, BA-Po Präsidialkanzlei 708/3, vol. 4.
[58] Parliamentary debates, HoC, 5th ser. clxxxviii, cols 419–34, 18 Nov. 1925. For the wide press coverage in Germany see BA-Po, Deutsche Botschaft Moskau 09.02, vol. 473.

ments. Moscow, isolated in face of the 'Locarno spirit', was looking for a new orientation, and seemed eager to improve relations with Britain despite renewed anti-British propaganda. London, however, saw no advantage in welcoming the Soviets with open arms. No new political direction had so far become apparent in Russia. Moreover, a rushed Russian *rapprochement* with the west would have overburdened the security scheme. Having to 'digest' Germany was a difficult task to master for the League. Coping with two countries at the same time would have been impossible. Also, quarrels with Germany and Poland could be tackled more easily if Russia remained outside the League. It would serve British interests best to continue its waiting policy.[59]

The same relaxed attitude did not apply to British policy towards Germany. The euphoria about Locarno soon gave way to a feeling of indignation. With a mixture of anger and disappointment Chamberlain and his colleagues noticed the – in their views excessive – German demands for complete evacuation of the Rhineland as well as serious opposition to the Locarno treaties on the part of right-wing German Nationalists, the DNVP. Chamberlain, who worried that his *opus magnum* was in danger, saw all his prejudices against Germany re-confirmed.[60]

> On every side in fact we have done our part to wipe out the war spirit and to co-operate with Germany in building up in common a new Europe on truly pacific lines. What has been Germany's reply? In hardly a single point have the German government come forward with any offer to meet our desires . . . Cannot Dr Luther and Dr Stresemann realise that M. Briand no less than themselves has a public opinion to deal with? We do not under-estimate the difficult position and indeed the weakness of the present German government but the conviction is inevitable that that weakness has been, and is being, deliberately used to squeeze concessions out of the western powers.[61]

There is no doubt that Chamberlain's complaints were partly justified. Germany's expectations as to what good might come from Locarno were exaggerated and highly unrealistic, and it was Stresemann's fault to have encouraged such hopes.[62] On the other hand, Chamberlain failed to understand that a major reason for Stresemann playing on Locarno's positive ramifications for Germany was his attempt to appease right-wing opposition to it. The British foreign secretary simply could not imagine what it meant for a German foreign minister to be confronted with an irrational opposition, that Stresemann was walking a tightrope to get the Locarno treaties passed in the

---

[59] Gregory memo, 1 Nov. 1925, *DBFP*, 1st ser. xxv, doc. 46.
[60] Chamberlain felt confirmed by an entirely negative report on the characteristics of the 'German race' by Addison, the counsellor in Berlin: Addison to Chamberlain, 10 Dec. 1925, ibid. doc. 141; Jacobson, *Locarno diplomacy*, 66–7.
[61] Chamberlain to D'Abernon, 1 Feb. 1926, *DBFP*, 1st ser. xxv, doc. 231.
[62] Orde, *Security*, 146–54; Jacobson, *Locarno diplomacy*, 66–8.

Reichstag. One slip that resulted in stronger than expected opposition from the right would result in Stresemann's and the government's political destruction, and the end of the 'Locarno spirit'.

Locarno was soon put to the test with Germany's entry into the League of Nations. Luther and Stresemann had managed to get their new government together just in time to submit the formal German application for the extraordinary session in March 1926. Major obstacles arose, however, when Warsaw, closely followed by Spain and Brazil, also demanded a permanent seat on the council. Briand and Chamberlain supported the Polish claim,[63] but Polish equality with the status of a great power was an anathema to Germany. The crisis was shelved temporarily by postponing German League membership until September, leaving all parties time for consideration. The first storm facing Locarno was thus weathered, but it was little more than a squall compared to the one that was already looming on the horizon.

The new storm confronting the Locarno powers was provoked by Russia and Germany announcing their intention to sign another bilateral treaty. This was a severe blow to the 'Locarnites' who had hoped to take the wind out of Rapallo's sails by wooing Germany into the western orbit. The Foreign Office was surprised at the news of Russo-German negotiations. Once again the British ambassador in Berlin was at fault. Schubert had informed D'Abernon about Soviet desires to put into writing the interpretation of article 16 reached at Locarno, as early as 22 December 1925. The following day the ambassador wired to London various other aspects of his conversation with Schubert, but was noticeably silent on the Soviet issue.[64] On 30 March 1926, the ambassador commented on Russian delight at the failure of Germany to enter the League[65] but also on the apparent confusion within Germany.

> Before Geneva there was a vague intention to give Russia some sort of consolation for her failure to prevent Germany's entry into the League of Nations. The idea is reported to have been discussed in various forms – one being a treaty of neutrality – but nothing very concrete was decided upon.[66]

This latter despatch, however, only reached the Foreign Office on 6 April. Officials were therefore completely taken aback when, on 1 April, D'Abernon transmitted Schubert's announcement that the treaty would be signed in the

---

63 Krüger, *Außenpolitik*, 312–15; Kimmich, *Germany*, 76–92; D. Carlton, 'Great Britain and the League council crisis of 1926', *HJ* xi (1968), 354–64; Pitts, *France and the German problem*, 112–14.

64 Aufzeichnung Stresemann on conversation with D'Abernon, 22 Dec. 1925, PA-AA, ORu, vol. 5. See also Aufzeichnung Stresemann on conversation with Laboulaye, 22 Dec. 1925, *ADAP*, ser. B, ii/1, doc. 1; D'Abernon to Tyrrell, 23 Dec. 1925, *DBFP*, 1A ser. i, doc. 158; Walsdorff, *Westorientierung*, 176.

65 D'Abernon to Chamberlain, 30 Mar. 1926, received at Foreign Office, 31 Mar. 1926, *DBFP*, 1A ser. i, doc. 383.

66 D'Abernon to FO, 30 Mar. 1926, received at Foreign Office, 6 Apr. 1926, ibid. doc. 384.

near future.[67] Foreign Office officials were not very happy about the announcement, but, as Tyrrell wrote, 'it would be a mistake on our part not to accept this as a *fait accompli* and make the best of it . . . by intensifying our present policy of encouraging Germany to look west and not east'.[68] They criticised the ill-chosen moment for the treaty's publication so soon after the abortive League meeting, but were grateful that the surprise caused by Rapallo was not repeated and were inclined to trust Stresemann's reassurances. Gregory pointed out that thankfully the treaty did not look like a Bismarckian reassurance treaty, and that Germany should be encouraged with 'every incentive and motive for entrenching herself more solidly under the Locarno shelter'.[69]

The Foreign Office worried, however, about French and Polish reactions to the Russo-German agreement and busily tried to limit the possible damage done to the Locarno spirit. Chamberlain immediately instructed D'Abernon that Stresemann must, under no circumstances, interpret the terms of article 16. 'He must please bear in mind that the German claim to be "neutral" was absolutely declined as quite inconsistent with the Covenant.' Moreover, the article's obligations were *against the aggressor* and applied to all members of the League.[70]

Chamberlain also briefed ambassador Crewe in Paris on the Foreign Office's attitude. Weighing advantages and disadvantages of either putting pressure on Germany to prevent the agreement being signed, or accepting the *fait accompli*, the foreign secretary strongly advocated the latter. Germany had given sufficient categorical assurances that the new treaty was no departure from Locarno. Moreover, by adopting this course,

> Russia's last effort to wreck the western *entente* would have come to nought; the position of the German government *vis-à-vis* the opposition to them in Germany on the extreme Right and Left would have been strengthened; and it would become easier with Germany in the solution of present problems, thus encouraging her to realise that her interests were best served by facing west rather than east.[71]

---

[67] D'Abernon to FO, 1 Apr. 1926, ibid. docs 391, 392.

[68] Tyrrell, Gregory minutes, 5, 6 Apr. 1926, PRO, FO 371/11791/N 1489.

[69] From the documents he quotes it is difficult to follow Gorodetsky's view that the Northern department suggested that Germany was trying to exert pressure on Britain to review its policy towards Russia. The department was very much in accord with Chamberlain's concern about the effect of the treaty on France, Poland and the League, and particularly on whether or not the treaty would damage Locarno. Officials also supported Chamberlain's policy of ignoring Russia to bring her to reason: Gorodetsky, *Truce*, 140.

[70] Chamberlain to D'Abernon, 7 Apr. 1926, *DBFP*, 1A ser. i, doc. 400; Aufzeichnungen Schubert, 9 Apr. 1926, *ADAP*, ser. B, ii/1, docs 117, 118 (original emphasis).

[71] Orde to Crewe, 10 Apr. 1926, *DBFP*, 1A ser. i, doc. 412. Gorodetsky overemphasises the importance of the treaty of Berlin being considered in France as anti-British. Only from the Soviet perspective was the treaty directed against Britain. Moscow was arguing constantly that Britain was organising an anti-Russian front and now claimed victory as these alleged

In addition, the Foreign Office worked hard to calm Czech and Polish fears.[72] Chamberlain, however, could not free himself from his doubts about Berlin's honesty or his annoyance at their renewed political double game. He resented the German ingratitude regarding Allied concessions and Berlin's continuing presentation of further demands without, however, giving anything in return, as the new Russo-German treaty demonstrated. Moreover, German outbursts against Poland in the context of the new agreement seemed to raise the worst fears about German intentions:

> If Germany makes a treaty with Russia he [Schubert] professes astonishment that anyone should suggest a doubt or a criticism. If Poland holds a conversation with Russia even though nothing results Poland is 'stirring up animosity and hatred against Germany' . . . Ask Stresemann what is the German equivalent for the English proverb sauce for goose is sauce for gander. As long as Germans persist in treating Poles as pariahs it does not lie in their mouths to complain of Polish ill-will to Germany. It is Germany's own fault if Polish–German relations do not improve.[73]

Chamberlain was even more alarmed when the Russo-German treaty was published on 26 April 1926. He agreed with his colleagues that both text and attached letters were 'full of obscurities', and their language 'extraordinarily ambiguous'.[74] Article 3 of the treaty seemed particularly objectionable and needed explanation. Chamberlain could barely conceal his anger. He complained to D'Abernon that 'Germany's chief preoccupation is "to run with the hare and hunt with the hounds" '.[75] As appropriate action, the Foreign Office suggested issuing a public declaration that the treaty's provisions did not run against the League covenant and Locarno.[76]

At the same time, the Foreign Office needed all its skills of persuasion to hold the French excitement in check. Before the treaty was published, Chamberlain and Briand had agreed on the inadvisability of lodging any

British endeavours had been frustrated by the new Russo-German agreement. No country in Europe took this irrational Soviet attitude seriously, and it influenced neither the French nor the British attitude towards the Russo-German treaty. What mattered both for Paris and London was the German attitude, and whether or not the new treaty was a departure from Locarno: Gorodetsky, *Truce*, 140.

[72] Max Muller to Chamberlain, 12 Apr. 1926; Chamberlain to Clerk, 13 Apr. 1926; Chamberlain to Max Muller, 13 Apr. 1926, *DBFP*, 1A ser. i, docs 414, 413, 420; Aufzeichnung Schubert, 22 Apr. 1926, *ADAP*, ser. B, ii/1, doc. 157.

[73] Chamberlain to D'Abernon, 24 Apr. 1926, *DBFP*, 1A ser. i, doc. 459. Chamberlain referred to Schubert's outburst reported in D'Abernon to Chamberlain, 23 Apr. 1926, ibid. doc. 450.

[74] Orde minute, 27 Apr. 1926, PRO, FO 371/11792/N 1928; Orde minute, 27 Apr. 1926, PRO, FO 371/11323/C 5162; Troutbeck memo, 22 June 1926, PRO, FO 371/11325/C 7180.

[75] Chamberlain to D'Abernon, 28 Apr. 1926, PRO, FO 371/11324/N 1954.

[76] Record of conversation between Lampson and the German ambassador, 28 Apr. 1926, PRO, FO 371/11323/C 5150; Sthamer to AA, 27 Apr. 1926, *ADAP*, ser. B, ii/1, doc. 178.

protest in Berlin.[77] Grahame, the British minister, now reported from Brussels that a committee of Quai d'Orsay officials had examined the treaty, found it execrable, and questioned whether Germany ought now to be admitted into the League of Nations.[78] This was very disquieting news. If the French raised objections against German entry into the League as a punishment for the Russo-German treaty, this would endanger Locarno, as its effectiveness hinged on German League membership. A co-ordinated Anglo-French response to the treaty was more vital than ever. Lampson told the French ambassador at a dinner that it was hardly for France to be too critical, since it was her ill-timed proposal to give Poland a permanent seat on the League council, which had set the Russo-German ball rolling. 'He [de Fleuriau] laughed and did not deny that to some extent it was true. I did *not* add (which we all know) that it was the transfer of M. Laroche from the *Quai d'Orsay* to Warsaw as ambassador last autumn which originally freed the train.'[79]

In the meantime Sir Cecil Hurst, the British legal adviser, had thoroughly examined the Russo-German treaty and found its text compatible with Locarno and the covenant in all controversial points.[80] Hence, when on 3 May the Foreign Office received the official French note containing the major French objections to the treaty and demanding precise written explanations from Berlin on the critical points, officials were at pains to convince France of the inopportunity of such action. Tyrrell and Hurst even went to Paris to calm tempers.[81] A detailed *aide-memoire* outlining the British legal views was handed to Briand on 5 May. Lampson was close to despair at the French attitude. He wrote to Eric Phipps, the envoy extraordinary in Paris, on 6 May:

Are the French really quite mad? Do they realise that (apart from pushing Germany further into the arms of Russia, which they seem set on doing) any failure to bring Germany into the League means the non-entry into force of our guarantee under Locarno? Do they realise that if they lose Locarno they lose *almost certainly* for all *time* all chance for a guarantee from us?[82]

In his reply Phipps had quite a simple and chauvinistic explanation for French behaviour:

I do not think the French are really mad, but they are very feminine. Perhaps you will be unkind enough to say that the two things are almost identical.

---

[77] Crewe to Chamberlain, 13 Apr. 1926, *DBFP*, 1A ser. i, doc. 421.
[78] Grahame to FO, 29 Apr. 1926, PRO, FO 371/11323/C 5205.
[79] Lampson minute, 30 Apr. 1926, PRO, FO 371/11324/C 5369.
[80] FO minute Hurst, 29 Apr. 1926, ibid.
[81] De Fleuriau to Chamberlain, received 3 May 1926, PRO, FO 371/11324/C 5334; Tyrrell minute, 4 May 1926, ibid; Stresemann to Brockdorff-Rantzau, 9 May 1926, PA-AA, R 28223k.
[82] Lampson to Phipps, 6 May 1926, PRO, FO 371/11324/C 5436 (original emphasis).

They are certainly at present in a very pettish frame of mind, but it must be admitted that things have not gone any too well for them lately.

Phipps referred to the long line of French diplomatic defeats – the Ruhr crisis, the Dawes plan, the fall of the franc and colonial problems:

> In the political sphere the recent Russo-German convention has been the bitterest pill of all for the French to swallow . . . We must not . . . take things too tragically, for after all Berthelot, brilliant and clever as he is, is only a tail, and seems with time, less and less able to wag the Briand dog, who, I feel convinced, having staked everything on Locarno, will continue to make every sacrifice in order to carry through that policy . . . If we 'nurse' frightened France, provided British public and parliamentary opinion permit such treatment until the entry of Germany into the League, I feel sure that we shall, in spite of all firebrands here, succeed in implementing the Locarno policy. Afterwards, . . . having tried the honey, we can, if need be, uncork our bottle of vinegar.[83]

Phipps's impression of Briand's attitude proved sound. The Foreign Office's reply to the official French note crossed with a letter in which the French government withdrew its demand for a formal declaration from Berlin, and proposed instead a meeting of the Locarno powers' legal advisers at Geneva to discuss the critical issues. Both the British and German governments readily consented, and the conversations, according to a British report, 'proved eminently satisfactory'.[84]

To British relief, the German attitude left little to be desired in the handling of the three critical weeks after the treaty's publication. Upon learning from D'Abernon of the very unfavourable impression the treaty had left in Britain, Stresemann gave the most categorical assurances that Locarno would continue to be the principal basis of his policy. 'I implore you, please tell Sir Austen Chamberlain that I am no less concerned with or less responsible for Locarno than he is himself . . . I should as soon entertain [word missing in original] of committing suicide as of abandoning that basis. Indeed to abandon it would practically be equivalent to suicide.'[85] Stresemann saw no difficulty in meeting the British request for further public assurances that the treaty did not run counter to the League, and immediately proposed both a radio broadcast and a *Reichstag* speech.

Despite considerable scepticism Chamberlain gave increasing credit to the German reassurances. In a speech at the Albert Hall on 30 April, the foreign secretary publicly declared his good faith in the German government. He was

---

83 Phipps to Lampson, 8 May 1926, PRO, FO 371/11324/C 5503.
84 Troutbeck memo, 22 June 1926, PRO, FO 371/11325/C 7180.
85 D'Abernon to FO, 30 Apr. 1926, PRO, FO 371/11323/C 5237; Stresemann to Botschaft London, 1 May 1926, *ADAP*, ser. B. ii/1, doc. 184.

also pleased with Stresemann's interview with the press and at first considered it unnecessary to demand the further assurances demanded by Briand.[86]

However, Briand's wishes were almost sacrosanct to the foreign secretary. If another German declaration assisted in appeasing France then it would have to be given. Chamberlain therefore changed his mind and sent a 'personal' telegram to D'Abernon:

> I . . . used all our influence to secure fair and even friendly consideration of the German action in other capitals. Stresemann owes me something in return and I rely on you to persuade him to make this time a speech directed to foreign audiences and calculated to reassure them. The trouble about Germany is that they never think of any public opinion but their own.[87]

Stresemann was surprised at this renewed request, since Tyrrell had reassured Sthamer, the German ambassador in London, the previous day that the British were satisfied with the German reconfirmations. As Stresemann told D'Abernon, he thought he had given sufficient proof of his good faith by his interviews with the *Berliner Tageblatt* and his broadcast. Nevertheless, he was willing to make another statement for British public opinion – did the ambassador think an interview in *The Times* would do?[88]

The proposed *Times* interview, the jurists' meeting, and a last formal German declaration that Gaus, the German legal adviser, had expressed governmental views, finally satisfied British and French demands. The French Senate's debate passed without causing too many obstacles for Briand. As the discussions both in Britain and France on the Russo-German treaty revealed, the Locarno agreement stood on shaky grounds. Germany and the Allies had concluded Locarno partly on different premises. For Berlin, Locarno was the beginning of both a serious revision of the treaty of Versailles, and the readiness to seek common peaceful solutions with the western powers. Locarno was the toilsome German attempt to overcome exaggerated nationalism, excessive demands of revisionism, the glorification of freedom of action and a lack of responsibility in international affairs, which all gave reason for the Allied lack of confidence.[89] For the Allies, by contrast, Locarno was rather a premature reward for Germany, of which she still had to prove herself worthy. In these circumstances the treaty of Berlin was hardly a step in the right direction.

Germany paid the price for the treaty of Berlin. One of the major repercussions was the French decision to postpone the withdrawal of occupying troops

86 Chamberlain minute, 3 May 1926, PRO, FO 371/11324/C 5387; D'Abernon to FO, 5 May 1926, FO 371/11323/C 5430; Stresemann to Brockdorff-Rantzau, 9 May 1926, PA-AA, R 28223k.
87 Chamberlain to D'Abernon, 7 May 1926, PRO, FO 371/11324/C 5403.
88 Sthamer to AA, 6 May 1926, *ADAP*, ser. B, ii/1, doc. 190; Aufzeichnung Stresemann, 10 May 1926, PA-AA, R 28223k; D'Abernon to FO, 10 May 1926, PRO, FO 371/11324/C 5565.
89 Krüger, *Außenpolitik*, 298.

from Germany. Britain, though with a bad conscience, accepted that it was most unwise to raise the question of occupying forces with Briand at that time. Chamberlain's mistrust of Germany and considerations of the French domestic situation held greater sway than the promises made in Berlin. He increased pressure on France only when continuing occupation otherwise seriously endangered Germany's entry into the League in September 1926. This, however, was well after the Russo-German treaty had retreated into the background of popular attention.

The agreement nevertheless left a bitter aftertaste. It served as a pretext and justification for France – now again ruled by Poincaré who was against evacuation anyway – to delay the unpopular decision to withdraw the troops. It also confirmed the scepticism of British officials towards German intentions – particularly on the part of Austen Chamberlain whose support for German wishes became increasingly half-hearted and reluctant, as German intentions remained ambiguous. The treaty of Berlin showed foreign statesmen that, despite her firm commitment to Locarno, Germany was not entirely prepared to sacrifice her eastern ties for a western agreement. While Germany did not succeed in playing this bargaining chip to speed up revision, its existence made western politicians more careful in their decisions. Locarno was supposed to re-establish peace in western Europe and peace was impossible without Germany. The treaty of Berlin reminded the western powers that a potential element of trouble persisted which would harm rather than benefit everyone. The agreement also served as steady reminder for the Allies that their bilateral relations with Russia would have an effect on – and possibly provoke a reaction from – Germany. Yet the combination of Locarno and the treaty of Berlin had potential for usefulness. Britain was the first to recognise this. British relations with the Soviet Union deteriorated sharply in 1927 to the point where diplomatic relations were ruptured. Due to German mediation, however, the damage to British policy could be limited.

6

Rapallo and the Rupture of Anglo-Soviet Relations

Locarno had unlocked the door to a new period of peace in Europe. The western powers found the subsequent path of conciliation sometimes stony, but nevertheless manageable and – at least at first – seemingly devoid of insurmountable obstacles. The close personal relationship between the three Locarnites, Briand, Chamberlain and Stresemann, and the informal 'Geneva tea parties' where they discussed politics, contributed to the new confidence.[1] Europe did its best to overcome the divisions of the First World War.

The Soviet Union, however, felt like an outcast. From the moment they learned that Germany was to sign an agreement with the western powers, the Russians firmly believed that Locarno was a British conspiracy against them. British aversion to Bolshevism was no secret, but this did not result in an openly hostile policy. Neither Austen Chamberlain nor other Foreign Office officials were fundamentally concerned about the ideological drivers behind Moscow's policy. The Foreign Office had pragmatically decided that the best way of 'taming' the Russians was to ignore them. London would wait until the need for diplomatic and economic contacts brought Moscow to reason.

While the western powers celebrated the success of Locarno, Soviet paranoia about a capitalist front grew. In the European capitals, Soviet diplomats complained that Britain was seeking to isolate Russia. Chamberlain's categorical assurances that there was 'not an atom of foundation' for these allegations had little effect. According to the report of Peters, the counsellor, dated early December 1925, the Soviet press was finding evidence of anti-Soviet designs everywhere and the Kremlin had still not made up its mind on how to respond to Locarno.[2]

Peters's observation was not quite correct. Soviet Russia was shaken by the domestic struggle for power between Stalin and Trotsky. At the same time it

---

[1] Jacobson, *Locarno diplomacy*, passim; Krüger, *Außenpolitik*, 301–74. I do not concur with Grayson's interpretation of the 'tea parties', as it was during these privately held talks that the important issues relevant to European stability were raised and progress on Germany's reintegration into Europe on the Versailles provisions took place, and not at the League of Nations council, as Grayson suggests: *Chamberlain*, 96–101.

[2] Chamberlain memo on conversation with Briand, 16 Oct. 1925, PRO, FO 371/11016/N 5812; D'Abernon to Chamberlain, 17 May 1925, FO 371/11027/N 5905; Chamberlain to His Majesty's *chargé d'affaires* to Moscow, 5 Nov. 1925, FO 371/11016/N 6213; cabinet meeting 3 (26), 3 Feb. 1926, CAB 23/52; Peters to Chamberlain, 4 Dec. 1925, FO 371/11022/N 6823.

was engaged in a fundamental debate about the future of communist ideology. The two conflicting positions were the continuation of the Leninist principle of world revolution on the one hand, and its replacement by Stalin's concept of 'socialism in one country' on the other. Stalin eventually won this battle.[3] Yet the resulting temporary instability on the domestic scene, and Moscow's fear that Russia's security was endangered by a capitalist front that possibly linked the security of Europe and Asia, seemed to demand foreign political action from the Kremlin. Moscow hence embarked on a dual, in fact contra-dictory, foreign policy in order to prevent a potential 'hostile capitalist en-circlement' along the frontiers of the USSR. Outside western Europe, Moscow actively encouraged nationalist, anti-imperialist movements in Asia.[4] At the same time, however, the Kremlin was anxious to improve re-lations with the west. Yet Soviet feelers remained unnoticed in London. Desperate about its isolation and eager for a British loan, the Soviet govern-ment had decided on a gradual *rapprochement* with Britain. The Soviet diplo-mats Rosengolz and Maisky complained to Hodgson, the British *chargé d'affaires* who was in London on leave from Moscow, that they were neither told about British grievances nor encouraged to improve relations between the two governments. Hodgson advised them privately to ask informally at the Foreign Office which strategy would be successful.

The Foreign Office had little enthusiasm for the Soviet initiative. Informal talks would serve no purpose. Furthermore, there had been too many unsuccessful Soviet advances in the past to inspire faith in their prom-ises. Since Moscow refused to acknowledge its pre-war debts in Britain, London was not prepared to ratify the trade agreement negotiated by the Labour government in 1924. Russia's recognition of her obligations was an essential Conservative prerequisite for any British loan to Moscow guaran-teed by the government.

Chamberlain, backed by the cabinet, retained this reserved attitude throughout the first months of 1926:

> The policy which . . . I have followed in regard to the Soviet Union has been to avoid a breach of the diplomatic relations established before we took office, and neither to court nor to show fear of that government, but to leave them alone in the expectation that sooner or later they would discover that they have more need of us than we have of them. This policy has been successful. Indeed . . . it has been too successful, for . . . it appears to have so frightened M. Chicherin as to have upset altogether his judgement . . . he has misunderstood this negative attitude, and . . . it has become an obsession with him that the whole policy of Great Britain is directed to the isolation of Russia, and even to the formation of an actively anti-Soviet *bloc*. This is foolish, but it is also dan-gerous . . . Whilst dealing as we think proper with communist agitation in this

---

3   E. H. Carr, *Socialism in one country, 1924–1926*, London 1964, ii/3; Jacobson, *Soviet Union*, 152–76.
4   Jacobson, *Soviet Union*, 177–9.

country, we should avoid denunciations of the Soviet government and its members, which only confirm Chicherin in his obsession.[5]

The Board of Trade and the Treasury shared Chamberlain's reservations towards Russia. Both warned of increasing business with Russia. The news that the German government had guaranteed a 300 million *Reichsmark* credit and the German suggestion that France, Britain and Germany should co-ordinate their trade and credits policy towards Russia deterred rather than encouraged the British.[6] The Board of Trade in principle welcomed the idea of a co-ordinated policy but warned of its impracticability, given that the foreign trade monopoly made Soviet business inelastic and expensive. The Board would have liked to see credit facilities for Russia decreased rather than increased, as the Soviet government was playing off the different countries against each other to get the best terms possible. As far as Russo-German trade was concerned, the Board of Trade found it natural and not even disadvantageous that Germany should be a larger exporter to Russia than Britain – given her geographical position. If Germany could sell to the Soviets she was a less active competitor for Britain in other markets.[7] The Treasury mainly objected to the granting of new credits to Russia because it would delay satisfactory relations between the Soviet Union and Europe, but the Foreign Office found this argument unconvincing.[8]

Confident of the support of these governmental departments, Chamberlain was uncompromising in his dealings with Moscow. Hodgson was instructed to wait for the Russians to bring up the topic of Anglo-Soviet relations rather than take the initiative himself. 'They [the Soviets] are really suffering from swollen heads. They are of less consequence to us than they suppose and they grossly flatter themselves when they suppose that British policy is dictated by thought of them.'[9]

However, the British were soon forced to think more of the Soviets than

---

5   Cabinet meeting 3 (26), 3 Feb. 1926, PRO, CAB 23/52; memo for the cabinet, 16 Feb. 1926, FO 371/11789/N 640. Gorodetsky's hypothesis of a thaw in Anglo-Soviet relations originating in the Foreign Office is incomprehensible: *Truce*, 134–44. Chamberlain and the Foreign Office unanimously adopted the same distant attitude towards Soviet overtures as they had done prior to Locarno. Russian endeavours to improve relations, desperate as they were, were bound to fail as long as Moscow did not accept the British terms as a basis for negotiations. Moreover Gorodetsky's interpretation of Stresemann's policy with regard to the treaty of Berlin is supported neither by the British documents quoted, nor from German material which he does not consider. On the consistency of Chamberlain's Russian policy see J. Haslam, 'Soviet foreign policy, 1924–1927', unpubl. MLitt. diss. Cambridge 1978, 48, 52, and Dutton, *Chamberlain*, 275–6.
6   Urquhart to Gregory, 18 Feb. 1926, PRO, FO 371/11787/N 833; D'Abernon to FO, 25 Feb. 1926, FO 371/11791/N 894; Orde to secretary of BoT, 5 Mar. 1926, ibid; Jacobson, *Soviet Union*, 199–200.
7   BoT to FO, 24 Mar. 1926, and minutes, PRO, FO 371/11776/N 1377.
8   Treasury to FO, 8 Apr. 1926; Orde to secretary of BoT, 30 Apr. 1926, PRO, FO 371/11776/N 1582. For further Treasury arguments see Gorodetsky, *Truce*, 138.
9   Chamberlain to Hodgson, 26 Apr. 1926, *DBFP*, 1A ser. i, doc. 465.

they liked. Russia's intervention in the British general strike of 3 to 12 May 1926 – though modest in providing only financial assistance while keeping a low profile in terms of propaganda – was grist to the mills of the anti-Bolsheviks in the cabinet.[10] The Foreign Office, preoccupied during the critical days with the reaction to the Russo-German treaty of Berlin, over-looked the few incoming reports on Moscow's involvement in the strike, and paid little attention to it. At the height of the crisis Hodgson sent a lengthy despatch suggesting that the negative attitude towards Moscow be aban-doned in favour of more co-operation.[11] The *chargé d'affaires* could not have chosen a more inconvenient moment. Moscow's interference in British dom-estic affairs had strengthened the anti-Soviet faction in the government. Russia's assistance in the strike would have been passed over without major Foreign Office attention, had it not been for home secretary Joynson-Hicks's heavy attack on the government's Russian policy in the cabinet meeting of 9 June, his fatal speech in the House of Commons on 10 June and a subsequent heated discussion about a rupture of Anglo-Soviet relations. This forced the Foreign Office to consider the international implications of such action.[12]

The cabinet unanimously agreed on 16 June that Moscow's interference in British domestic affairs justified a diplomatic breach. Chamberlain, however, defended his Russian policy against strong attacks from Joynson-Hicks, Churchill and other die-hards and temporarily managed to prevent a rupture of relations. The Foreign Office had compiled a memorandum stressing that the political and economic advantages of diplomatic ties with Moscow outweighed the practical disadvantages. This ultimately convinced the cabinet that the moment for such action was inopportune.[13] But the number of government members and high officials who were increasingly and publicly outspoken in favour of abandoning the Soviet connection grew.

During the summer of 1926, Chamberlain succeeded in defending his view that a British breach with Russia would harm rather than serve European politics. This was particularly the case in respect of Germany, which had to enter the League of Nations in order to put the Locarno treaty finally into effect. The foreign secretary, who had linked his personal political fate so closely with Locarno, did not want to endanger his *opus* by forcing Germany to choose between Rapallo and Locarno in the event of escalating Anglo-Soviet controversies. The competitiveness of British trade on the Russian market, especially in comparison with Germany, would equally suffer. Hodgson sent Russian statistics showing that British imports of Russian goods

---

[10] Gorodetsky, 'The Soviet Union and Britain's general strike of May 1926', *Cahiers du monde russe et soviétique* xvii (1976), 287–310.

[11] Hodgson to Chamberlain, 6 May 1926, *DBFP*, 1A ser. i, doc. 504.

[12] Cabinet meeting 37 (26), 9 June 1926, PRO, CAB 23/53; Parliamentary debates, HoC, 5th ser. clxxxvi, cols 1673–6; Gorodetsky, *Truce*, 171–4.

[13] Cabinet meeting 40 (26), 16 June 1926, PRO, CAB 23/53; Gregory memo, 11 June 1926; FO memo regarding Anglo-Soviet relations, 16 June 1926, *DBFP*, 1A ser. ii, docs 56, 62.

were valued at 159 million roubles compared to Germany's 89 million roubles; British exports to the Soviet Union were 109 million roubles against Germany's 153 million roubles.[14] A diplomatic breach would increase Germany's advantages disproportionately.

Sharply increasing Anglo-Russian tensions in China since the autumn of 1926 brought the issue of diplomatic rupture back on the Foreign Office agenda.[15] Beginning in May 1925, student protests in Shanghai against imperialist powers, followed by sixteen months of massive strikes and boycotts in major Chinese cities, had led to two years of urban demonstrations, rural rebellions and military conflicts – what has become known as the national revolution in China. Moscow actively supported this unrest right from the start by sending advisers from the Red Army and Comintern to China. As Jacobson points out, never before or afterwards did the leadership of the USSR get so actively involved in a revolutionary movement outside the direct reach of the Red Army. And, to Whitehall's greatest displeasure, Soviet involvement in China was a military success.[16] Contrary to many of his cabinet colleagues and against a wavering Foreign Office mood on this issue, Chamberlain wanted to postpone the rupture of relations with the Soviet Union as long as possible as he feared the implications for European politics. On 3 December 1926 at Geneva, he told Briand that the time was ripe for something in the nature of a new departure towards Moscow, but he would try to secure unanimity among the powers first. At the same time, the Soviets launched a trade offensive and sought to place large orders for industrial equipment in Britain. These endeavours, however, came to an abrupt standstill with the sudden death of Krassin, the head of their London mission and the most conciliatory of Soviet officials. The Foreign Office, preoccupied with what it regarded as an inevitable deterioration of relations with Moscow neither noticed nor responded to these overtures.

Chinese problems and Anglo-Soviet tensions absorbed a great deal of Foreign Office attention. Chamberlain appointed Miles Lampson, the long-standing head of the Central department, as the new British *chargé d'affaires* to Beijing. No action against Moscow was to be taken, however, until Lampson had reviewed the Chinese situation.[17] Continental affairs also did not develop as smoothly as Britain had hoped after Locarno and required greater attention than expected. Hence, a rupture of Anglo-Soviet relations could have very negative consequences for peace and stability in Europe. In the week between 3 and 10 December 1926, the Foreign Office produced no

14 Hodgson to Chamberlain, 24 Sept. 1926, *DBFP*, 1A ser. ii, doc. 80, n. 9.
15 See O'Malley's memo (with a definition of British interests in China and the Pacific), 10 June 1926, and Strang's reply, 5 Aug. 1926, Strang papers, CCAC, STRN 4/4. On the German evaluation of British policy in China see unsigned and undated memo (1927), BA-Po, Deutsche Botschaft Moskau 09.02, vol. 259.
16 Jacobson, *Soviet Union*, 188–97.
17 Chamberlain to Tyrrell, 3 Dec. 1926, *DBFP*, 1A ser. ii, doc. 318.

fewer than five memoranda discussing the pros and cons of diplomatic action against Moscow.[18]

The list of disadvantages, particularly for British trade, was long. More serious, however, would be the effects of a breach on the situation in east central Europe. Gregory, meanwhile, promoted to assistant under-secretary, argued that Germany's already embarrassed position between Rapallo and Locarno would be rendered even more troublesome. Poland, after Marshal Piłsudski's *coup d'état*, might make fresh demands for safety guarantees. Finland and the Baltic states, finally, would also be seriously alarmed. Gregory left no doubt that the international situation had to be weighed against moral and domestic arguments, and that he by no means excluded a diplomatic rupture. Nevertheless, he saw great dangers for British policy arising from such action.

Moreover, there were the sensational revelations of the *Manchester Guardian* in December 1926 and Social Democrat Philipp Scheidemann's speech in the *Reichstag* about German–Soviet secret military co-operation.[19] Subsequent government communiqués confirmed the report, although the Wilhelmstraße immediately declared that these contacts had been terminated. The Foreign Office remained relatively calm. Nevertheless, it is not unlikely that these reports subconsciously strengthened the views of those officials who argued against a breach with Russia, given that this would increase the difficulty of controlling this aspect of Russo-German relations. Information about Russo-German military relations increased during 1927.[20]

In January and February 1927, Chinese unrest grew dramatically, thus increasing pressure from cabinet die-hards to draw a line under relations with Moscow. From the Foreign Office's point of view, however, the moment was more inopportune than ever. Not only had the overall international situation worsened, Chamberlain was also worried about the bellicose policy of Piłsudski in Poland, which might upset east central Europe and drive Lithuania into Soviet arms. Chamberlain's concern was not unfounded, given that Piłsudski contemplated the annexation of Lithuania to solve the Vilna question in Poland's favour and get further access to the Baltic sea.[21] Developments in Germany were no less disquieting due to yet another severe government crisis. In January 1927, Briand had to bow to severe domestic

---

[18] Gregory memos, 3, 10 Dec. 1926; Tyrrell memo, 4 Dec. 1926; Hamilton-Gordon memos, 7, 9 Dec. 1926, ibid. docs 317, 319, 332, 344, 350.

[19] Lindsay to Chamberlain, 7, 10 Dec. 1926, PRO, FO 371/11281/C 12969; Lindsay to FO, 16 Dec. 1926, FO 371/11281/C 13237; Hodgson to Chamberlain, 19 Jan. 1927, FO 371/12598/N 520. For the extent of Russo-German military relations see *ADAP*, ser. B, ii/2, 'Sowjetunion, Militärische Beziehungen', passim; M. Geyer, *Aufrüstung oder Sicherheit. Die Reichswehr in der Krise der Machtpolitik 1924–1936*, Wiesbaden 1980, 58–76; Zeidler, *Reichswehr*, 143–53.

[20] Lindsay to Chamberlain, 22 Feb. 1927, *DBFP*, 1A ser. iii, docs 20, 24; Lindsay to Sargent (on conversation with Schlesinger), 19 May 1927, PRO, FO 371/12595/N 2343; Sir F. Hall, parliamentary question, 29 June 1927, FO 371/12150/C 5662.

[21] See chapter 7 below.

pressure against concessions in the military control of Germany and made it clear that he would not meet Stresemann's demands for troop reduction in the Rhineland. After the enthusiasm of the Franco-German *rapprochement* at Thoiry, this decision brought relations between Paris and Berlin to their lowest point since Locarno, a situation which continued well into 1928.[22]

Chamberlain, concerned about Briand's political vulnerability, refused to add to his difficulties and, to Stresemann's great frustration, backed Paris unconditionally. The effect of this decision on the German domestic situation could not yet be foreseen. But there was disturbing news from Berlin that the Deutsch-Nationale-Volks-Partei (DNVP) was once again about to enter the government coalition. Without a doubt they would increase their revisionist demands, thereby further antagonising France. Since Locarno, Chamberlain had discovered the historical reasons for the German Nationalists' close relations with Moscow and now used this argument at every occasion:

> The Nationalists of Germany have throughout based their opposition to the Locarno policy on the thesis that good relations with Russia are, as Bismarck held, of vital consequence to Germany, and that Locarno was a British trap to involve Germany in Britain's quarrel with the Soviet Union. I cannot doubt that an open breach between Russia and ourselves would gravely embarrass Dr Stresemann in the pursuit of his policy of reconciliation with the west. It would certainly encourage the Nationalists in their hope that presently with the aid of Russia they will be able to challenge the settlement of the eastern frontiers.[23]

In contrast, Chamberlain did not expect the breach with Russia to weaken the Soviet government seriously and thought it unlikely that Moscow would change its European policy.

The issue of China left Chamberlain very little time or mind for other issues on the political agenda. In the meantime, the Chinese revolution had split into two factions, which fought for ideological supremacy and control of the national revolution. Moscow supported the Guomindang. Its strategy was to stir up sentiments against Great Britain, the principal foreign power in China. Anti-British rallies in Shanghai, the centre of British economic interests, forced London to make significant concessions to the Chinese Nationalist authorities in early 1927.[24] Hence, pressure on Chamberlain to break off diplomatic relations with Moscow grew further. Still, he sought to delay an Anglo-Soviet diplomatic rift as long as possible, but needed further support for this position in the cabinet. Various British missions were consulted about their views and none of the replies was entirely in favour of a

---

[22] Jacobson, *Locarno diplomacy*, 101–19; Krüger, *Außenpolitik*, 356–66; Pitts, *France and the German problem*, 180–96.

[23] Chamberlain memo, 24 Jan. 1927, *DBFP*, 1A ser. ii, doc. 422; Sthamer to AA, 16 Feb. 1927, PA-AA, Deutsche Botschaft London, vol. 713.

[24] Jacobson, *Soviet Union*, 218–20.

breach. Sir Ronald Lindsay, D'Abernon's successor as ambassador to Berlin since October 1926, was definitely against it. He believed that an Anglo-Soviet breach would place Germany in an awkward position between Moscow and London. This was undesirable at a time when Polish–Lithuanian tensions were increasing, Moscow's position in this quarrel remained unclear and German–Polish commercial negotiations had also just collapsed.[25]

Anglo-Soviet relations further deteriorated. Under severe pressure from the hardliners, the cabinet decided, on 18 February, that a rupture of relations was inevitable within the next few months. Chamberlain succeeded again in delaying action because of the unstable situation in Europe and the fact that Britain was unprepared for such a step. However, a stern note was handed to the Soviet *chargé d'affaires* in protest at Moscow's activities.[26]

The negative effects on Germany of a rupture of relations continued to be a powerful argument in Chamberlain's plea to postpone action against Moscow. They were even specifically mentioned in the cabinet meeting of 23 February 1927.[27] Lindsay again transmitted German worries on 26 February and quoted Schubert's regret at the German inability to mediate between Moscow and London. *Reichskanzler* Wilhelm Marx was reported to have hinted that Germany would remain neutral in the case of an eventual breach of relations. In reply to Lindsay, Chamberlain wrote that the fear of German, Polish and Baltic reactions had so far prompted him to adopt a more restrained attitude towards Moscow than he would have taken otherwise.[28] For the House of Commons debate on 3 March 1927, the cabinet instructed the foreign secretary to inform parliament about objections to a breach with Russia from a foreign policy perspective, but to bear in mind the importance of not giving the impression to Soviet Russia that Britain was powerless and tired.[29]

The countdown of worsening relations had begun: it was only a question of finding the appropriate pretext before London would break off diplomatic relations with Moscow. Chamberlain was anxious to discuss the issue with both Stresemann and Briand at Geneva. He was relieved that Germany took Anglo-Soviet tensions increasingly calmly. The *Reichstag* debates after Geneva showed that all parties supported German neutrality in case of a

[25] Lindsay to Gregory, 3 Feb. 1927, *DBFP*, 1A ser. iii, doc. 3.
[26] Cabinet meeting 12 (27), 18 Feb. 1927, PRO, CAB 23/54. For the British note to Moscow see Chamberlain to Rosengolz, 23 Feb. 1927, *DBFP*, 1A ser. iii, doc. 21; Sthamer to AA, 24 Feb. 1927, PA-AA, Deutsche Botschaft London, vol. 767.
[27] Cabinet meeting 13 (27), 23 Feb. 1927, PRO, CAB 23/54.
[28] Lindsay to Chamberlain, 26 Feb. 1927; Chamberlain to Lindsay, 1 Mar. 1927, *DBFP*, 1A ser. iii, docs 29, 32; Lindsay to Chamberlain, 4 Mar. 1927, PRO, FO 371/12590/N 1577; Jacobson, *Soviet Union*, 221.
[29] Cabinet meeting 14 (27), 3 Mar. 1927, PRO, CAB 23/54; Sthamer to AA, 3 Mar. 1927, PA-AA, R 28233k.

breach, although for different reasons.[30] This moderation was even more appreciated since the results of the Geneva meeting had otherwise been disappointing for Stresemann. He had made no progress in his demands for evacuation of the Rhineland, and was under heavy pressure from his opponents. Briand had been more obstinate on the issue of troop reductions than ever before because of his domestic difficulties. Chamberlain disapproved of French policy but backed down out of fear of seeing his friend fall. He appreciated that Stresemann had equally recognised Briand's precarious situation and had not pressed him.[31]

The pretext for a British breach with Russia was finally found in May 1927. Evidence of Soviet espionage in Britain accumulated during March 1927 and made the die-hards anxious to bring the issue to a head. On 11 May, the Home Office used information of Arcos's (the All-Russian Co-operative Society's) involvement in espionage to order a police raid both on Arcos and the Russian trade delegation for the following morning. The illegitimate search – as the Russian trade delegation was considered extra-territorial – lasted three days and the evidence found was insufficient to justify the raid. Nevertheless, the Conservative government broke off diplomatic relations with Moscow on 26 May 1927, proving Moscow's bad faith by quoting from intelligence decrypts and thereby gravely compromising the SIS's work against Soviet Russia.[32]

The Arcos raid took the international community by surprise. The Foreign Office and British missions abroad were also unprepared. The Russians immediately looked to Berlin where Stresemann, anxious to offend neither London nor Moscow, declared strict German neutrality in the affair. He could not help but wonder, however, whether the British really had the limited goals which they professed, or whether they would compromise Germany's relations with Russia. Stresemann agreed to take charge of Soviet interests in Britain and notified London of this decision immediately. Chamberlain, in turn, told Sthamer that he would have asked Berlin to take over British affairs in Russia if he had not feared to cause the Germans embarrassment by doing so.[33]

Chamberlain was relieved at Berlin's reasonable reception of the Anglo-Soviet quarrel. He told Lindsay: 'Dr Stresemann need have no fear that I shall misinterpret the German government's acceptance of the charge

---

[30] Lindsay to Chamberlain, 22 Mar. 1927, PRO, FO 371/12138/C 2766; Reichstag debate, 22 Mar. 1927, FO 371/12138/C 3036; Troutbeck memo 'The German nationalists and the situation in China', 16 Mar. 1927, FO 371/12190/C 2706.
[31] Chamberlain to Tyrrell, 9 Mar. 1927, Austen Chamberlain papers, PRO, FO 800/260, 283–7; Jacobson, *Locarno diplomacy*, 114–15.
[32] C. Andrew, 'British intelligence and the breach with Russia in 1927', *HJ* xxv (1982), 957–64 at pp. 962–4; Gorodetsky, *Truce*, 219–31. The Arcos raid, with its debate about extra-territoriality, had its precedent in the search of the Soviet trade mission in Berlin in 1924, where an escaped communist prisoner had taken refuge: Krüger, *Außenpolitik*, 267.
[33] Sthamer to AA, 23, 31 May 1927, PA-AA, R 28224k.

of Russian interests here.' Berlin was reassured that the move 'was solely confined to the immediate object we proclaimed. It was in no sense whatever the prelude to some wider policy. We had no ulterior motives.'[34] At no time, however, had Chamberlain been prepared either to actively encourage or to honour a moderate German attitude in the Anglo-Russian controversy by looking more favourably at some of the German political demands. When he discussed the rupture of relations with Briand in London on 18 May, Chamberlain did not conceal his concern about the possible repercussions of the breach for Berlin and tried to convince Briand of the necessity of settling the outstanding questions between the Locarno powers – viz. the evacuation of the Rhineland – amicably and quickly:

> I [i.e. Chamberlain] said to him [i.e. Briand] before Locarno that we were battling with Soviet Russia for the soul of Germany. We had won a success at Locarno . . . but the more difficult our relations with Russia became the more important it was that we should attach Germany solidly to the western powers . . . It was absolutely necessary that we should give the Germans the satisfaction to which they were entitled in this matter [i.e. evacuation] and that we should prevent them from succumbing to the temptation offered by the redoubled efforts to win them which the Soviet government were certain to make.[35]

Briand listened politely but did not move an inch in his refusal to consider evacuation. Chamberlain, despite the feeling that the Allied powers did not have clean hands with regard to the evacuation issue, did not press him further because, by May 1927, Briand's political position was too precarious to risk aggravating the situation.[36] The Chamberlain–Briand meeting resulted in a joint communiqué referring to the 'solidarity of the *entente cordiale*' rather than the 'spirit of Locarno'.

The rupture of Anglo-Soviet relations also dominated the Geneva League session in June 1927. Chamberlain was questioned intensely about the implications of the British move for international relations. In the meantime, the situation was aggravated by the murder of Voikov, the Soviet *chargé d'affaires* in Warsaw, by a young White Russian. Moscow immediately suspected British complicity.

Moscow retaliated for Voikov's murder by executing alleged British spies without trial and issuing a sharp protest note to Warsaw.[37] These developments increased worries among the foreign ministers at Geneva that this Russo-Polish quarrel could turn into a larger conflict, especially since

---

34 Chamberlain to Lindsay (twice), 31 May 1927, *DBFP*, 1A ser. iii, docs 224, 225.
35 Conversation between Chamberlain and Briand, 18 May 1927, ibid. doc. 201.
36 Pitts, *France and the German problem*, 202–4.
37 Phipps to Chamberlain, 13 June 1927, *DBFP*, 1A ser. iii, doc. 231; P. S. Wandycz, *The twilight of French eastern alliances, 1926–1936: French–Czechoslovak–Polish relations from Locarno to the remilitarisation of the Rhineland*, Princeton, NJ 1988, 95; J. Korbel, *Poland between east and west: Soviet and German diplomacy towards Poland, 1919–1933*, Princeton, NJ 1963, 217–19.

Moscow continued to believe in a British-organised conspiracy behind it. Chamberlain, eager to remove this source of friction, asked Stresemann to use his special relationship with Russia and, on behalf of the League powers, urge moderation on Moscow. Stresemann had spoken to Chicherin just before his trip to Geneva and was therefore an important partner for conversation with Chamberlain. Stresemann had no choice but to agree and Wilhelmstraße officials accordingly made their representations to Moscow.[38]

There the matter rested. It remains a matter of speculation whether Chamberlain realised how awkward the situation was into which he had manoeuvred Stresemann by making him abandon his neutral attitude in the Anglo-Soviet conflict and use his intimacy with Russia for a defence of Poland, of all countries. Stresemann had no choice but to accept Chamberlain's request if he wanted to avoid suspicions at Geneva that some secret Russo-German understanding about Poland existed, and thus endanger what was left of the Locarno spirit. Chamberlain was more grateful for Stresemann's action than he showed to the German foreign minister. Neither his nor Stresemann's record of their final conversation mentions a word of appreciation by Chamberlain for the German action. To Tyrrell, however, Chamberlain wrote that Stresemann had been 'most reasonable and conciliatory, and he showed in my opinion an increasing appreciation of other people's difficulties and an increasing tact in handling them'.[39]

Chamberlain could not compensate Stresemann for his support of British policy towards Russia by honouring the outstanding promise of troop reductions in the Rhineland immediately, and was careful not to show publicly a connection between the two issues. The French cabinet was divided, with Briand on the one side in favour of a small reduction of troops, and Poincaré on the other against any kind of concession. Neither side dared to advance their positions too openly for fear of bringing down the government. Chamberlain, aware of the precarious French situation, hesitated to press the issue too strongly, given the danger of thus sacrificing Briand and risking the re-emergence of Poincaré. The furthest Chamberlain could go at Geneva in June 1927 was to issue a public statement implicitly disapproving of French resistance to fulfilling the legitimate German claims. This declaration helped Stresemann to return from Geneva not completely empty-handed and was thus important for his domestic position. Chamberlain continued to press the French for troop reductions in accordance with the November 1925 promises. His firm *démarche* in Paris in August 1927 finally resulted in French consent to withdraw a total of 10,000 Allied troops, bringing their number in

[38] Chamberlain to Tyrrell, 16 June 1927, *DBFP*, 1A ser. iii, doc. 240; Aufzeichnungen Stresemann, 7, 15 June 1927, *ADAP*, ser. B, v, docs 209, 236; Addison to FO, 7 June 1927, PRO, FO 371/12598/N 2929; record by Chamberlain of conversations with Stresemann, 14, 18 June 1927, *DBFP*, 1A ser. iii, docs 234, 244; H. L. Dyck, 'German–Soviet relations and the Anglo-Soviet break, 1927', *Slavic Review* xxv (1966), 67–83 at pp. 79–83.
[39] Chamberlain to Tyrrell, 17 June 1927, Austen Chamberlain papers, PRO, FO 800/261, 55–64.

the Rhineland down to 60,000 – the minimum number considered necessary to ensure French security.[40]

'The English will approach us only so far as this is possible without encroaching on Anglo-French relations,' observed Wilhelmstraße official Dirksen in September 1927.[41] His appreciation of Chamberlain's policy was correct. London favoured conciliation with Berlin, but the *entente* with France came first, beyond all doubt. In critical situations, Germany remained the vanquished nation, which had to comply with Anglo-French demands, no matter what diplomatic action she offered in return. Germany had no choice. She needed western rather than Russian support for the realisation of her revisionist aims. German revisionism, however, implied the weakening of the French security system. Germany asked Paris to make concessions on issues vital to French security, which were far greater than anything Stresemann could offer as recompense. Chamberlain was well aware of this. Apart from his undoubtedly strong personal sympathy for Briand and his affinity for France, Chamberlain had to guarantee that the bargain with Germany was not to the disadvantage of France. Locarno was Berlin's attempt to speed up revisionist goals. The price was diminished intimacy with Moscow despite the treaty of Berlin. Britain did not like Russo-German relations, but she did not fear them. Berlin's reaction to the rupture of Anglo-Soviet relations had once again confirmed German priorities.

---

[40] Jacobson, *Locarno diplomacy*, 132–4; Pitts, *France and the German problem*, 208–14.
[41] Dirksen memo, 29 Sept. 1927, quoted from Dyck, 'German–Soviet relations', 82.

7

Rapallo and the Decline of the Locarno Spirit

After the rupture of Anglo-Soviet diplomatic relations, British foreign policy returned to normal. The British legation in Moscow was closed and Sir Robert Hodgson and his staff recalled to London. Soviet Russia retreated into the background of British attention. Western European problems once again dominated British foreign policy. Until its fall from power in June 1929, the Conservative government focused on disarmament and a further revision of the treaty of Versailles. The evacuation of the Rhineland and reparations were the predominant issues.

Germany had joined the preparatory disarmament conference in November 1927. The principal problem throughout the many years of negotiation was how to combine the German demand for revision of the peace treaty and equality of rights with the French request for security. The question of security equally overshadowed the negotiations for the evacuation of the Rhineland. A withdrawal of Allied troops deprived Paris of her last opportunity to control Germany's military strength[1] and prevent a future German attack on French territory. The recurrent French nightmare of a third German invasion within a lifetime was deep-rooted, and made France's demand for security almost impossible to satisfy. An additional problem was the reparations issue. To make Germany pay for the lost war was a means of controlling her economic recovery and of preventing her from regaining the position of the predominant economic power in Europe.

With the years that passed since the end of the war, Germany's demand for revision became increasingly outspoken and impatient. After Locarno and the noticeable improvement of Germany's economic and political situation, Berlin's pressure on Britain and France grew, first as the result of Locarno's expected effects, but also due to the increasing intervention of popular opinion and sectional interest groups. An additional factor from May 1928 was Stresemann's failing health, which increased his sense of urgency in obtaining his foreign policy goals. Germany's apparent economic stability raised hopes for a return to her former independent great power status. In this foreign policy objective the German foreign minister was not driven by outside pressure alone. He was clearly a revisionist himself, convinced that he had to accomplish his task of liberating Germany from the shackles of Versailles – and he wanted to harvest the fruits of his labour before he died. It

---

[1] This had originally been the task of the IMCC which had been dissolved in January 1927. For the French position see Pitts, *France and the German problem*, passim.

was the means, not the ends that distinguished Stresemann from his political opponents.

Between the clashing political objectives of France and Germany, Britain retained the role of a more or – increasingly – less impartial mediator. In retrospect it is obvious that this self-appointed role was too heavy a burden to carry for Britain. By signing Locarno, Chamberlain had committed himself to bringing about reconciliation between Paris and Berlin. He could not, however, solve the dilemma that German and French aims were essentially incompatible.

The framework of British global policy, with its limited interests in Europe and the principle of not taking sides, made it impossible for Chamberlain to offer France a British guarantee in compensation for her diminished security. He recognised, however, that the French claims were not without justification. Paris had nothing to gain and much to lose from German revisionism. His mediation was directed by a strong personal sympathy for France and particularly for his counterpart, Briand. This stood in stark contrast to Germany, which he disliked and distrusted, and the complex domestic situation of which he did not understand. Chamberlain's attitude towards the German foreign minister, Stresemann, was ambivalent. Although Chamberlain gradually developed a personal liking and appreciation for Stresemann and respect for his endeavours at reconciliation, he felt that Stresemann did not personify the German nation. The more uncompromisingly revisionist the Wilhelmstraße became after 1928, the less inclined Chamberlain was to distinguish between Stresemann and 'the Germans'. His impatience with Berlin's failure to comply with his requests therefore steadily grew. Chamberlain over-estimated his impartiality and personal influence in Paris and Berlin as well as the role which Britain could assume in the process of European reconciliation. In critical situations Chamberlain tended to side with Briand; French considerations always took precedence over German desires. If domestic pressure determined the fate of his two colleagues, Chamberlain would rather have seen Stresemann fall from power than Briand. He would do nothing that might compromise the Anglo-French *entente*.[2]

---

2 My own view of Chamberlain concurs with Dutton's more reserved attitude (Dutton, *Chamberlain*, 263–6), rather than with the optimistic evaluation of B. J. C. McKercher ('Austen Chamberlain's control of British foreign policy, 1924–1929', *IHR* vi [1984], 570–91 at pp. 580–5), and fundamentally disagrees with that of R. Grayson. Grayson points out, correctly, that Chamberlain disliked a number of French politicians, for example Poincaré (Grayson, *Chamberlain*, 58–9). From this observation it cannot be concluded, however, that Chamberlain was not a convinced Francophile. Chamberlain's attitude was strongly determined by considerations that suited him and his policy personally at a certain moment, as he was ambitious to have his political objectives realised. Poincaré, for instance, was a political opponent whose country, language and culture Chamberlain clearly appreciated. With Stresemann it was the opposite. Grayson's conclusion concerning Chamberlain's attitude towards the Germans is equally misleading (p. 57). The quote he presents does not reflect adequately the political importance of Stresemann and Luther in German foreign relations. Nor is his allegation supported by other British, German or French

Despite the slow progress in the revision of Versailles, Germany's return to full great power status was no longer debatable. After Locarno and her entry into the League, Germany's equality was merely a question of time. Britain noted with concern that in striving for a speedy recovery outside the restrictions of Versailles, Berlin was tempted to take the line of least resistance and was searching for support in eastern Europe and especially the Soviet Union. This, however, was little appreciated in London and even less in France. Both countries regarded eastern Europe as a potential future trouble-spot due to the numerous conflicting interests in this region, which had barely been glossed over by the Paris peace treaties. Thus, while Britain would have preferred to leave the small nations to themselves, continuing unrest made a certain British attention necessary.

Within the overall framework of British policy, east central Europe was always of limited importance. The amount of attention given to the different countries of the area therefore varied. Poland, the French _protégé_ which loudly claimed great power status, had waged a war against Russia in 1920/21 and found itself in permanent antagonism with Germany over Danzig, Upper Silesia and the Polish Corridor. As such, it was as a constant potential troublemaker that Poland received British attention. The three small Baltic states, in contrast, served as an economic springboard for Britain into Soviet Russia.

Since the end of the First World War, British interest in the Baltic had continually diminished. In 1918–19 London's involvement in the region had been determined by the desire to oppose all German influence on Russia's western border and to prevent a Russo-German _rapprochement_. The three states could also serve as a transit area for future British trade with Russia, and as a strategic military base for British intervention in the Russian civil war. At the Paris peace conference, however, London had already subordinated her Baltic policy to her general interests in the USSR. The border states were now regarded as a _cordon sanitaire_ against the spread of communism beyond Soviet Russia, and as an anti-German buffer to curtail Berlin's influence in Russia.[3]

The end of the Russian civil war and British policy in the Russo-Polish war of 1920/21 illustrate, however, that London had drawn the border of her political sphere of interest along the Rhine.[4] The Baltic states were no longer of direct political importance to Britain but remained economically – and

archival sources. Chamberlain's numerous expressions privately and in parliament after June 1929 equally confirm his dislike and mistrust of the Germans.

3   E. Sundbäck, 'Finland, Scandinavia and the Baltic states viewed within the framework of the border state policy of Great Britain from the autumn of 1918 to the spring of 1919', _Scandinavian Journal of History_ xvi (1991), 313–34; M.-L. Hinkkanen-Lievonen, _British trade and enterprise in the Baltic states, 1919–1925_, Helsinki 1984, 54–76.

4   F. R. Bryant, 'Lord D'Abernon, the Anglo-French mission and the battle of Warsaw 1920', _JbfGO_ xxxviii (1990), 526–47.

hence indirectly politically – significant by serving as a potential springboard into the Soviet market.

British hopes for Russian trade did not materialise. Soviet Russia replaced economic liberalism with a state-planned economy and the Baltic states gained limited economic importance in their own right. Britain and Germany competed closely in the Baltic region, but the trade balance was usually slightly in Germany's favour. Britain sought to curtail the German predominance in the border area and keep the three states within the British sphere of influence. However, the increase in German political and economic power became inevitable as the Foreign Office, unlike its German counterpart, refused to back British economic engagement politically.[5]

Britain's limited involvement in the Baltic states did not mean a complete lack of interest in the region situated precariously between Poland, Germany and Soviet Russia. Open territorial disputes existed between Lithuania and Poland over Vilna,[6] and between Germany and Lithuania over Memel.[7] Moscow and Berlin shared an interest in the Baltic area as part of a ring around Poland. They therefore sought to curtail Franco-Polish ambitions to enlarge the *cordon sanitaire* designed to separate Germany and Russia and to prevent a security scheme along the lines of what was later called an eastern Locarno. After Rapallo, the British feared that Berlin and Moscow harboured aggressive intentions to satisfy their territorial demands against both the Baltic states and Poland.

Within the limits of the attention that could be given to a sideshow in European politics, the Foreign Office followed the events in the Baltic closely. Unwilling to get involved themselves, the British knew that the conflicting interests of many different factions in this area might easily upset the *status quo*. German moderating influence in the area was therefore a useful stabilising counterbalance against the rise of Bolshevism outside Russia and hence less objectionable than might otherwise have been the case.

German politicians were aware that their policy in the Baltic was followed with a critical eye in Whitehall. The credibility of Stresemann's western orientation depended upon the extent of his intimacy with Moscow. His policy in the Baltic, which contained a considerable anti-Polish element, thus had its limits.[8] When Locarno was followed by the German–Russian

---

5 This account of British policy in the Baltic states is based on Hinkkanen-Lievonen, *British trade*, 141–7. For German–Baltic relations see J. W. Hiden, *The Baltic states and Weimar Ostpolitik*, Cambridge 1987, and 'The "Baltic problem" in Weimar's Ostpolitik', in Berghan and Kitchen, *Germany in the age of total war*, 147–70. See also J. W. Hiden and P. Salomon, *The Baltic nations and Europe: Estonia, Latvia and Lithuania in the twentieth century*, London–New York 1991, ch. iii.

6 The contemporary terminology was 'Vilna' instead of today's 'Vilnius'.

7 A. E. Senn, *The great powers, Lithuania and the Vilna question, 1920–1928*, Leiden 1966, and 'The Polish–Lithuanian war scare 1927', *CEA* xxi (1961), 267–84; I. Röskau-Rydel, 'Polnisch-litauische Beziehungen zwischen 1918 und 1939', *JbfGO* xxxv (1987), 556–81.

8 Hiden, *Baltic states*, ch. vi.

neutrality treaty in 1926, the British knew that Berlin would not sacrifice her eastern ties for a western *rapprochement*. With growing confidence that Germany's policy was now oriented towards the west, Britain accepted that Berlin, despite and because of its eastern ties, could serve as a stabilising factor in the Baltic. This was all the more necessary as it was not the Rapallo partners, but the small states themselves that conducted an aggressive foreign policy.

Lithuania had 'solved' the Memel problem, pending since the Paris peace conference, by invading the area on 10 January 1923. Berlin could not retaliate as her hands were tied because of the Ruhr occupation. The conference of ambassadors officially approved the Lithuanian *fait accompli* on 16 February 1923. The Allied Memel convention of 8 May 1924 formally transferred the sovereignty of the Memel area to Lithuania.[9] More problematic in British eyes was the Polish–Lithuanian dispute over Vilna. Lithuania claimed ownership of the town for historical reasons, Poland on ethnic grounds as the population was mainly Polish. Vilna had changed hands several times between Lithuanian, Russian and Polish authorities during 1919/1920 and remained Polish-occupied after its invasion by a dissident Polish general in October 1920. Polish–Lithuanian tensions delayed Lithuanian diplomatic recognition by the Allied powers until 1922. The Vilna question proved impossible to solve in the following years as Lithuania categorically refused to retreat in this question of prestige and renounce her claim to the traditional capital.[10]

British concern that German grievances over Memel might lead to tensions in the Baltic turned out to be unfounded. Berlin was too preoccupied with her animosities against Poland and careful to prevent any Polish alliance with the Baltic states. Hence, the Germans were interested in reasonable relations with Lithuania and grudgingly acquiesced in the loss of Memel. In 1928 the two countries concluded a treaty confirming their frontiers, followed by a commercial agreement in 1929.

Polish–Lithuanian relations were more disturbing. The proposed Soviet guarantee of the Baltic states' borders in 1924, the Soviet–Lithuanian non-aggression pact of 28 September 1926 with the explicit Soviet recognition of Lithuania's claim on Vilna, and Kovno's[11] obvious attempts after Locarno and Augustinas Voldemaras's *coup d'état* in Lithuania in December 1926 to improve relations with Germany, raised fears in Warsaw and made Britain suspicious of renewed hostilities against Poland.[12] An alternative

---

9   G. von Rauch, *Geschichte der baltischen Staaten*, 3rd edn, Munich 1990, 105; Hiden, *Baltic states*, 148.

10 Hiden, *Baltic states*, 101–5; Senn, *Great powers*, 105–57; Korbel, *Poland between east and west*, ch. x.

11 Kovno, today Kaunas, was the Polish name for the Lithuanian capital.

12 Collier minutes, 4 Oct. 1926; Chamberlain, 7 Oct. 1926, on a report on German–Polish relations, PRO, FO 371/11281/C 10479; Max Muller to Chamberlain, 7 Oct. 1926, FO 371/11725/N 4551; Carr to Chamberlain, 16 Oct. 1926, FO 371/11726/N 4887; Chamberlain to Max Muller, 16 Oct. 1926, with enclosed reprint of Chamberlain to Max Muller and

scenario, which occurred after Piłsudski's *coup d'état* in Poland in May 1926, was a Polish occupation of Lithuania.[13] Speculative reports about various forms of German–Lithuanian–Russian–Polish combinations at the expense of one country or another circulated and disquieted the Foreign Office throughout 1927.[14]

With deteriorating Anglo-Soviet relations and Chamberlain's worries about Berlin's position in the dispute, German and Russian activities in the Baltic area received closer attention. At the height of the Arcos crisis in May 1927, Vaughan, the British envoy at Riga, wrote that 'it is difficult to estimate here how far a state of civil war and anarchy in Lithuania might prove an irresistible temptation to Marshal Piłsudski; and if the Poles marched on Kovno, the quiescence of Germany and the Soviet Union could obviously not be counted on for long'. Senior Foreign Office officials agreed that the outlook for this 'dangerously tempting situation both for the Poles and the Germans' was indeed grim.[15] This shift in attention is noticeable, given that previously senior Foreign Office officials had usually turned a blind eye towards warnings of trouble in the region. Now even the foreign secretary took a certain interest in the Baltic area.

Much to Britain's relief, the summer crisis passed without escalation. Polish–Lithuanian relations appeared to improve over the summer of 1927 but sharply deteriorated again from October. Piłsudski's attendance at the anniversary celebrations of the Vilna occupation, which were accompanied by anti-Lithuanian demonstrations, prompted the Lithuanian prime minister Voldemaras to complain to the League of Nations. The dispute seemed to escalate when on 24 November the Soviet minister in Warsaw officially warned Piłsudski that Moscow would not tolerate any Polish action against Lithuanian independence.

Britain was displeased with this development of affairs. From early November, Chamberlain and Briand contemplated sending a collective note to the Lithuanian government urging moderation. While this note should be co-signed by the Italians, they were divided about whether or not to include Berlin. Briand favoured a German participation but Chamberlain appeared reluctant. The Wilhelmstraße did not fail to notice the lack of comments on Polish–Lithuanian relations from Sir Ronald Lindsay, the British ambassador.[16]

---

others, 12 Apr. 1926, FO 371/11723/N 5803; Chamberlain to Max Muller, 26 Oct. 1926, FO 371/11281/C 11370; Rauch, *Baltische Staaten*, 118–20.

[13] FO memo Chamberlain, 24 Jan. 1927, PRO, FO 371/12589/N 342; Krüger, *Außenpolitik*, 320.

[14] Lindsay to Chamberlain, 18 Feb. 1927, PRO, FO 371/12127/C 1526; Vaughan to Chamberlain, 11 Mar. 1927, FO 371/12540/N 1288; Max Muller to Chamberlain, 20 Mar. 1927, FO 371/12546/N 1425; Vaughan to Chamberlain, 7 Sept. 1927, FO 371/12546/N 4462.

[15] Vaughan to FO, 6 May 1927, and minutes, PRO, FO 371/12537/N 2263.

[16] Stresemann to Botschaft Paris, 3 Nov. 1927; Stresemann to Botschaft Moskau, 5 Nov. 1927; Schubert to Botschaft Paris, 10 Nov. 1927; Hoesch to AA, 15 Nov. 1927, *ADAP*, ser.

Briand had good reasons to be interested in German participation in a solution of the Polish–Lithuanian dispute. In the conflict he saw the opportunity to tackle territorial disputes in east central Europe once and for all. Supported by Poincaré, Briand had developed plans for a Corridor–Memel exchange. Briand equally renewed his attempt at a revision of the Franco-Polish military convention to give Paris more influence over Polish policy in Lithuania, and other conflicts, which threatened to provoke a Soviet–Polish war.

Whitehall kept a low profile in the dispute. London feared an escalation and dreaded the possibility of being dragged in. Unlike France, whose Polish ally was involved, or Germany, which harboured resentments against both Warsaw and Kovno but backed Lithuania as the 'lesser evil' since the Corridor was more important than Memel, Britain had no direct interest in either party to the conflict. The Foreign Office therefore welcomed Lithuania's appeal to the League for a solution of the 'state of war', since League involvement had the advantage of not committing Britain directly.[17]

The western powers were not alone in their concern for the development of Polish–Lithuanian relations; Moscow was equally severely irritated. The Soviet–Lithuanian non-aggression treaty recognised the legitimacy of Kovno's claim to Vilna. Soviet diplomats, interested in Lithuania's independence, feared that her insistence on the validity of her demands might one day force her into union with Poland. This had to be prevented. Moreover, Berlin feared a definite settlement of the Vilna question as this might prejudice a decision on Germany's eastern borders and the Polish Corridor. Lithuania's independence was also vital to prevent the extension of the Franco-Polish *cordon sanitaire*. Hence, both Moscow and Berlin sought to eliminate the immediate danger of an armed conflict between the two countries but were highly interested in postponing a definite solution of the Vilna problem for the time being, as there was little chance that they would ever agree on a settlement of the question that was favourable to Poland.

By trying to keep their distance from the Polish–Lithuanian dispute, British officials risked doing justice to none of the conflicting parties. The lack of official relations with Soviet Russia increased Britain's difficulties as she could only guess at Moscow's intentions. Still, British officials mistrusted both German and Russian objectives and their impartiality as mediators. German officials declared on several occasions that they fully backed Lithuania over Vilna, but, for the moment, sought to prevent the outbreak of hostilities.

Britain could not ignore German interests in the Baltic area. The Foreign Office realised that all sides could only benefit from German participation in

B, vii, docs 68, 73, 88, 109; Senn, 'Polish–Lithuanian war scare', 267–8; Röskau-Rydel, 'Polnisch-litauische Beziehungen', 568–9; Keeton, *Briand's Locarno policy*, 278–84.
17 Schubert to Botschaft Paris, 10 Nov. 1927; Schubert to Botschaft Moskau, 13, 14 Nov. 1927; Hoesch to AA, 15 Nov. 1927, *ADAP*, ser. B, vii, docs 88, 98, 103, 109.

the search for a peaceful solution, and German contacts to the Lithuanian prime minister. Voldemaras spoke differently to different people, was interested in assistance from Berlin and Moscow and lent his ear more to their views than to British or French advice.[18] The Foreign Office learnt with satisfaction that Kovno's political course was no less clear to the Germans than to themselves. Officials were reluctant to formulate the British position in the conflict. They still hoped for international co-operation within the framework of the League, as this would involve the least British commitment.

The League council meeting in December 1927 in Geneva succeeded in removing major frictions between Kovno and Warsaw by shelving the issue of Vilna.[19] Yet Voldemaras continued to play the role of troublemaker. Polish–Lithuanian tensions reached a new height at the end of June 1928. The League was unable to solve the problem. Voldemaras was so obstructive that even Britain now agreed to a joint Anglo-French-German *démarche* in Kovno despite persisting mistrust of German intentions. But these joint representations equally proved futile. Voldemaras ignored the council. Angry and frustrated, Chamberlain wrote to Harold Nicolson, now the first secretary at the Berlin embassy, enquiring whether Stresemann could have another stern word with Voldemaras, 'who, I feared, was being encouraged by the Soviet government or at least by their agents, in spite of what Dr Stresemann had said to M. Litvinov in December'.[20]

British suspicions of Soviet interference only gradually diminished. Germany and France made 'very strong' representations in Kovno; Britain joined only informally. The repeated representations in Lithuania finally showed an effect. The Poles, fed up with Voldemaras, publicly toyed with a military intervention but reassured London privately that they would not resort to force.[21] Kovno's readiness to continue the negotiations was the sign for London to resume her former uninterested attitude in the affair, given that the Foreign Office was convinced that Poland would never resort to force without Allied consent. Lithuania could be brought to reason by international pressure as the German and Russian interventions had shown. The Polish–Lithuanian talks dragged on for years. Few results were achieved in endless negotiations about border traffic and economic issues. The Vilna problem remained the major obstacle to a bilateral settlement. German and Russian support for Lithuania was, however, now regarded as so unlikely that London could once again afford the luxury of turning a blind eye to future developments in the area.[22]

18 Voldemaras spoke several times to German diplomats about his intentions. There is no indication, however, that he ever consulted British officials: Schubert to Botschaft Moskau, 1 Nov. 1927; Aufzeichnung Dirksen, 5 Dec. 1927, *ADAP*, ser. B vii, doc. 103, 175.
19 For the proceedings at Geneva see Senn, 'Polish–Lithuanian war scare', 280–3; Keeton, *Briand's Locarno policy*, 280–4.
20 Chamberlain to Nicolson, 4 July 1928, PRO, FO 371/13268/N 3517.
21 Chamberlain to Erskine, 20 July 1928, PRO, FO 371/13268/N 3609.
22 Röskau-Rydel, 'Polnisch-litauische Beziehungen', 569–70.

Another aspect of the Rapallo relationship continued to occupy Foreign Office attention. Russo-German military ties persisted in flagrant violation of the treaty of Versailles. London did not expect an outbreak of hostilities in the immediate future, but resented the effect which the news of this collaboration would have on France and, as a result, on the process of reconciliation between the Allied powers and Germany.

Since Rapallo, the Foreign Office had attentively followed reports about Russo-German military co-operation but had never found them sufficiently alarming to demand an official British protest. The Foreign Office completely underestimated the extent of the Russo-German military relationship. This is all the more astonishing as London's information was very accurate and – pieced together – would have made a formidable case for protest.

London neither knew nor expected that Locarno had two sides. The agreement not only tied the Berlin government to the west, but also intensified contacts between the Reichswehr and the Red Army.[23] Moscow's attempts to prevent the Germans from signing Locarno resulted in a remarkable number of concessions to the Reichswehr, notably the surprisingly speedy and uncontroversial conclusion of a number of agreements concerning the establishment of test sites for planes and tanks, manoeuvre visits and exchange programmes for officers as well as contacts between the navies and general staffs. These agreements formed the basis of the intensive co-operation between the two armies from 1928 to 1932.

British mistrust towards Russo-German military co-operation nevertheless persisted and increased during 1927. On 26 December 1926 the *Manchester Guardian* sensationally revealed Russo-German military activities. The series of articles, combined with further discoveries by the Social Democratic organ *Vorwärts* and Philip Scheidemann's speech in the *Reichstag* on 16 December 1926, forced the German authorities into gradually confirming the allegations. At the same time, they declared however, that the contacts had been terminated.[24] British officials were irritated by the different incoming evaluations of Russo-German activities. Contradictory reports from Britain's missions in Moscow and Berlin left the Foreign Office confused.

Hodgson, the *chargé d'affaires* in Moscow commented on the *Manchester Guardian* revelations that

> the subject is one which has come up from time to time during the last five years. It has, however, invariably been surrounded by so many contradictions and uncertainties that I have never felt competent to express an opinion as to what proportion of the rumours in circulation is founded on fact and what is pure myth . . . On the whole I give it as my opinion that the recent campaign has a certain substratum of fact, but not much. There have been Germans over here, representatives of various political groups, and these Germans have been

---

23 Zeidler, *Reichswehr*, 130–3.
24 Lindsay to Chamberlain, 22, 25 Feb. 1927, PRO, FO 371/12589/C 1768/N 919; Zeidler, *Reichswehr*, 145–53.

in contact with Russian officials. It is quite likely – and I think, probable – that large plans for co-operation have been discussed. Yet I believe that very little except talk has really ensued and that the campaign regarding the 'Soviet grenades' is, in the main, a journalistic *feu d'artifice*.[25]

Hodgson's observations here are typical of his evaluations of Russo-German activities. The British *chargé d'affaires* tended to believe in the myths rather than the facts behind the rumours and continually played down Russo-German military co-operation. His views, misleading over so many years, played a pivotal role in influencing the Foreign Office's attitude. The former ambassador, D'Abernon, who had equally played down military relations, had in fact enhanced Hodgson's credibility. Sir Ronald Lindsay, D'Abernon's successor, was a more attentive and critical observer in this respect. His reports therefore overthrew a good deal of the longstanding Foreign Office views and as such were discomfiting.

Information confirming the existence of Russo-German military co-operation continued to arrive at the Foreign Office. Randal of the British legation to the Holy See, reported a conversation with the principal Vatican authority on Russia who, during a visit to Moscow, learnt of the activities of German technicians in key Soviet industrial positions.[26] An increasing number of reports pointed to the shipment of war material from German ports via Russia to China. This was the last thing Britain could tolerate, given the strategic importance of a non-communist China to the British empire and the British–Russian struggle over this issue. The Foreign Office seriously contemplated an official protest in Berlin as this not only violated the Versailles treaty, but also impacted on British vital interests. Yet there was an obstacle: Britain had no proof that the weapons were produced in Germany. British officials eventually refrained from taking action because Stresemann promised to stop the transportation of arms and ammunition from German harbours on German ships to China, hence unknowingly fulfilling British demands.[27]

In late June 1927 the Foreign Office had to deal with a parliamentary question enquiring about the truth of imports of poison gas from Russia into Germany and whether this constituted a breach of the treaty of Versailles. Officials squirmed when trying to find a diplomatic formula for the reply. 'An awkward question. . . . We don't want to go into details especially as our information is scanty', minuted Charles Howard-Smith.[28] The Foreign Office had information about a gas factory at Troitsk near Samara on the Volga. Consul-general Moritz Schlesinger of the Wilhelmstraße, in an interview with Lindsay, equally confirmed the existence of chemical warfare

25 Hodgson to Chamberlain, 19 Jan. 1927, PRO, FO 371/12598/N 520.
26 Randall to Chamberlain, 3 Mar. 1927, PRO, FO 371/12597/N 1033.
27 Warsaw Chancery to Central department, 8 Apr. 1927, PRO, FO 371/12139/C 3560.
28 Howard-Smith minute, 28 June 1927, PRO, FO 371/12150/C 5662; Jacobson, *Soviet Union*, 212–15.

co-operation on 19 May.[29] In his reply to parliament, Chamberlain admitted that these reports constituted a violation of the peace treaty, but declared his faith in German reassurances that the contacts had been terminated.

The Foreign Office's proclaimed faith in Germany was soon put to the test. In late July London received information about the employment of German aeronautical and naval instructors by the Soviet government.[30] The War Office had evidence showing that Germany was making plans for an army in excess of what she was allowed under the treaty of Versailles.[31] Nothing was done or, as Howard-Smith correctly noted, could be done. Not only would Britain's intelligence sources be compromised – with the consequence that information channels might be endangered; overly detailed references to the violations of the peace treaties would attract French attention and provide a useful pretext for further delays in the negotiations on disarmament, evacuation of the Rhineland, and reparations. Yet Britain was careful not to increase German frustration over these issues, as this might help to drive her into Moscow's arms.

The British dilemma had turned full circle. A solution to the problem continued to be remote, despite an increasing number of reports concerning Russo-German co-operation. Moreover, the information available to British officials showed the extent to which Germany managed to circumvent the restrictions imposed upon her by Versailles. For instance, Russia had placed large orders for war material at Venlo in the Netherlands, where the Dutch firm Nedinsco used the patents of Zeiss of Jena to manufacture periscopes, artillery range-finders, and other essential equipment. Large orders for hides and glycerine had likewise been placed in the Netherlands, doubling the prices over a year.[32] Already during 1926 and 1927, Russia had imported raw materials such as copper, lead, zinc and rubber on a large scale from Germany, Czechoslovakia and the Netherlands. Moscow, the Foreign Office concluded, was obviously building up a modern army with up-to-date equipment although, for the moment, nothing indicated that Moscow was preparing for aggressive action.[33]

In the first half of 1928, most attention was paid to further weapon shipments from Germany to China via Russia. Chamberlain was 'rather alarmed

---

[29] Perowne minute, 28 June 1927, PRO, FO 371/12150/C 5662; Lindsay to Sargent, 19 May 1927, FO 371/12595/N 2343. 'Troitsk' should probably read 'Tomka', which was the key testing plant for chemical weapons between 1928 and 1931. The establishment of the Tomka plant had been agreed by *Reichswehr* and Red Army officers in March 1927: Zeidler, *Reichswehr*, 198–204. In previous years the German firm Stolzenberg had made experiments with poison gas in Russia: ibid. 97–100.

[30] This information points to Lipeck, the air fighter school and test site, which was established in early 1926: ibid. 179.

[31] Howard-Smith minute, undated (end of July 1927), PRO, FO 371/12595/N 3744; WO to FO, 23 Aug. 1927, FO 371/12123/C 7066.

[32] Grenville to Chamberlain, 30 Dec. 1927, PRO, FO 371/13311/N 30.

[33] Lindsay to Chamberlain, 22 May 1928, PRO, FO 371/13311/N 2846.

at the serious development', as the weapons were used to support the Chinese National government seeking independence from Britain. British authorities examined the issue of whether these exports were compatible with German obligations under the peace treaty, but did not arrive at a definite conclusion. Carl von Schubert had reassured them that legislation would be changed if the British could bring confirmation of the various allegations.[34] British hands were tied, however. A Committee of Imperial Defence (CID) report on the military situation in Germany concluded that despite the arms traffic to Russia and China, Berlin was in no position to wage an aggressive war because it lacked the necessary armaments and equipment. Hence, no action was required and the Foreign Office could not even protest against the appointment of Colonel Bauer as military adviser to the Chinese national government.[35]

Russo-German political relations were abruptly frozen after the arrest of German engineers in the Donez basin in Russia in March 1928.[36] However, military contacts nonetheless continued and increased. In December 1928 London learnt that General von Blomberg, the chief of the Truppenamt, attended Soviet army manoeuvres.[37] The Foreign Office was at pains to find an interpretation, which would not make the issue an infraction of article 179 of the treaty of Versailles. Howard-Smith minuted that

> The word 'mission' is not defined in the article and I should have thought that it might be contended that the word 'mission' used in connection with military measures can only mean a number of officers appointed after agreement between two governments for the instruction of the military forces of one of them. . . . This is surely different from the presence of certain German officers at foreign manoeuvres. However, we need not raise this point.[38]

[34] Central department to Berlin Chancery, 21 Feb. 1928, PRO, FO 371/12889/C 1433; Sargent to Wills, 9 Mar. 1928, FO 371/12889/C 1635.
[35] CID report, 17 Dec. 1928, PRO, FO 371/12889/C 9467; Lampson to FO, 26 Feb. 1929, FO 371/13956/F 2558; Howard-Smith to FO, 12 Mar. 1929, FO 371/14045/N 1737. Bauer died, however, before he could take over his post: Ashton-Gwatkin minute, 28 May 1929, FO 371/13936/F 1679.
[36] Jacobson, Soviet Union, 242–3.
[37] The reference is to Blomberg's journey through the Soviet Union between 19 August and 17 September 1928: Zeidler, Reichswehr, 337. The German government refused to allow Allied officers to observe German army manoeuvres: Nicolson to Chamberlain, 13 July 1928, DBFP, 1A ser. v, doc. 90. The British military attaché, Cornwall, attended Reichswehr manoeuvres unofficially as Schlachtenbummler (cheerleader). He gained the impression that the Reichswehr contained the nucleus of a very formidable fighting organisation, although its equipment, its tactics and the standard of training seemed backward: Cornwall to Rumbold, 28 Sept., and Rumbold to Cushendun, 3 Oct. 1928, ibid. doc. 174. This evaluation was still held in 1930: chief of the imperial general staff memo, 11 Feb. 1930, DBFP, 2nd ser. i, appendix 2.
[38] Rumbold to Chamberlain, 7 Dec. 1928; Howard-Smith minute, 13 Dec. 1928, PRO, FO 371/12889/C 9232.

The true extent of Russo-German military co-operation remained hidden from British officials. Despite the fact that the years 1928–32 marked the height of the collaboration, Britain faced difficulties in following it as most of the contacts took place in the Soviet Union. The lack of diplomatic relations with Moscow severely hampered British observations about Russo-German military links. Nevertheless, the information available in London was accurate and surprisingly detailed. Officials made no use of it because they did not wish to recognise its importance. London was preoccupied with disarmament and nothing was more disturbing to the negotiations than secret German rearmament. The recognition that there was no way of stopping the Russo-German contacts led the Foreign Office to turn a blind eye to inconvenient military reports.

At the end of the 1920s, the Rapallo alliance, i.e. German–Russian secret co-operation, ceased to be threatening to most of Germany's and Soviet Russia's neighbours. The shadows of Versailles receded, Germany's revisionist ambitions were satisfied step by step. The Rapallo treaty no longer held its original significance as Germany came to realise that a modification of the peace treaty could be achieved only with the co-operation of the western powers. A close alliance with Moscow was counterproductive in this respect, given Moscow's economic difficulties and diplomatic isolation. Nevertheless, Berlin would not go as far as to sacrifice her ties with the Soviet Union just for the sake of an alliance with the west. Moscow was always useful as a counterweight against the former victors. From a pragmatic point of view, the Soviets were indispensable to the Germans because of the contacts between the *Reichswehr* and the Red Army. Moreover, the threat of a revival of Rapallo remained a powerful bargaining card.

This bargaining card had more weight in Paris than in London. Britain, refused to be affected by a Russo-German alliance but could not completely ignore it because of its impact on the French as well as on certain limited parts of the empire. The Foreign Office, in many cases, ignored Russo-German co-operation. Officials were convinced that this relationship did not pose a sufficient threat to the *status quo* to justify an intervention. Even in such cases as military co-operation, officials refrained from any action in order not to irritate France and thereby endanger the process of reconciliation between Paris and Berlin. A renewed conflict between these two powers would only increase the British commitment in Europe, and this was a situation the Foreign Office was determined to avoid.

8

An Economic Rapallo?

'That the Russian threat is economic rather than political in character seems now to be recognised on all sides', minuted a high-ranking Foreign Office official on 3 March 1931.[1] This remark was made at a high point in the Anglo-German rivalry for business in the Soviet Union, which had been ongoing since the end of the First World War. Germany's position at this time was more favourable for a variety of reasons: her pre-war trade experience with the tsarist empire, the most-favoured nation clause in the Rapallo treaty and the trade agreement of October 1925. Wherever they could, British diplomats therefore tried to follow in the paths which Germany had paved.

International economic co-operation in Russia did not materialise in the 1920s. Germany, Britain and also the United States remained close competitors, not least because the Soviet authorities objected to any form of international co-operation for fear that this would turn into a capitalist front against them.[2] Yet on 4 February 1930 consul-general Moritz Schlesinger, the leading expert on Soviet Russia in the German ministry of foreign affairs, suggested to John Thelwall, the commercial counsellor at the British embassy in Berlin, that there should be closer Anglo-German economic co-operation in the Soviet Union, on the understanding that it should be kept secret from the Moscow government. According to Sir Horace Rumbold, Britain's ambassador in Berlin since 1928, Schlesinger had offered to furnish any information desired about the general trend of business between Germany and Russia, about the amount and length of credit given as well as its terms, 'in fact anything that we might care to ask, provided, of course, that we gave him similar information if he wanted it'.[3]

This German move might seem extraordinary at first sight. Yet Russo-

---

1 Nichols minute, 3 Mar. 1931, PRO, FO 371/15224/C 1357.
2 H. James, *The Reichsbank and public finance in Germany, 1924–1933: a study of the politics of economics during the great depression*, Frankfurt-am-Main 1985, 306–8. The Soviets pursued a policy of peaceful coexistence in their economic relations with the capitalist states. Their foreign trade monopoly allowed them to choose where and what to buy: W. Beitel and J. Nötzold, *Deutsch-sowjetische Wirtschaftsbeziehungen in der Zeit der Weimarer Republik. Eine Bilanz im Hinblick auf gegenwärtige Probleme*, Baden-Baden 1979, 54–5; R.-D. Müller, *Das Tor zur Weltmacht. Die Bedeutung der Sowjetunion für die Wirtschafts- und Rüstungspolitik zwischen den Weltkriegen*, Boppard 1984, 188, 199.
3 Rumbold to Henderson, 7 Feb. 1930, PRO, FO 371/14371/C 1156. On Schlesinger see H. von Dirksen, *Moscow, Tokyo, London: twenty years of German foreign policy*, London 1951, 92; G. Hilger and A. Meyer, *The incompatible allies: a memoir history of German–Soviet relations, 1918–1941*, New York 1953, 24–5; Dyck, *Weimar Germany*, 50–6.

German relations had rarely been worse than at the time of Schlesinger's initiative.[4] Since the 1925 commercial treaty between Berlin and Moscow, the Soviets had been pressing Berlin for a large credit in order to finance Russian orders in Germany. In 1926, the German government eventually granted an export credit guarantee for 300 million *Reichsmark* in order to secure closer links between the two economies. At the same time Berlin attempted to interest British and American capital in business with Russia, believing that it was vital to arrange and control the influx of foreign capital into Russia to ensure that the dominant German position in the Russian market would not be endangered.[5]

Although the German export industry benefited considerably from the 1926 credit line as well as from the rupture of Anglo-Soviet relations in 1927, German business circles were nevertheless disappointed with developments in Russo-German economic relations. The Soviet policy of granting concessions to western firms operating in Russia was considered to be too restrictive, leaving these companies insufficient freedom of action. Complaints about harassment by Soviet authorities were frequent. Stresemann informed Soviet diplomats that further German credits to Moscow were dependent on greater consideration of German business needs. Russo-German relations suffered further with the arrest of German engineers and specialists in the Donez basin on suspicion of 'counter-revolutionary activities' in the summer of 1928.[6] As a result, the ongoing trade negotiations for a new 600 million *Reichsmark* credit were abruptly frozen. Russia also attempted to play off the capitalist states – notably her largest trading partners, Britain and Germany – against one another in order to get the best credit terms possible, to the point of purchasing British goods with German money.

German businesses were consequently reluctant to concede further credits to the Soviet Union, unless the Berlin government guaranteed them. They argued that there was growing uncertainty as to the amount of Soviet debt to other countries as Russia's domestic situation deteriorated, and the country faced a new food crisis. The Germans feared that this crisis would force Moscow to spend her small hard currency reserves on importing foodstuff during the crucial period between November 1928 and March 1929 when large Russian repayments to Germany – 160 million out of the 300 million *Reichsmark* credit – were due.[7] Given this economic and political scenario, German politicians were reluctant to guarantee new credits to Russia unless her political and economic relations improved. Moreover, there had been a

4   Rumbold to Henderson, 31 Jan. 1930, PRO, FO 371/14371/C 940; Dirksen to AA, 29 Dec. 1930, Dirksen papers, BA-Po, vol. 50; James, *Reichsbank*, 305–16; J. Haslam, *Soviet foreign policy, 1930–1933*, London 1983, 28–31, 58–70.
5   Schäffer diary entry, 24 May 1926, Schäffer papers, IfZ, ED 93/2.
6   E. H. Carr, *Foundations of a planned economy, 1926–1929*, iii/1, London 1970, 51–3; Jacobson, *Soviet Union*, 243.
7   Schubert to Brockdorff-Rantzau, undated (June 1928), PA-AA, R 94538.

sharp downward trend in German economic activity since the autumn of 1928, resulting in high unemployment rates and an even higher budget deficit.[8] As German liquidity problems grew, the country's credit crisis reached a peak in 1929. In the negotiations prior to the Young plan, the Germans referred to their financial weakness in order to get the final reparations sum fixed at the lowest level possible. The issuing of further credits to Moscow would have undermined this argument.

These economic strains hardly encouraged the granting of further large-scale credits to Russia. Yet the German economy was dependent on trade with Moscow, if only to prevent a further increase in unemployment, which would place an even greater burden on the budget. Opinions among German politicians were divided as to whether to take the risk and attempt to revive Russo-German commercial relations by permitting new credits, or whether to refrain from further involvement given the Soviet economic situation.[9] For its part, Moscow continued to press for new credits from Berlin and continued to play the Germans off against the British.[10] The German government faced a balancing act as it tried to calculate the advantages and risks attached to further credit issues. It was obvious, however, that for economic and particularly for financial reasons the terms which Germany had granted in the 1926 credit scheme could not be maintained.

Schlesinger, in charge of Russian economic affairs at the Wilhelmstraße and a protagonist of Soviet–German economic co-operation, was officially among those urging caution in dealings with Moscow, although he was aware of the importance of the Russian market to the German economy. Earlier attempts to co-ordinate German economic interests with those of other countries, notably France, had been unsuccessful and had been put on ice during the negotiations for the Young plan. So Germany had to go it alone for the sake of her own economic and financial stability, which made trade with Russia imperative. For its part, the Soviet economy and Stalin's first five-year plan depended on imports which could be financed only by credits. The German government had to guarantee these credits because it relied on Moscow repaying the money. The government knew that if credits were stopped as a result of Soviet failure to meet its liabilities, the Soviets' whole process of forced industrialisation would collapse, making the credit repayment even less likely.

The Foreign Office did not understand this mutual Russo-German economic dependence. Officials mistrusted Berlin's credit policy and were

8   Müller, Tor, 200; H. James, The German slump: politics and economics, 1924–1936, Oxford 1986, ch. iii.
9   Müller, Tor, 200–4; W. Gosmann, 'Die Stellung der Reparationsfrage in der Außenpolitik der Kabinette Brüning', in J. Becker and K. Hildebrand (eds), Internationale Beziehungen in der Weltwirtschaftskrise 1929–33, Munich 1980, 237–63 at pp. 244–5.
10   Lindsay to Chamberlain, 27 Nov. 1927; Tyrrell/Palairet to Lindsay, 29 Nov. 1927, PRO, FO 371/12582/N 5644.

concerned about Moscow's ability to repay the loans.[11] William Peters, the British counsellor in Moscow, was the only Briton who recognised the driving considerations behind the Russo-German credit agreements:

> I personally consider that the Soviet government would not hesitate, if it were a case of meeting foreign liabilities, to falsify bank statements or to doctor them so as to conceal the use of gold reserves for the liquidation of foreign obligations . . . Abroad Soviet credit would disappear in a night were a single foreign obligation to remain unfulfilled. No one appreciates this better than the Soviet government, and for that reason it may be confidently stated that should Soviet concerns get into financial difficulties the very last people to suffer would be foreign creditors.[12]

London had little idea about the ruthlessness of the Soviet rulers. British officials could not believe that the Soviets would rather see their population starve than fail to pay their bills. The Foreign Office applied the standards of western business negotiations and the behaviour of gentlemen to a dictatorship in which the individual counted for nothing. This British inability to understand the Bolshevik mentality, a consequence of Britain's continuing misapprehension of communist ideology and its impact on Soviet policy, eventually caused her to lose out to Germany economically.

In February 1930, Schlesinger approached the British with a suggestion for German–British economic co-operation in Russia because he believed British and German interests to be compatible. Until 1930 Berlin had been Russia's only creditor (and on a large scale) but German officials knew that the British had been negotiating for a credit agreement with Moscow in 1927 before the rupture of diplomatic relations.[13] As the Germans hoped to reduce their credit involvement in Russia without giving it up completely, the possibility of co-ordinating their efforts with the British made good sense.

The Foreign Office was surprised by the German initiative, as the Rapallo partners had never before permitted anyone else to participate in their economic relationship. Schlesinger, however, was only pursuing an idea, which the former head of the Northern desk of the Foreign Office, Gregory, had raised as early as 1926.[14] The immediate British reaction to the German offer

---

[11] FO minute, 30 Mar. 1927, PRO, FO 371/12585/N 1570; Lindsay to Chamberlain, 11 Apr. 1927, FO 371/12595/N 1715; Lindsay to Sargent, 19 May 1927, FO 371/12595/N 2343.

[12] Peters to Chamberlain, 21 April 1927, PRO, FO471/12585/N 2014. On Anglo-Soviet trade relations see A. Williams, *Trading with the Bolsheviks: the politics of east–west trade, 1920–1939*, Manchester 1992, 80–9.

[13] Brockdorff-Rantzau to AA, 19 May 1927, PA-AA, R 94463; Schubert to Brockdorff-Rantzau, undated [June 1928], PA-AA, R 94538; unsigned and undated *Aufzeichnung* about a talk with Rosengolz, Soviet *chargé d'affaires* in London, PA-AA, R 28295k; Schäffer diary entry, 23 Nov. 1929, Schäffer papers, Jft, ED 93/7; Dalton diary entries, 22 Jan. 1930, 3 Mar. 1930, Dalton papers, BLPES, I/13.

[14] Unsigned despatch to AA, 30 June 1926, PA-AA, Deutsche Botschaft London, vol. 712; Dufour to AA, 11, 28 Aug. 1926, PA-AA, R 28409k, R 31591–4k.

was not unfriendly but also not free from *Schadenfreude*. 'We have known for some time that the German commercial treaty was not working at all well. It is, to say the least, gratifying to hear from the Germans themselves . . . that our policy in refusing to give the Soviet government a full commercial treaty was the right one', commented Charles Bateman, chiefly responsible for economic issues in the Northern department.[15] Before any reply could be given to Berlin, the Board of Trade and the Department of Overseas Trade had to be consulted, as the procedure for decisions of economic nature that lay outside the Foreign Office's competence demanded. As will be shown, it was precisely because of this division of responsibility and the limited liaison between the different Whitehall departments that the Schlesinger initiative was doomed to failure. The British response to Berlin was delayed for so long that, by the time an exchange of views was resumed, Germany had arranged matters directly with Russia, much to the displeasure of the Foreign Office.

Schlesinger could not have chosen a more inconvenient moment to make his offer to Britain, as the disastrous economic effects of the October 1929 Wall Street crash and the beginning of the Great Depression began to show. Britain was severely hit by the economic crisis and faced a sharp rise in unemployment with severe consequences for the budget. The Labour party, back in office since the May 1929 elections, had yet to realise its election promise to revive trade with Russia and had only started bilateral commercial negotiations with Moscow in January 1930. Opinions not only between Conservatives and Labour, but also within the Labour party were divided as to the speed with which contacts with Moscow should be resumed.[16] While William Graham, president of the Board of Trade, advocated a slower approach, foreign secretary Arthur Henderson urged prime minister Ramsay MacDonald to take rapid action. This departmental disagreement 'set the tone for a Foreign Office/Board of Trade enmity on the Russian question for the rest of the negotiations'.[17] Another problem on which departmental views diverged was the distinction drawn between trade and finance. Without British credits trade with the Russians could not be financed. The chancellor of the exchequer, Philip Snowden, had conservative views on what constituted 'sound finance' and opposed too generous credits. The situation was further complicated because the commercial attaché at the Moscow embassy reported to the Board of Trade, whereas the Foreign Office received economic information from Sir Edmund Ovey, the British ambassador.[18]

Anglo-Soviet trade negotiations progressed slowly. Whitehall departments

15 Bateman minute, 17 Feb. 1930, PRO, FO 371/14371/C 1368.
16 Sthamer to AA, 10, 26 Feb. 1930, PA-AA, R 94389, R 35902; Parliamentary debates, HoC, 5th ser. vccxxxiv, cols 1927–86, 5 Feb. 1930; vccxxxv, cols 1854–8, 24 Feb. 1930; Aufzeichnung Schlesinger, 24 Mar. 1930, PA-AA, Deutsche Botschaft Moskau, vol. 33/3.
17 A. Williams, *Labour and Russia: the attitude of the Labour party to the USSR, 1924–1934*, Manchester 1989, 110–12 at p. 111.
18 Williams, *Trading*, 192; D. G. Boadle, 'The formation of the Foreign Office economic relations section, 1930–1937', *HJ* xx (1977), 919–36.

could not agree on the terms for export credits. The compromise reached in the cabinet on 5 March 1930 was largely prime minister MacDonald's work and permitted an export credits guarantee for a maximum of twelve months. On 1 April, almost seven weeks after Schlesinger had first spoken to Thelwall, the Department of Overseas Trade approved an exchange of views between British and German officials.[19] This decision illustrates the department's dissatisfaction with the present state of Anglo-Russian trade relations and the cabinet decision. The department believed that it was worth examining whether the Anglo-Soviet deadlock in the trade negotiations could be improved with German assistance.

Despite the Department of Overseas Trade's consent to an exchange of views, another seven months were to elapse before communications with the Germans were renewed. At the end of October, Schlesinger again approached the commercial counsellor in Berlin and told him about the present state of Berlin's commercial relations with Moscow. Schlesinger not only mentioned that the German government's export credits guarantee had been increased from 60% to 70% of the value of goods, but also that the Russians were still endeavouring to play Britain and Germany off against each other with regard to credit terms. He considered it inadvisable to increase the present length of credits beyond twenty-four – but preferably only eighteen – months. He was also concerned that the Soviets' dumping policy could lead to export restrictions on Russian goods, which, in turn, might make it difficult for Moscow to fulfil its obligations to her creditors.[20]

The contrast between Schlesinger's renewed effort to seek out the British and the lack of interest shown in London, embarrassed the Foreign Office. Officials realised that the German offer had both political and economic advantages for Britain. This was a unique opportunity not only to get the long desired entry into the Russian market, but also to influence Russo-German relations indirectly. A letter was sent to the Export Credits Guarantee Department, the Board of Trade and the Department of Overseas Trade, urging all departments to provide information which could be passed on to Berlin.[21] On 26 November Schlesinger again asked Thelwall whether Britain had granted an export credits guarantee to Russia that exceeded eighteen months, for Moscow had repeatedly informed the German government that she could receive longer credits in Britain.[22]

In mid-January 1931, almost one year after Schlesinger's first initiative,

---

[19] DOT to FO, 1 Apr. 1930, PRO, FO 371/14371/C 2577.

[20] For a general description of German credit terms to the Soviet Union see Beitel and Nötzold, *Deutsch-sowjetische Wirtschaftsbeziehungen*, 60–73. For the specific German decision-making process in the summer of 1930 concerning an increased term for the credits see H.-W. Niemann, 'Die Russengeschäfte in der Ära Brüning', VSWG lxxii (1985), 153–74 at pp. 156–8.

[21] Rumbold to Henderson, 31 Oct. 1930; Seymour to Stirling (Export Credits Guarantee Department), 22 Nov. 1930, PRO, FO 371/14883/N 7950.

[22] Newton to Henderson, 26 Nov. 1930, PRO, FO 371/14886/N 8316.

the Export Credits Guarantee Department sent Nixon on an informal visit to Berlin to discuss the issue.[23] Schlesinger told Nixon that Germany had to reconsider her export credit terms to Russia because of her tight financial situation and the growing problem of unemployment. He sought co-operation with London because it was difficult to withdraw from conditions already granted – such as the length of credits – while the Russians continued to play Germany off against Britain. Nixon, in turn, described the British credits scheme in general terms, but no arrangement was made at this meeting.

Berlin was highly interested in an agreement with Britain, which was given priority over an agreement with France. From May 1931, the already crumbling German financial situation sharply deteriorated. After the Austro-German customs union affair, German business and foreign creditors withdrew capital on a large scale, while the *Reichsbank* and ministries were insufficiently informed about the seriousness of the situation.[24] A reshuffling of German debts and reparation payments in order to counter the shortage of financial reserves in German banks became increasingly urgent and was finally achieved by the Hoover moratorium and at the London conference in July 1931. The situation was so precarious that, had Russia defaulted on the repayment of her credits to Germany, the effects on German finances would have been disastrous. During the visit of *Reichskanzler* Heinrich Brüning and foreign minister Julius Curtius to Chequers in early June 1931,[25] as well as during prime minister MacDonald's and foreign secretary Henderson's return visit to Berlin in July 1931,[26] the question of Anglo-German economic co-operation in Russia was discussed. However, it was agreed that this aspect of the respective talks – which was only a small part of a bigger picture – should remain secret in order to prevent Moscow from becoming suspicious.

Unanimously, British officials of various government departments took an interest in what the Germans had to say about the Russian credit issue. However, they failed to understand that Germany's motivation was primarily financial and that Germany was trying to slow down the meltdown of her currency reserves. Economic considerations came second and, for the first time, even political issues were subordinated to financial problems.[27] The

[23] Nixon memo, 22 Jan. 1931, PRO, FO 371/15602/N 968; Stirling to Seymour, 1 Jan. 1931, PRO, FO 371/15599/N 55.

[24] The Bank of England was considerably more sympathetic to German financial problems than the Banque de France: G. Schulz, *Von Brüning zu Hitler*, Berlin 1992, 394–411.

[25] Newton to Sargent, 19 June 1931; Brown (BoT) to Nichols, 3 July 1931, PRO, FO 371/15622/N 4994; Aufzeichnung Curtius, 10 June 1931, PA-AA, R 28229k. The German version of the talks is that British officials suggested to them some form of co-operation in Russia, whereas British officials claimed that they had been approached by Curtius. From the overall German situation and the general British attitude it seems more likely that the Germans had raised the issue first.

[26] Neville Butler's notes on the prime minister's visit to Berlin, July 1931, MacDonald papers, PRO, 30/69/292. On the Chequers meeting see E. W. Bennett, *Germany and the diplomacy of the financial crisis, 1931*, Cambridge, MA 1962, 122–31.

[27] Rödder's otherwise excellent study is unaware of the British involvement in the

Foreign Office incorrectly assumed that Germany had lost faith in the stability of the present regime in Russia and therefore sought an arrangement over the credit terms. Officials did not understand the complex structural shortcomings of the German economy, which had led to the financial crisis and suspected that Germany had let her financial situation deteriorate deliberately in order to achieve political concessions.[28]

The revised May 1931 edition of Vansittart's memorandum 'An Aspect of International Relations' is a classic example of this British view.[29] It described the German economy as a state-controlled structure deliberately serving nationalist ambitions. Germany's overall policy seemed to be subordinated to economic imperialism, as indicators for which served: her reparations policy, the Customs Union proposal, the seemingly excessive military budget, German demands for equality in armaments and the revision of her eastern frontier. Vansittart was convinced that the Brüning government had provoked the German financial crisis deliberately to achieve the abolition of reparations. He also predicted that admitting the German financial weakness too candidly would lead to a panic withdrawal of foreign capital.

The British interest in maintaining German financial stability was guided by the overriding desire to save her own shattered credit system and to secure the repayment of British short-term credits to Germany, which amounted to seventy million pounds sterling. Officials saw a solution to the German financial crisis primarily in terms of French and American financial assistance. The former, however, could only be attained if Germany made substantial political concessions to French demands for security. British officials therefore tried to convince Berlin of the necessity of meeting French demands – unsuccessfully as it turned out.[30]

The British view that the financial crisis was politically motivated affected its perception of the German drive for an agreement over Russia. British officials totally underestimated the *Reich's* desperate financial situation, including that of the *Reichsbank*. Even after the crash of the Vienna *Creditanstalt*, the governor of the Bank of England failed to anticipate the collapse of the German banking structure. Because they underestimated the seriousness of the German financial situation, British negotiators approached the Schlesinger offer from a purely economic point of view. They attributed much more importance to information on the questions of trade quantities

Russo-German credit issue: A. Rödder, *Stresemanns Erbe. Julius Curtius und die deutsche Außenpolitik 1929–1931*, Paderborn 1996, 158–64.

[28] James, *German slump*, 50–73; J. von Kruedener (ed.), *Economic crisis and political collapse: the Weimar Republic, 1924–1933*, New York–Oxford–Munich 1990.

[29] Original memo, 1 May 1930, revised memo, Mar., May 1931, Vansittart papers, CCAC, VNST 1/1. Vansittart's change of mind in his attitude towards Germany between March and May 1931 is interesting.

[30] K. Jaitner, 'Deutschland, Brüning und die Formulierung der britischen Außenpolitik Mai 1930 bis Juni 1932', *VfZg* xxviii (1980), 440–86 at pp. 463–5; Link, *Amerikanische Stabilisierungspolitik*, 502.

and the proportion of British and German trade in Russia – i.e. how much would go to Germany and how much to Britain – than to the German financial situation. The visit of German industrialists to the Soviet Union in March 1931 was observed principally to determine whether this would further increase the German share of trade in Russia at Britain's expense.[31]

It was not easy for British officials to form a clear opinion of the German situation. The main problem was the division of competencies within Whitehall. The Foreign Office had little knowledge of economic and financial issues and no influence on them at all.[32] The Treasury, Board of Trade and Department of Overseas Trade, on the other hand, often failed to grasp the political side of economic questions. In the case of credits to the Soviet Union, the discussion between German and British authorities was complicated by the fact that, unlike the British, the German ministry of foreign affairs had established an economic section after the First World War.[33] When German diplomats approached the British embassy in Berlin on economic questions, reports normally went first to the Foreign Office in London, which would register them and pass them on to the departments in charge. It could take no action but also showed no desire to be consulted in economic affairs: 'Interdepartmental co-operation on economic questions was haphazard and burdened by petty jealousies.'[34]

From the outset, the Foreign Office had welcomed the possibility of Anglo-German co-operation in Russia. Britain could only benefit economically from the German offer, because she too needed new markets.[35] Despite a cabinet decision to proceed with economic talks with Germany, the mechanisms to allow the exchange of views so urgently desired by the Germans were barely put into gear.[36] Neither the Department of Overseas Trade nor the Export Credits Guarantee Department nor the Treasury provided the relevant information to the Germans. Angrily, Orme Sargent, head of the Central department wrote to the Department of Overseas Trade on 21 July 1931:

> You may remember that early last year we wrote to you regarding the proposal that Thelwall should exchange information, particularly on the subject of trade with the Soviet Union, with the Commercial department of the German ministry of foreign affairs, and that you replied that you entirely favoured such an exchange of opinion . . . while the Germans have been very forthcom-

---

31 Ovey to Henderson, 3, 13 Mar. 1931, PRO, FO 371/15224/C 1360/C 1746; Ovey to Henderson, 23 Mar. 1931, FO 371/15612/N 2151. On 2 April Schlesinger had informed the commercial counsellor about the outcome of the recent visit of German industrialists to the USSR: Rumbold to Henderson, 2, 17 April 1931, FO 371/15224/C 2305/C 2668.
32 Boadle, 'Economic relations section', passim.
33 Krüger, Außenpolitik, 27.
34 Boadle, 'Economic relations section', 920–1.
35 P. Williamson, National crisis and national government: British politics, the economy and the empire, 1926–1932, Cambridge 1992, 58–78.
36 Conclusions of cabinet meeting 36 (31), 1 July 1931, CAB 23/67.

ing Thelwall has not yet been in a position to give anything in return. This seems rather unsatisfactory and I wonder whether you can suggest any remedy.[37]

The Foreign Office had every reason to be apprehensive about its failure to achieve an exchange of views with Germany. Although Germany, unable to pay reparations, was under pressure from its creditors and had arranged a first standstill agreement with them on 17 September, there was no sign that she was altering her liberal credit policy towards Russia.[38] Part of the Hoover moratorium had been a German promise to cut expenditure,[39] but this obviously did not apply to credits to Russia. British officials knew that Russia was concerned about the precarious German financial situation and feared that Germany would cut back her credit involvement.[40] They did not know that, at the height of the financial crisis in mid-July, Moscow had urged Berlin to release some frozen Russian accounts in German banks so that Moscow could meet maturing bills and would not lose her credit-worthiness. The German government had secretly agreed to meet the Russian demand, because Reich and Länder did not have the financial means to pay the 70% export credits guarantee in the case of Soviet default.[41] Moreover, in September 1931 the *Reichsbank* approved a new rediscount credit worth 150 million marks to the Russians.

It certainly seems extraordinary that the Germans should be able to grant credits of this amount and duration after the events of recent months. Clearly the negotiations have not been easy: the press has contained vague statements for some time past about them. The result shows again the immense bargaining powers of the Soviet government in giving orders of this size,[42]

minuted junior official R. M. A. Hankey who, despite his subordinate status, had remarkably sound judgement. Bateman even went a step further: 'Should it not be advisable to make the point raised by Mr Hankey with the Treasury? It is extraordinary that Germany can afford these enormous credits to Soviet

[37] Sargent to E. Crowe, 21 July 1931, PRO, FO 371/15622/N 4994.
[38] Schulz, *Brüning*, 463. On the international financial crisis of 1931 see Bennett, *Financial crisis*, passim; Carlton, *MacDonald versus Henderson*, 197–217; H. James, 'The causes of the German banking crisis of 1931', EcHR xxxvii (1984), 68–87, and *German slump*, passim; B. Eichengreen, 'The origins and nature of the great slump revisited', EcHR xlv (1992), 213–39; Williamson, *National crisis*, 255–426.
[39] FO memo on Hoover scheme and proposed gesture by Germany, 13 July 1931, PRO, FO 371/15187/C 5172; Tyrrell to FO, 16 July 1931, FO 371/15187/C 5295.
[40] Ovey to Henderson, 21 July 1931, PRO, FO 371/15195/C 5728; Ovey to Henderson, 26 July 1931, FO 371/15191/C 5687.
[41] Aufzeichnung Meyer, 22 July 1931; Aufzeichnung zur Frage der Russenkonten, unsigned, Dietrich (minister of finance) to Chintschuk (Soviet ambassador in Berlin), 23 July 1931, PA-AA, R 94387; Strang to Henderson, 10 Aug. 1931, PRO, FO 371/15211/C 6366.
[42] R. M. A. Hankey minute, 16 Sept. 1931, PRO, FO 371/15224/C 7106.

Russia when a good deal of our present trouble is caused by Germany's inability to let us have our cash back.'[43]

The question of Russian credits suddenly became an urgent subject for British officials. Treasury and the Export Credits Guarantee Department were now as concerned as was the Foreign Office. The standstill agreement had frozen foreign short- and long-term credits in Germany for six months. As the Russian financial situation looked ever more grim, the Foreign Office had received numerous indications that the Soviet financial system was on the brink of collapse. William Strang, the counsellor in Leningrad, reported that the Soviet adverse balance of trade for the first eight months of 1931 was 211 million roubles, a sum as great as the total adverse balance for the five fiscal years of 1925–6 to 1929–30.[44] Strang further argued that it was difficult to see how Moscow could meet the growing volume of her obligations at a time when the prices of the goods she exported had fallen to an all-time low, and when her best customer, Great Britain, had left the gold standard. A Russian failure to meet maturing German bills, moreover, would provoke a new financial crisis in Berlin, which in turn would affect the German repayment of British short-term credits worth seventy million pounds sterling. With this scenario in mind, British officials heavily criticised the Germans, who argued that the Soviet economy was not in danger and who showed no sign of halting their reckless lending to Russia.[45] The British, by contrast, felt that the risks already taken by the *Reich* were enormous and would finally fall not on Germany but on Germany's creditors, notably on Britain.

Nixon of the Export Credits Guarantee Department was again sent to Berlin, this time however, with the explicit task of coming to an agreement with the German government over the Russian question.

> Mr Nixon's negotiations are primarily concerned not so much with the restriction of Germany's commitments in respect of Russian trade, as in putting a stop to the competition between the British and the German governments in the matter of the credit facilities which they are respectively offering to the Soviet government. In the somewhat improbable event of Mr Nixon succeeding in reaching an arrangement on these lines, it will naturally have the effect of checking somewhat Germany's future commitments.[46]

For domestic reasons Britain was extremely interested in adjusting British and German credit terms to Moscow. In fact, the whole British attitude towards Russo-German relations had changed during the credit discussions.

---

[43] Bateman minute (on report of Rumbold to Reading, 10 Sept. 1931), 22 Sept. 1931, PRO, FO 371/15224/C 7106.

[44] Strang to Reading, 27 Oct. 1931, *BDFA*, II/A: *The Soviet Union*, x, doc. 250, and also docs 251, 260; Strang to Reading, 6 Oct. 1931, PRO, FO 371/15604/N 6780.

[45] Bateman memo, 19 Oct. 1931, PRO, FO 371/15224/C 7829; *BDFA*, II/A, *The Soviet Union*, x, doc. 251.

[46] Sargent minute, 21 Oct. 1931, PRO, FO 371/15226/C 7829.

When the topic was first raised in London the general tenor of British comments was satisfaction that the Russo-German special relationship was not as smooth as the two countries would like to make others believe. Now, however, Britain increasingly resented the possibility of falling victim to an 'economic Rapallo' at British expense. In July 1931 the Labour government had found itself obliged to guarantee Soviet credits for thirty months – far beyond any previous length of credits to Russia – in order to secure six million pounds of orders for heavy material for British industry. Up to that time the Export Credits Guarantee Department had refused to approve guarantees for credits of more than eighteen months for Soviet orders. This new approach was largely due to the long credits obtainable by the Soviet government in Germany. British officials argued that Moscow would be able to manoeuvre London into the dangerous course of guaranteeing increasingly long credits in the absence of an agreement with Berlin on the subject.[47] In view of the critical Soviet economic situation such an extended length of credits was not thought justifiable.

The objectives of Nixon's visit to Berlin – namely to reach an under-standing with Berlin on reducing the length of credits granted and to secure comparable terms of British and German offers – were precisely those of Schlesinger when he first approached the British in February 1930, but which were then left unanswered. However, now that some seventy million pounds sterling – or 922 million *Reichsmarks*[48] – deposited in German banks were at stake, British diplomats sprang into action. They blamed Berlin for having unreasonably extended its length of credits and for having granted excessive insurance premiums on the bills, which the German government in its present financial situation would hardly be in a position to honour.[49] British diplomats forgot, however, that Schlesinger's initial proposal had had the purpose of avoiding just this situation, in which a government would have to bow to pressure from Moscow and concede credit terms more generous than it could actually afford. Moreover, Schlesinger would have liked to reduce the length of credits with British co-operation.

Meanwhile Berlin had declared that, despite the end of the standstill agreement in February 1932, it would not be able to resume the repayment of

---

[47] Bateman memo, 19 Oct. 1931, ibid.

[48] James, *Reichsbank*, 221.

[49] In his memo Bateman pointed out that German business and banking circles would probably welcome an understanding designed to shorten credit for the Soviet Union, whereas Schlesinger and other German government officials argued that if the length of credit and insurance premiums were equalised between London and Berlin, Britain would probably enjoy considerable advantage over Germany, more especially now that British production costs were being lowered: Bateman memo, n. 45. The shift in Schlesinger's argu-ment must be seen in the context of the deterioration of the German economic situation since February 1930. Whereas at the beginning of the great slump co-operation had been possible for the German economy, by the summer and autumn of 1931 this was no longer the case. For domestic reasons Berlin was too dependent on Soviet orders.

reparations and credits, given that its financial situation remained precarious.[50] London, by contrast, erroneously suspected that Germany refused to repay British short-term credits only because of the danger of Russia failing to return German loans, and not because of any more fundamental problems with the German economy. This view seemed to coincide with Britain's impression that the risk of a Russian failure to fully meet her obligations in Germany had increased. The British were therefore irritated that their view of Russia's serious financial situation was still not shared in Berlin and that the Germans would draw no conclusions with regard to their credit policy to Russia. 'In the case of the Germans the wish may well be father to the thought, and though no doubt in their heart of hearts they realise the Russian business is very risky, yet they prefer to take this risk rather than face further unemployment with its threat of social upheavals.'[51] The British shook their heads about Germany's credit policy towards Russia but could not make up their minds about which strategy to adopt in order to bring about a change in Berlin:

> The fact is that H.M. government are not in a position to say whether or not these governmental guarantees are a help or a hindrance to German solvency and capacity to pay; on the information available we incline to the latter view but it is possible that if we had further facts at our disposal we might modify that view.[52]

The credit topic was briefly raised at the special advisory committee's meeting in December 1931 but played only a marginal role in the committee's report on Germany's present situation and none at all in its proposals for a solution to the crisis.[53] Nevertheless, credits continued to play a considerable role in Anglo-German relations during 1932. Rumours of a Russian demand for a standstill of repayments to Germany constantly worried British officials, particularly as they observed that Moscow increasingly paid for its imports of German goods by deliveries in kind instead of cash. But still there was no sign of a change of attitude towards Moscow in Berlin. On the contrary, Brüning was reported to have remarked that 'the Russians could pay in wheat and rye, which the Germans wanted. If they did not meet their bills in some form or other, their credit would be destroyed for good and all.'[54]

As much, however, as British officials were interested in the question of Russian solvency, 'what we [the British] really wanted was a transference

---

[50] Bülow to Rumbold, 31 Oct. 1931, DBFP, 2nd ser. ii, doc 286.

[51] Nichols minute, 14 Nov. 1931, ibid; Newton to Simon, 13 Nov. 1931, BDFA, II/A, The Soviet Union, x, doc. 256.

[52] Nichols minute, 30 Nov. 1931, PRO, FO 371/15224/C 8850.

[53] Report of the special advisory committee convened under the agreement with Germany concluded at The Hague on 20 January 1930, 23 Dec. 1931, DBFP, 2nd ser. ii, appendix iii.

[54] Rumbold to Simon, 15 Jan. 1932, DBFP, 2nd ser. viii, doc. 148; Gosmann, 'Reparationsfrage', 256.

from Germany to the UK of a portion of the "short credit" orders now placed in Germany'.[55] The British trade balance with Moscow remained adverse because the Soviets preferred to buy from Germany, which granted longer credits. Moreover, ·in a further desperate attempt to secure long-term large-scale business with Russia, Berlin began to grant the Soviets special trade conditions, including a moratorium on customs duties for Russian imports to Germany. This was formalised in a new customs tariff agreement with Russia on 28 May 1932.[56] Britain objected to this preferential treatment, especially of Russian oil imports to Germany, because it would disadvantage companies with British share holdings in the German market.[57]

> It seems to me to be all wrong that Germany (whose credit position is, to say the least, not quite sound) should be able to set the pace in this question of credits for Russia. That is what she is doing and what she apparently intends to do irrespective of the appalling, and indeed dangerous situation in the USSR at the present moment,

minuted Bateman.[58] Various means of resolving or at least of improving this situation were considered: one of them was exerting pressure on both Germany and the Soviet Union to buy British rather than German goods. Another was the use of the Anglo-Soviet adverse balance of trade as the reason for limiting Russian imports into Britain. For Moscow it would be a severe blow to lose her largest export market and the opportunity to acquire hard currency. The effect on Germany would also be serious. During his third visit to London on 15 April 1932, Schlesinger admitted that changes in the British attitude towards sales from Russia in the United Kingdom might endanger the payment of Soviet bills in Germany and that Berlin was already contemplating preventative measures should Britain enforce her threat. At present Berlin was examining the possibility of importing more Russian products such as oil, rye and wheat, but if things came to the worst it would replace Canadian wheat, which accounted for a large share of imports, with Russian.[59]

British officials' endeavours to increase their trade with Russia and to bring German and British credit terms into line did not go beyond a verbal exchange of views between the different Whitehall departments. Reports in the spring and summer of 1932 indicated a slight change in the German credit policy towards Russia. Berlin guaranteed new credits only to the same

---

55 Bateman minute, 22 Feb. 1932, PRO, FO 371/16318/N 1088.
56 Schäffer diary entry, 6 Feb. 1932, Schäffer papers, Jft, ED 93/13; Newton to Simon, 31 May 1932, PRO, FO 371/16328/N 3400.
57 Ovey to Simon, 16 Feb. 1932, PRO, FO 371/16318/N 1008; Rumbold to Simon, 22 Feb. 1932, FO 371/16327/N 1181; MacDonough to J. Balfour, 1 Mar. 1932; J. Balfour minute, 2 Mar. 1932; Balfour to BoT, 2 Mar. 1932, FO 371/15949/C 1698; BoT to FO, 7 May 1932, FO 371/15949/C 3793.
58 Bateman minute, 20 Sept. 1932, PRO, FO 371/16328/N 5373.
59 Third discussion with German officials, 18 Apr. 1932, PRO, FO 371/16327/N 2731.

extent as old bills were met and reduced its guarantees from 70% to 60%. The major obstacle to more British trade with Russia remained the categorical British refusal to consider credits of more than twelve months' duration, or to give guarantees in excess of £1.6 million. Not even the news of a new Russo-German arrangement regarding orders to be placed in Germany, received on 15 June, changed British attitudes.[60] Business and members of parliament kept up the pressure on the Export Credits Guarantee Department and the secretary of the Department of Overseas Trade for additional facilities. They argued that the Soviet authorities were willing to place substantial orders if given credit, but that – failing further guarantees – these could not be accepted. Large numbers of men would thus lose employment. When foreign secretary John Simon met Litvinov at the disarmament conference in Geneva, the Russian confirmed that further orders in Britain depended on larger credits.[61]

Whitehall did not bow to Soviet–German pressure on the credit issue. Although Russo-German commercial relations seemed to cool when Franz von Papen replaced Brüning as *Reichskanzler*,[62] British officials would no longer accept German leadership in the trade question. The Foreign Office was convinced that Germany had deliberately undercut Britain in the amount and the length of the credits offered to Moscow but recognised that there was little chance of coercing Berlin into altering its policy. Hence, British leverage had to be applied to Russia, thus indirectly exerting pressure on Germany. On 17 October 1932, Britain renounced the Anglo-Soviet trade agreement of 16 April 1930. At the same time she declared her willingness to increase and consolidate trade with the USSR on the basis of a much better balance of imports and exports, security of payment and safeguards against dumping.[63] No reference was made in the official British statements to Germany or the credit issue, but this certainly had been the trigger.

> If . . . we have no intention of competing with the Germans in either the amount or the length of our Russian credits, and in fact regard the whole German credit policy as highly dangerous, it must follow, as far as I can see, that we cannot rely solely, or even mainly, upon credits to secure a better balance of trade with Russia, but must make serious use of the threat to curtail the indispensable Russian market here [in Britain].[64]

[60] Bateman minute, 27 June 1932, PRO, FO 371/16328/N 3737; Rumbold to Simon, 25 Apr. 1932, FO 371/16327/N 2730; reply to parliamentary question put by Mr Carlton, 5 July 1932, FO 371/16320/N 4065; Thelwall to Nixon, 17 June 1932; Rumbold to Simon, 18 June 1932, and minutes, FO 371/16328/N 3737.
[61] British delegation, Geneva, to FO, 22 July 1932, PRO, FO 371/16320/N 4419.
[62] Rumbold to Simon, 10 Aug. 1932, PRO, FO 371/15949/C 7108; H. M. Adams and R. K. Adams, *Rebel patriot: a biography of Franz von Papen*, Santa Barbara, CA 1987, 126–7.
[63] Simon to Ovey, 17 Oct. 1932; Ovey to Simon, 19 Oct. 1932, *DBFP*, 2nd ser. vii, docs 165, 166.
[64] Collier minute, 4 Oct. 1932, PRO, FO 371/16320/N 5575; FO memo (on the policy to be

British diplomats steered a risky course when contemplating the reduction of Russian sales in Britain. Admitting that Soviet difficulties in meeting their obligations in Germany were increasing, Berlin was making every effort to secure the repayment of outstanding bills by granting Moscow further guarantees.[65] Nixon of the Export Credits Guarantee Department had warned the Foreign Office that

> if you brandish the revolver you will . . . be one day forced to shoot and if you start shooting, i.e. prohibiting imports, you may possibly balance Anglo-Russian trade but rather on the motto of Tacitus' famous tag 'Solitudinem faciunt, pacem appellant'. You may reach an equilibrium by reducing both sides to zero and that I do not conceive to be the object aimed at.[66]

Such a development, Nixon argued, would inevitably have repercussions for the repayment of German credits to Britain. They would be made impossible if the German financial situation was disrupted by a Russian default.

After a violent anti-British press campaign in Moscow as a result of the denunciation of the trade agreement, negotiations between London and Moscow for a new treaty were resumed on 15 December 1932. Soon, however, the credit question was back on the agenda. A memorandum by Nixon, compiled after a visit to Berlin in early January 1933, again pointed to the impossibility of Russia paying cash for her imports from Germany. The Foreign Office concluded from this report that if Moscow could not pay cash to Germany it would be equally impossible to pay for British goods. Thus, 'if Russia cannot pay cash to us, except by defaulting on existing commitments, then her purchases from us under the new commercial agreement will have to be on credit. This brings the credit question to the very front of our forthcoming negotiations.'[67]

The Anglo-German rivalry for trade with, and credits to, Russia had turned full circle. British officials had struggled in vain to avoid any development whereby business with the Soviets was possible on the basis of credits only. The whole situation had developed into a vicious circle. As Collier, the head of the Northern department, minuted,

> the Germans are determined at all costs to keep their present lion's share of Russian orders and, whatever the risk, to give as much credit as the Russians choose to insist on, in order to maintain their position. They will not join with us in a policy of keeping credits within the limits dictated by ordinary

pursued in the forthcoming commercial relations with the Soviet Union), 22 Nov. 1932, Baldwin papers, CUL, vol. 118.
[65] Rumbold to Vansittart, 16 Nov. 1932, *DBFP*, 2nd ser. vii, doc. 182; Rumbold to Simon, 24 Nov., 1 Dec. 1932, PRO, FO 3712/16328/N 7024, N 7189.
[66] Nixon to Collier, 10 Oct. 1932, PRO, FO 371/16320/N 5575.
[67] Nixon memo, 17 Jan. 1933; Ashton-Gwatkin minute, 24 Jan. 1932, PRO, FO 371/17249/N 415 (memo also printed in *BDFA*, II/A: *The Soviet Union*, xi, doc. 12).

commercial prudence, but hope to force us to extend our credits to their level and so make us share the risk with them.[68]

From the German perspective, the argument looked different. Schlesinger, back in 1930, had proposed a joint Anglo-German credit policy in Russia, but his suggestions had fallen on deaf ears in London. Moscow – at first deliberately but eventually out of necessity – exploited German economic weakness and forced Berlin to grant increasingly large and long credits. When Britain finally realised the importance of consultations with Germany over credits to Russia, Germany was already too deeply involved as a creditor to Moscow and too weak politically, economically and financially to force through a change in policy, however much German officials would have liked to do so. This German dilemma was never fully understood in Whitehall. London consequently regarded Berlin officials as being as dishonest and unreliable personally as the country was financially.

If, in early 1930, Britain had responded positively to the German offer of adjusting its strategy regarding Russian credits, the Anglo-German controversy could possibly have been avoided. However, fortunately for both countries, the dispute had no lasting negative effect on their respective situations. The Russian economy did not collapse, and Germany's finances gradually recovered. The catalysts that did fundamentally alter Anglo-German–Russian trade relations came from rather different sources. Anglo-Russian negotiations for a new trade agreement in particular were abruptly interrupted by the arrest of British engineers in Russia in the so-called Metropolitan–Vickers case. Similar to the arrest of the Germans in the Donez basin in 1928, it resulted in a British embargo on all imports from Russia.[69] In Germany, Hitler's advent to power finally terminated Russo-German intimacy. Special treatment of the Bolsheviks was now out of the question although economic relations continued on a lower level right until 1939.

---

[68] Collier minute, 25 Jan. 1933, PRO, FO 371/17249/N 415.
[69] For the Metropolitan–Vickers case see *DBFP*, 2nd ser. vii, ch. v; W. Strang, *Home and abroad*, London 1956, 78–120; Haslam, *Soviet Union*, 16–19.

9

Rapallo and the Disarmament Conference

The end of the First World War left many states with feelings of deep insecurity. Germany's neighbours looked anxiously towards her as a potentially formidable military power, despite her defeat. By signing the treaty of Versailles, Berlin had to accept an extensive restructuring and curtailment in the armaments and manpower of the *Reichswehr*, as well as Allied supervision. The victorious powers recognised, however, that European stability did not depend solely on Germany. Rather, peace required general disarmament of victors and vanquished alike. General disarmament was therefore supposed to create a stable international order under the auspices of the League of Nations where 'natural' relations between states would no longer guarantee this order.[1]

These were ideal objectives which would hardly pass the reality test. Such was the state of international uncertainty that no country was willing to contemplate disarmament as long as its own needs for security remained unsatisfied. For the time being the definition of 'national security' turned out to be almost always incompatible with the interests of other states. From the outset, the unbridgeable differences in the interpretation of 'security', and the League resolution XIV of September 1922, which inextricably linked 'disarmament' and 'security', made the likelihood of achieving international disarmament virtually impossible.[2]

The definition of 'security', however, not only widened the gap between victors and vanquished, but also strained relations between Britain and France. Paris suffered from a traumatic inferiority complex *vis-à-vis* Germany and feared that a revitalised, revanchist Germany might once again advance onto French soil. It was clear that France would only accept disarmament once her security needs had been met in the framework of an alliance with Britain or collective security under the shelter of the League of Nations.

This French claim of security stood in stark contrast to the overriding German desire for equality in armaments. Ultimately, Germany hoped to be permitted rearmament to the Allied level again. However as long as this remained impossible, the Germans supported the concept of general disarmament down to the low level that had been imposed on them, provided they

---

[1] M. Geyer, 'Die Konferenz für die Herabsetzung und Beschränkung der Rüstungen und das Problem der Abrüstung', in Becker and Hildebrand, *Internationale Beziehungen*, 155–202 at p. 158.
[2] Northedge, *League of Nations*, 118.

were granted securities against aggression by her militarily superior French and Polish neighbours.

British hopes centred on re-establishing a certain balance of power on the continent, with France and Germany being more or less equally strong and applying the principle of checks and balances against each other without constant British involvement.

British interests concerning disarmament and international security seemed to be pulling in two directions. Despite being in the same post-war boat as France, Britain was by no means convinced of the justification of French requests for security, and was unwilling to support them. Still, London could not afford to alienate Paris by too obviously favouring universal disarmament and the German position. Britain's interest was to avoid continental engagement as far as possible. She would contribute to European stability only as much as was necessary to maintain peace and the *status quo*. British support for the League of Nations must be seen in this context.[3]

The principal British role during the tiresome disarmament negotiations was to mediate between the irreconcilable French and German positions. For Britain it was difficult to acquiesce in France's uncompromising insistence on 'security before disarmament'. To a certain extent, British sympathies with regard to security had turned in Germany's favour soon after the end of the war, although the German violations of the disarmament clauses of the peace treaty were a constant source of irritation. Many officials were convinced of the necessity of revising parts of the treaty of Versailles and of securing German economic and financial stability as a balancing factor in Europe. With such diverging initial interests, disarmament seemed almost impossible. It took the 'phase of rehabilitation and of return of confidence'[4] following the Locarno regional security guarantees for France and Belgium, and Germany's admission to the League of Nations, to brighten up the prospects for successful disarmament negotiations.

The September 1925 League of Nations' assembly established a 'Preparatory Commission for the Disarmament Conference' and invited not only various League member states, but also a number of non-members including Germany, the United States and the Soviet Union. Everyone except for the USSR accepted the invitation. Moscow declined formally on the grounds that Russian relations with Switzerland – strained because of the murder of a Soviet delegate to the 1923 Lausanne conference – would not permit Russian participation in the conference. However, Russia's true reason for abstention

---

3   For the different disarmament positions see R. C. Richardson, *The evolution of British disarmament policy in the 1920s*, London 1989; S. Nadolny, *Abrüstungsdiplomatie 1932/33. Deutschland auf der Genfer Konferenz im Übergang von Weimar zu Hitler*, Munich 1978; Geyer, *Aufrüstung oder Sicherheit*, passim; M. Vaïsse, *Sécurité d'abord: la politique française en matière de désarmement: 9 décembre 1930 à 17 avril 1934*, Paris 1981; E. W. Bennett, *German rearmament and the west, 1932–1933*, Princeton, NJ 1979, 92–101.
4   J. Wheeler-Bennett, *The disarmament deadlock*, London 1934, 36.

appears to have been her dislike of the League, the much-hated symbol of capitalism and the organ of the 'Principal Allied Powers', notably Britain.[5]

Soviet participation, however, was considered essential for successful disarmament. Thus, some form of *rapprochement* between Moscow and Bern had to be achieved. After French representatives had tried in vain to reconcile Russia and Switzerland, British officials approached Moscow's Rapallo partner with a request for mediation. Albert Dufour, formerly at the London embassy and now German League representative in Geneva, turned out to be successful, and Russia and Switzerland officially terminated the dispute on 18 April 1927.[6]

British officials had mixed feelings even about this limited revival of Russo-German relations. Although they appreciated Germany's mediation, without which the Soviet presence at Geneva would have been impossible, they realised that the price to be paid could well be a renewal of the same Russo-German co-operation which had been so obstructive at the Genoa conference. A cabinet committee report of 23 November 1927, one week before the conference opened, discussed the likelihood of being confronted with a combination of German and Russian delegates in opposition to France and her friends at Geneva, and emphasised the need for detailed instructions for the British representatives.[7] Britain '[regarded] the German contention that German disarmament must be applied to France, [as] unreasonable and impracticable', but considered the French demands to be equally exaggerated.[8] Officials feared that Russo-German co-operation might not only stiffen the uncompromising French attitude, but that Germany, with Soviet backing, would be equally implacable. Such a stalemate would force Britain to side openly with one party or the other, something she wished to avoid at all costs. British policy therefore faced a dilemma. There was no doubt that the preservation of close Anglo-French relations was vital. But Locarno and British attempts to appease Germany would be in serious danger if London's support for one particular side was too explicit. Moreover, Britain had broken off diplomatic relations with Moscow in May 1927 following the 'Arcos raid' and had, at the time, been anxious to secure German neutrality and moder-

5   A. J. Toynbee (ed.), *Survey of international affairs, 1927*, Oxford–London 1929, 4–5, 315–21. See also the generally questionable interpretation of W. M. Chaizman, *Die UdSSR und die Abrüstung zwischen den beiden Weltkriegen*, Berlin (East) 1963.
6   Cecil FO minute, 26 Nov. 1926, PRO, FO 371/11889/W 11114; Bernstorff/Aschmann to AA, 17 Mar. 1927, PA-AA, R 32067; Drummond to Chamberlain, enclosing Dufour to Drummond, 27 Mar. 1927, PRO, FO 371/12590/N 1571; Sperling to Chamberlain, 22 Mar., 2, 18 Apr. 1927, FO 371/12601/N 1421; Toynbee, *Survey, 1927*, 319; Richardson, *Evolution*, 45.
7   Report of the cabinet committee on policy for reduction and limitation of armaments, 23 Nov. 1927, *DBFP*, 1A ser. iv, doc. 229.
8   Chamberlain minute, 27 May 1927, PRO, FO 371/12667/W 4575; Cadogan memo, 17 May 1927, ibid. For a synopsis, showing the difference between the French and British proposals, see Wheeler-Bennett, *Disarmament*, 58–61.

ating influence on Russia in the matter.[9] An Anglo-German estrangement over disarmament would therefore not only destroy the opportunities for London to communicate with Moscow via Berlin; it would also wreck previous efforts to reconcile Germany with the west, consequently re-establishing the post-war blocks of victors and vanquished.

Anglo-French worries about the possibility of Russo-German co-operation during the conference were realistic given that Russian and German diplomats had indeed agreed on consultations. On 14 May 1927 Berlin learned that the Russians firmly intended to take part in the next preparatory meeting for disarmament. Moscow was therefore provided with the printed material from the previous meetings. Moreover, Litvinov had told a journalist of the *Vossische Zeitung* that he would certainly talk over the disarmament question with German officials before going to Geneva.[10]

Nevertheless, the Wilhelmstraße had no intention of tying itself to the Russians in Geneva. For one, Germany did not need to. In 1927 she was not as politically isolated as she had been in 1922 and she could expect at least some support for her disarmament views from Britain and America. Moreover, German officials recognised that Russia's economic decline and political isolation weakened her support for German revisionism.[11] Berlin was therefore careful not to offer consultations but to wait for the Russians to suggest preparatory talks. Ernst von Weizsäcker, in charge of League matters in Berlin and one of the German delegates to Geneva, noted on 14 August 1927:

> We will be able to use the Russian delegation as a pace maker during the next meeting of the Commission Préparatoire. But we have to avoid the impression of creating a Russo-German extremist position, given our need for Anglo-American support particularly on the issue of army disarmament. It will be necessary, therefore, to conduct our preparatory talks with the Russians in such a way that we can shake off the Russian delegation at Geneva, if necessary.[12]

On his way to Geneva, Litvinov briefly stopped for consultations in Berlin. When he suggested active Soviet–German co-operation at Geneva, Stresemann's reply was evasive.[13]

The fourth meeting of the preparatory disarmament conference opened in

---

9 J. Heideking, 'Vom Versailler Vertrag zur Genfer Abrüstungskonferenz. Das Scheitern der alliierten Militärkontrollpolitik gegenüber Deutschland nach dem Ersten Weltkrieg', *MGM* ii (1980), 45–68 at p. 60; Jacobson, *Locarno diplomacy*, 23.

10 Dufour to Bülow, 14 May 1927, PA-AA, R 32608.

11 Dyck, *Weimar Germany*, 109.

12 Aufzeichnung Weizsäcker betr. Vorbesprechung mit russischen Sachverständigen über die im November d.J. bevorstehende 4. Tagung der Commission Préparatoire, 10 Aug. 1927, PA-AA, R 32068.

13 Aufzeichnung unsigned and undated (end Nov. 1927); Aufzeichnung Wiedner, 8 Dec. 1927, PA-AA, R 32070; Runderlaß des AA, 19 Dec. 1927, *ADAP*, ser. B, vii, doc. 217.

Geneva on 30 November 1927. Those countries which had hoped to limit general discussions by only establishing a committee to examine the French bid for security, were soon disappointed. The German demand for a full debate on disarmament gave Litvinov the opportunity to startle the audience with his proposals for complete disarmament.[14] All countries were unanimously opposed to the scheme, given that it went far beyond anything that could reasonably be discussed or remotely realised at the present time. In its surprise and irritation the conference seemed inclined just to ignore the motion. It was Count Bernstorff, the German delegate, who prevented a stalemate by suggesting that the debate be postponed until the next meeting to give everyone time to cool off and examine the Russian proposals. According to a German report, this suggestion was greeted with widespread relief.[15]

German–Soviet collaboration was handled with great discretion during the fourth session of the disarmament conference. In Lord Cushendun's reports to London there is no reference to any obstructive behaviour by the Rapallo partners. Only the *Times* correspondent commented on Bernstorff having invited the Soviet delegate for dinner after Litvinov presented his disarmament proposals.[16]

The eventual stalemate in the negotiations was not caused by Germany or Russia, but by French insistence on considering security before disarmament. This brought the conference to the verge of breakdown. To many British observers, France seemed to deliberately obstruct progress in disarmament, thereby blocking the restoration of peace in Europe which was so much in Britain's interest.

British officials were by no means convinced of French weakness. On several occasions, Cushendun, the leader of the British delegation, pointed out to Boncour that France these days was politically and militarily considerably stronger than it had been in 1914, and that the Franco-German frontier was guaranteed by Locarno. If France insisted on her alleged vulnerability, Germany and Russia could exploit this argument at the subsequent disarmament conferences, placing France in an awkward position *vis-à-vis* world opinion. It was essential, therefore, that France and Britain developed a joint programme for the forthcoming negotiations.[17]

The 1927 preparatory disarmament negotiations were adjourned without any feasible result. No *rapprochement* of the diverging French, British and German views seemed in sight, which would have ensured a positive outcome of the fifth session of the committee. The delegates returned to Geneva on

[14] Litvinov proposal, PRO, FO 371/12677/W 11178; A. C. Temperley, *The whispering gallery of Europe*, London 1939, 75; Richardson, *Evolution*, 152–4.
[15] Runderlaß des AA, 19 Dec. 1927, *ADAP*, ser. B, vii, doc. 217.
[16] Sthamer to AA, 1 Dec. 1927, PA-AA, R 32070; J. Bernstorff, *The memoirs of Count Bernstorff*, London–Toronto 1936, 302.
[17] Cushendun to Chamberlain, 12 Dec. 1927, PRO, FO 371/12677/W 11629; Cushendun memo, 24 Jan. 1928, FO 371/13370/W 645.

15 March 1928 in a mood of 'remarkable listlessness'.[18] In addition to the continuing disagreement on 'security' and 'equality' following the report of the commission on arbitration and security, the commission had to deal with Russia's radical disarmament proposals which were deemed impracticable by virtually all states, most of which wanted to see them summarily rejected.

Britain and France had developed a joint strategy of approval to the Russian draft, thereby reducing its destructive impact.[19] British officials were loath to examine the Russian plans but withstood heavy pressure from other delegations to reject them outright. 'It was not for us [i.e. Britain] in view of our special relations – or absence of relations – to bell the Russian cat', Chamberlain told Briand on 10 March 1928.[20] But London defended this attitude also for other reasons. If the Soviet proposals were not given at least brief consideration this would enable Moscow to launch a massive propaganda campaign accusing all western states of being against effective disarmament. Moreover, Soviet participation in League affairs would become impossible for a long time to come.

The Soviet proposals, now elaborated by Litvinov in a draft convention of sixty-three articles, met with almost unanimous disapproval. However, only Cushendun, in a crushing speech, subjected the proposals to a detailed, if negative, examination. Germany and Turkey, by contrast, welcomed a general discussion of the draft convention. The result was a storm of criticism in the foreign press, which alleged a Machiavellian conspiracy between Bernstorff and the Soviets.[21]

German–Russian co-operation during the fifth session was again hardly discernible to outside observers. In Cushendun's summary of the meetings, Germany is occasionally mentioned but never in connection with Russia. Bernstorff and Litvinov had continued to consult, but less intimately than during the previous session, given that Russo-German diplomatic relations were somewhat strained following the arrest and trial of German engineers in the Donez basin.[22] When, on 23 March, the Russians conjured up their second disarmament proposal, the Germans were as surprised as everybody else.[23]

---

[18] Aufzeichnung Bernstorff, 30 Mar. 1928, PA-AA, R 32072; Cushendun to Chamberlain, 2 Apr. 1928, PRO, FO 371/13376/W 3343. See also Toynbee, *Survey, 1928*, 57–8.

[19] British delegation, Geneva, to Western department, 4 Mar. 1928, with enclosures from Cushendun, 10 Mar. 1928; Chamberlain to Mr London (Geneva), 13 Mar. 1928, *DBFP*, 1A ser. iv, docs 295, 304, 309.

[20] British delegation, Geneva, memo, 10 Mar. 1928; Mr London (Geneva) to Chamberlain, 2 Mar. 1928, ibid. docs 304, 292; Temperley, *Whispering gallery*, 82.

[21] Weizsäcker diary entry, 8 Apr. 1928, in *Die Weizsäcker-Tagebücher 1900–1932*, ed. L. Hill, Berlin 1982, 385.

[22] Dyck, *Weimar Germany*, 114; Dirksen, *Moscow, Tokyo, London*, 69–70; Hilger and Mayer, *Incompatible allies*, 217–22; K. Rosenbaum, 'The German involvement in the Shakhty trial', *The Russian Review* xxi (1962), 238–60.

[23] Köpke to Botschaft, Moskau, 11 Apr. 1928, ADAP, ser. B, viii, doc. 202 n. 2.

German officials were increasingly irritated by the Soviet conduct of affairs at Geneva. They resented Litvinov's insistence on extensive discussion of his radical disarmament proposals, because they regarded them as pure propaganda. Increasingly, Russo-German co-operation became a liability rather than an asset to Germany's position *vis-à-vis* Britain and France in the negotiations. Bernstorff therefore refrained from taking part in the general political discussions between Litvinov and delegates of other countries.

As the previous gatherings, the fifth session ended inconclusively. The committee had dealt mainly with the draft of the 'convention for the limitation of armaments' which was a record of different agreements rather than a draft proposal. So far it had been impossible to bridge the gulf between the dissenting British and French views. For this reason it seemed futile to carry on with general discussions as long as private negotiations so obviously failed to change the conflicting opinions.

More than a year elapsed between the meetings of the fifth and sixth sessions of the preparatory disarmament conference. The outlook for the forthcoming discussion looked gloomy. The year preceding the sixth session had generated initiatives for international reconciliation such as the Kellogg pact and the Litvinov protocol. However, these initiatives had been overshadowed by the abortive 'Anglo-French compromise on the limitation of armaments'.[24] A key element of this deal was concession to British views on naval matters that would enable her to withdraw her opposition to the French view on military land reserves.[25] Once the Anglo-French compromise received its *coup de grâce* at the hand of the Americans, Britain was 'under no obligation'[26] to continue her support for the French view on trained reserves. Until the very opening of the sixth session, Britain was undecided on which line to pursue during the negotiations.

> Our difficulties seem to arise from the fact that we are leading a double life, as it were, in this affair of disarmament. In public, and at Geneva, we preach disarmament and we refer with satisfaction to the guarantees for peace afforded by the Covenant, Locarno and the Kellogg Pact, while at home and in secret we seem to use much the same language as we did in 1913

wrote Alexander Cadogan, the Foreign Office member within the British delegation at Geneva.[27] British officials looked to Geneva with serious misgivings, given that this time they might be forced to take sides in the

---

[24] Toynbee, *Survey, 1928*, 61–81; Wheeler-Bennett, *Disarmament*, 127–42; Jacobson, *Locarno diplomacy*, 187–92; Richardson, *Evolution*, 169–84; D. Carlton, 'The Anglo-French compromise on arms limitation, 1928', *JBS* viii (1969), 141–62.

[25] Chamberlain, in a conversation with Berthelot, 29 June 1928, quoted in Jacobson, *Locarno diplomacy*, 188.

[26] Cushendun, House of Lords, 7 Nov. 1928, quoted from Wheeler-Bennett, *Disarmament*, 141. See also Cushendun memo, 20 Feb. 1929, *DBFP*, 1A ser. vi, doc. 370.

[27] Cadogan memo, 15 Mar. 1929, *DBFP*, 1A ser. vi, doc. 379.

question of land armaments. As much as they would not endanger their close relations with France, they could not afford to alienate either the Americans or the Germans.

Lord Cushendun, acting foreign secretary while Chamberlain recovered from ill-health, was particularly uneasy about the prospects facing Britain in Geneva. He had received a letter from the chief of the imperial general staff pointing out the dangers if Germany was too harshly rebuffed. 'If the efforts of the Preparatory Commission on Disarmament to reach agreement prove to be unsuccessful, Germany will claim to be absolved from the disarmament clauses of the treaty of Versailles . . . little time would elapse before Germany would again become a first class military power.'[28] Since neither a German nor a French conciliatory attitude could reasonably be expected, the British position was anything but enviable.

Cushendun arrived in Geneva in an extremely bad mood. The second reading of the draft convention, and a final debate of the Soviet disarmament proposals were the principal items on the agenda. Regarding the Soviets, Cushendun had so far urged moderation. This time, however, he favoured a blank rejection, being so impatient that other delegates had to persuade him that a *refus brutal* would be counterproductive as it would encourage subsequent Russian propaganda.

The majority of the delegates supported Cushendun's distant attitude towards the Soviets. When, on 17 April 1929, great confusion arose concerning voting procedure on the Soviet proposals, the Dutch president, Loudon, panicked and postponed the vote to the next day. Both the Soviets and the committee worked on compromise formulae during the night. On this occasion the Germans supported the committee's rather than the Soviets' draft. Cushendun recalled in his report to London that 'The bureau were not unaffected, in settling the terms of their draft, by the possibility – in my opinion, a remote one – that the Soviet delegation might, if denied satisfaction, leave the committee, followed, conceivably, by the German delegation.'[29]

Cushendun was right to assume that Germany would not follow the Soviet example should Russia leave the committee in the wake of a rejection of the Soviet proposals. The two delegations were in serious disagreement about future co-operation. The Germans, trying to avoid being taken in tow by the Russians, had urged them to adjust their proposals to the general discussions rather than to 'parade them in Geneva'.[30] Bernstorff told Litvinov that the Russian delegation was of course not obliged to listen to German advice but if it did not, Germany would no longer feel bound to support the Soviet proposals. During the critical days between 17 and 19 April, the German delegation refused to bow to Russian pressure although the Soviet delegate,

---

28 Cushendun memo, 3 Mar. 1929, ibid. doc. 376.
29 Cushendun to Chamberlain, 20 Apr. 1929, PRO, FO 371/14113/W 3731.
30 Weizsäcker to Krauel, 19 Apr. 1929, *ADAP*, ser. B, xi, doc. 181.

Boris Stein, told Weizsäcker that disarmament was a test of Soviet–German friendship. The Soviets countered Germany's lack of faith by refusing to inform them about their forthcoming policies.[31]

Germany's cautious attitude towards Russia was noted but not rewarded during the sixth session. The re-examination of the draft proposals proved to be even more tiresome than the discussion of the Soviet plan, with Germany categorically opposing the Anglo-French–American agreement on trained reserves, and on the limitation of war material. The negative impression made by Berlin's pursuit of its disarmament goals overshadowed anything that might have been interpreted in Germany's favour. British delegates at Geneva were tired of the disarmament talks and frustrated at the slow progress – if progress at all – of the negotiations. The looming general elections did not revive their spirits.

British disarmament policy received a new breath of life when Ramsay MacDonald's second Labour government took office in June 1929. The new political appointments in the Foreign Office – foreign secretary Arthur Henderson, parliamentary under-secretary Hugh Dalton, and Lord Robert Cecil, the specialist League adviser to the government – were ardent supporters of European reconciliation.[32] European *détente*, including both Germany and Russia, was a longstanding Labour aim. It was to be achieved via disarmament and a strong League of Nations, and would involve concessions by Britain, and particularly France. Francophobia was strong among Labour members. To them, Paris was the principal obstacle to peace. This attitude made the new government more responsive to German grievances.[33] With the exception of their Russian policy, Labour and the Conservatives diverged less in their overall objectives than in their methods. The Conservatives sought European pacification in co-operation with France, whereas Labour preferred the tactics of pushing France into making concessions.

As far as the new government's policy towards the Soviet Union was concerned, Labour had looked forward to resuming diplomatic relations with Moscow in order to secure trade and constructive participation in the disarmament conference. One of its first acts of foreign policy was therefore to re-establish diplomatic relations with Russia.[34] William Strang, the new

---

31 Bernstorff to AA, 25 Apr. 1929, PA-AA, R 32076. Russo-German relations had suffered from Germany's more western-orientated policy between 1929 and 1930, combined with a crackdown by the German government on communist disturbances in Berlin: Weizsäcker diary entries, 16 Feb., 16 Mar. 1930, in *Weizsäcker-Tagebücher 1900–1932*, 400–1; Rumbold to Henderson, 21 May 1930, PRO, FO 371/14371/C 4140; Dyck, *Weimar Germany*, 152–98; T. Weingartner, *Stalin und der Aufstieg Hitlers. Die Deutschlandpolitik der Sowjetunion und der kommunistischen Internationale 1929–1934*, Berlin 1970.

32 H. Dalton, *Call back yesterday: memoirs, 1887–1931*, London 1953, 218–58; R. Cecil, *A great experiment*, London 1941, 199–201, 205; C. Wrigley, *Arthur Henderson*, Cardiff 1990, 172–3; F. M. Leventhal, *Arthur Henderson*, Manchester 1989, 152; Carlton, *MacDonald versus Henderson*, 75; Marquand, *MacDonald*, 489–91.

33 Dalton, *Call back yesterday*, 252; Leventhal, *Arthur Henderson*, 152.

34 Williams, *Labour and Russia*, 125–6; Carlton, *MacDonald versus Henderson*, 33.

British counsellor in Leningrad, used one of his first meetings with foreign commissar Litvinov to discuss disarmament. However, Labour's enthusiasm for better relations with Soviet Russia was short-lived. *Rapprochement* turned out to be more complicated than anticipated and was dogged by misunderstandings and mutual distrust. Russian co-operation was, however, vital for progress in European reconciliation. It was therefore the declared Labour policy to 'show [the Russians] that we are reasonable with them if they are reasonable with us'.[35]

Labour officials went to the final meeting of the preparatory commission in November 1930 with the best intentions of working with Germany and Soviet Russia. However, it did not take long for Robert Cecil, a longstanding League enthusiast, to become deeply disillusioned:

> I have done my best to get into relations with the Russians as far as I can bring myself to do so, but I must say they give me a shiver down my back whenever I look at them . . . They are on the whole behaving well [marginal note: Tuesday: Not very well today] though they and the Germans persist in saying at intervals about any amendment they propose that if that is not adopted they take no further interest in the proceedings. It is rather like the man in the pantomime rehearsal, if you ever saw that work, who is always throwing up his part.[36]

In the face of Soviet–German obstruction, Cecil's patience was tried hard. British diplomats were equally embittered about the Germans. Since the commission's last meeting Stresemann had died, the Müller government had been replaced by *Reichskanzler* Heinrich Brüning and foreign minister Julius Curtius, and the new administration had embarked on a rigid course of revisionism which appeared to make trouble with the French at Geneva inevitable. The tone of German demands suddenly became increasingly blunt and the German delegates at Geneva were noticeably less ready for constructive co-operation. The German slogan 'equality of arms' implied that if general armaments were not brought down to the German level, the Berlin government would feel free to rearm, improving its standing with regard to Germany's neighbours. If the Allied powers did not meet their obligations under the treaty of Versailles, Germany would equally no longer feel bound by it.[37]

In the ranking of Brüning's priorities, disarmament came merely third, behind reparations and the worsening financial crisis. Regarding disarmament the *Reichskanzler* was moreover under heavy domestic pressure from *Reichswehr* circles. The *Reichswehr*, having pulled many strings to secure Brüning's appointment, only reluctantly approved of his strategy of putting

---

35 Cecil to Noel-Baker, 11 Nov. 1930, Noel-Baker papers, CCAC, NBKR 4X/98, pt i.
36 Williams, *Labour and Russia*, 126–7.
37 Bennett, *German rearmament*, 53. For the German position see Rödder, *Stresemanns Erbe*, 136–9, 143–9.

reparations before disarmament. German officers were no longer willing to comply with the restrictions of the treaty of Versailles, and – with the secret political and financial approval of the cabinet – had embarked on their first large-scale secret rearmament programme in 1928. Co-operation between the *Reichswehr* and the Red Army reached its peak between 1928 and 1932. The *Reichswehr* and cabinet thus expected the disarmament conference either to concede or, by failing to do so, to provide an excuse for German rearmament. In pressing for 'equality' they intended to accuse the Allied powers of not meeting their obligations under the peace treaty, thereby shifting the blame for a failure of the disarmament conference onto France.

In 1930, the flagrant violation of the treaty of Versailles represented by German rearmament did not yet overly bother British officials. It therefore had little impact on the British position at Geneva. London possessed a considerable amount of intelligence material pointing to secret German military activities and to large-scale military co-operation with Russia, but these reports were either not taken seriously, or officials failed to piece the information together to draw the correct conclusions. Britain also disparaged French intelligence and belittled the value of the French material although – viewed with the benefit of hindsight – it was accurate. When, by the end of 1931, British officials eventually came to realise that Germany was in fact heavily rearming, they decided to turn a blind eye to it in order not to endanger the general disarmament conference due to open in February 1932:

> The view that the Foreign Office have consistently maintained is that a policy of pin-pricks against Germany on account of these minor infractions [*sic*] was to be avoided. Now that the disarmament conference is in session, it is presumably less than ever desirable to pick a quarrel with the Germans over any infractions which are not of fundamental military importance. The French have not asked us to associate ourselves with any protest, or even asked for our views, and we are perfectly free to adopt any attitude we like in this case.[38]

The final session of the preparatory disarmament conference in November 1930 was again dominated by Franco-German antagonism over security or equality in armaments. The success of the National Socialist Party in the September 1930 general elections in Germany had aroused great resentment in France and stiffened their attitude. The Germans countered by reconfirming their well-known position. British officials still hoped that the Nazi success would be seen in France as a warning to be more conciliatory. On 31 October Cecil noted:

> There are . . . a variety of new factors which improve the prospects of a successful result: 1. The success of the Hitler Movement in Germany has had for its immediate effect an increase of suspicion and chauvinism in France. It has,

[38] R. M. A. Hankey minute, 28 June 1932, PRO, FO 371/15948/C 5153; Carsten, *Weimar Republic*, 261.

however, also had the effect of placing quite plainly before France the choice between general disarmament or rearmament of Germany. . . . The Hitler Movement has had therefore at least its favourable, if not fortunate side.[39]

Cecil's hopes proved futile. His patience was once again taxed by Bernstorff's uncompromising attitude towards France as well as constant minority votes by Russia, Germany and, for the first time, Italy.[40] Anglo-French relations were markedly close and cordial throughout the session which concluded by completing a draft convention for the general disarmament convention on French lines which was strongly opposed by Germany and Russia.

The preparatory disarmament conference left British officials with a feeling of dissatisfaction. They knew that the last word had not been spoken in the matters of security, disarmament or rearmament. A decision had only been postponed, for the draft convention was neither binding upon the general disarmament conference nor did it contain figures. For the moment Britain had only satisfied France, by supporting her on issues like land-armament, which were not of immediate British interest. British officials had no doubt that a final disarmament convention had to meet some German demands if they were not to further fuel German nationalism. The existence of strong German nationalism increased French insistence on security guarantees which London was by no means ready to back.

The Foreign Office became convinced that it was not the German demand for equality of rights and the possibility of rearmament, but rather the French bid for security that was blocking the way to disarmament. Britain could satisfy French interests only by giving certain guarantees. But this London was hesitant to do. British wavering, or lack of decisive policy in this context, was also the outcome of a fundamental inter-departmental struggle about Britain's future foreign political orientation. Was primacy to be given to European or imperial problems? In the relatively stable context of the 1920s, a number of dominions had pressed for increasing independence from Britain. The result had been intense debates about imperial preference, Balfour's report of 1926, and heated discussions about an 'empire foreign policy'. The state of Anglo–dominion relations can best be described as volatile, as the future structure of the British empire was at stake. At the same time it became clear that the Locarno system had failed to stabilise European relations permanently and that the chances for further reconciliation between France and Germany were dim. Against this background, and the imperial difficulties, the number of voices that were no longer prepared to sacrifice British interests for the sake of Europe grew. As R. F. Holland points out, it was not a

---

39 Cecil minute, 31 Oct. 1930, BL, Cecil papers, MS 51081. On Germany's policy see M. Salewski, 'Zur deutschen Sicherheitspolitik in der Spätzeit der Weimarer Republik', *VfZg* xxii (1974), 121–47.
40 Toynbee, *Survey, 1930*, 123–30.

crude attempt to 'get out of Europe' or 'return to empire'. Rather it can be said that after 1930 all areas of British policy were affected by the desire to regain some unilateral influence over affairs, an influence which since the war had been mortgaged to the unlikely success of League Assemblies, the meetings of European statesmen and imperial conferences.[41]

It is against this background that both British reservations towards meeting French security demands, and Briand's proposal for European political union have to be seen. Briand had first presented his ideas in a speech at Geneva on 5 September 1929 and delivered them in writing to all members of the League of Nations in May 1930. The objective of Briand's plan was a short treaty by which the signatories would accept the peaceful organisation of Europe as a community of sovereign states. The new Europe should be governed by a European conference, a small, permanent political executive committee, and a secretariat. Details should be clarified at a later stage; a first working programme primarily dealt with economic and financial issues. However, the key provisions were that economic questions were subordinated to political issues. And the political concept contained a further expansion of collective security and the Locarno system as well as guarantees for all European states. The Whitehall departments that were consulted were sceptical, not only because Briand's scheme appeared very nebulous, but also because it seemed incompatible with British interest in areas such as free trade, London's special relationship with the United States, and the work of the League of Nations. Moreover, it threatened imperial unity and contained provisions which Germany in particular was unlikely to accept.[42] Britain's long silence before replying to France was thus a mixture of lack of interest and the desire not to get involved, given the numerous potential conflicts of interest. Moreover, in the absence of Soviet League membership, Moscow was not part of the proposed scheme, which made German consent to French proposals even less likely and provided Britain with an elegant way of concealing her own unease.

There was yet another reason for British hesitation concerning 'the Europe which France is organising'.[43] Vansittart's famous 'Old Adam memorandums'[44] referred to the French 'obsession' with security and her

41 R. F. Holland, *Britain and the Commonwealth alliance, 1918–1939*, London 1981, 87–116 at p. 116.
42 C. Schwarte, 'Le Plan Briand d'Union Européenne: sa genêse au Quai d'Orsay et la tentative de sa réalisation à la commission d'étude pour l'union européenne (1929–1931)', unpublished mémoire de D.E.A. (Institut des Etudes Politiques de Paris), 1992; R. T. White, 'Cordial caution: British policy towards the French proposal for the European federal union', unpubl. PhD. diss. Salford 1981; R. W. D. Boyce, 'Britain's first "no" to Europe: Britain and the Briand Plan, 1929–1930', *ESR* x (1980), 17–45.
43 Tyrrell to Henderson, 8 Jan. 1930, PRO, FO 371/14365/C 230.
44 Vansittart memos, 'An aspect of international relations' 1930, March, May 1931, Vansittart papers, VNST 1/1; D. Wächter, 'The British view on Germany, 1928–1933: Sir Horace Rumbold and the Foreign Office', unpubl. MPhil. diss. Cambridge 1991, 40–51.

attempt to establish hegemony over Europe with her eastern European satellites. Britain dreaded the possibility of being excluded from a Franco-German *rapprochement* at Soviet expense, as proposed by some German and French industrialists and Catholic circles including the later *Reichskanzler* Franz von Papen. Britain was unsure about how seriously to take these ambitions or how to react to them. Germany's attitude to Briand's European plan was therefore considered one possible test of the extent of Franco-German relations.

Officials were soon reassured, however, that nothing had to be feared. The Wilhelmstraße received Briand's proposals with caution and, before formulating a reply, attached great importance to assessing British and Soviet attitudes. German officials deplored Russia's exclusion from the scheme, and kept Moscow constantly informed about their views.[45] Britain even came to see advantages in including Russia in the negotiations because 'the setting up of a European group with interests and ambitions of its own – especially if it perpetrated the, at present voluntary, exclusion of Russia – would create new lines of friction and conflict and thereby make disarmament impossible'.[46]

Under a British compromise formula, Russia was eventually invited to join the negotiations of the economic committee for the Briand plan. The Quai d'Orsay, in the meantime, had shifted the focus of his scheme to its economic elements, realising that Europe was not ready for political union. For Britain, Germany's reactions to the Briand plan had illustrated that Franco-German interests were still incompatible, and that she had no reason to fear an alliance against herself; nor did she need to fear Germany's turning on Russia. The inter-departmental discussions in Whitehall about the Briand plan, as well as parallel ongoing negotiations at the imperial conference, had also had the effect of reaffirming that British priorities were imperial rather than European.

With time advancing towards the final disarmament conference in February 1932 the chances for real disarmament became increasingly unlikely. As early as 12 February 1931 Henderson instructed Rumbold, the ambassador in Berlin, to tell the German government that 'the ideal of complete, or anything like complete, disarmament, is not at the present moment within the sphere of practical politics'.[47] British officials had come to realise that the definition of 'security' had to be dealt with on two different levels, as it had to be applied to France and Germany alike. Hence, the crucial question was whether or not the disarmament conference would be

45 Rumbold to Sargent, 13 Feb. 1930, and minutes, PRO, FO 371/14365/C 1358; Mr Norton FO memo, 19 May 1930, FO 371/14980/W 5192; Bülow to Dirksen, 15 Aug. 1929, Dirksen papers, vol. 5; Köpke to Deutsche Botschaft Moskau, 3 Jan. 1931, BA-Po, Deutsche Botschaft Moskau 09.02, vol. 277; W. Lipgens, 'Europäische Einigungsidee 1923–1930 und Briands Europaplan im Urteil der deutschen Akten', *HZ* cciii (1966), 46–89, 316–63.

46 Labour party international department, Briand's pan-Europa memo, July 1930, MacDonald papers, PRO, 30/69/280; Cecil to MacDonald, 18 Aug. 1930, Cecil papers, BL, MS 51081.

47 Henderson to Rumbold, 12 Feb. 1931, *DBFP*, 2nd ser. i, doc. 348.

able to establish a basis of security for both Berlin and Paris. Given the international situation in 1931 it was doubtful whether France would be susceptible to arguments in favour of German calls for equal rights. Franco-German antagonism – as strong as ever – had temporarily shifted away from disarmament to financial problems and particularly the ill-fated Austro-German customs union project.[48] Still, British officials, when looking ahead, saw the broader consequences of a failure to adjust French and German security needs:

> Can Poland be expected to subject herself to disarmament when she knows that, failing a settlement by peaceful methods, her quarrel with Germany might lead to hostilities? Again, so long as Russia is an unknown factor, can Poland be expected to disarm at all, and, if Poland does not disarm, does France expect Germany to remain disarmed, and, if so, for how long?[49]

Hence, in the context of French and German security, suddenly the old 'ghost' of Rapallo reappeared on the horizon. The danger of Germany and the 'unknown factor', Russia, uniting and advancing against Poland, seemed a serious obstacle to Polish and French disarmament and the establishment of some form of security for Germany. The inter-departmental sub-committee of the Committee of Imperial Defence, in charge of reconsidering the British position on all issues referred to in the preparatory commission's draft proposals, discussed at length the 'colossal and unsolved [Russian] problem'.[50] According to committee member Lord Lothian, the question of 'whether Germany and Russia were to be driven together, or whether they were to remain rivals . . . was the chief factor that anyone in Europe who talked about security had to take into account'.[51]

Worrying in this context was a memorandum by the chief of the imperial general staff referring to plans for military co-operation between the Russian and German general staffs, probably directed against Poland. Although it assumed that a Russo-German attack on Poland was unlikely for the moment – as this would leave Germany completely at the mercy of France – the memorandum pointed out that Russia was too erratic for any reliance to be placed upon her promises to disarm materially.[52] It was again Lord Lothian who linked the possible Rapallo front to the problem of security, and warned of the far-reaching consequences if Britain were to support the French

---

[48] Bennett, *German rearmament*, 96–7; Krüger, *Außenpolitik*, 531–9; Vaïsse, *Sécurité*, 104–14.

[49] Rumbold to Henderson, 26 Feb. 1931, *DBFP*, 2nd ser. vi, doc. 352; FO memo 'The Soviet Union and disarmament', 7 Apr. 1931, PRO, FO 371/15614/N 2476. For Germany's ambitions as regards Poland see Salewski, *Sicherheitspolitik*, 130–2.

[50] WO memo, 'A military appreciation of some of the world situation', Jan. 1931, MacDonald papers, PRO, 30/69/284.

[51] CID, disarmament sub-committee, meetings of 23 Apr., 14 May 1931, Templewood papers, CUL, C vii: 1.

[52] Chief of the imperial general staff memo, 31 May 1931, ibid.

position. '[This] meant that we were subscribing to the thesis that Germany should have no security, and should not be allowed sufficient forces even to be able to resist an attack.' If, in such a case, Germany left the League of Nations, 'the result might be military alliances between Germany and Italy, and even conceivably Russia as well, thus re-establishing the old system of a balance of armed power'.[53]

In the months before the disarmament conference, the issue of growing German revisionism and the question of the eastern frontier remained troublesome. British diplomats discussed the possibility of Germany being driven into the arms of Russia by growing internal right-wing pressure. When foreign minister Curtius mentioned to the British the German attitude towards disarmament, he also referred to the possibility of the German right and the Bolsheviks advancing on a common front. Sargent, the head of the Central department, was unimpressed by this statement and believed that the German government was once again using the Bolshevik threat as propaganda in respect to disarmament and the 'principle of equality'.[54] However, in December 1931 it was British policy not to undertake any fresh commitments with regard to French security as long as no amicable solution to the question of the eastern frontier of Germany was visible. Matters had been further complicated for Britain by the advent of the national government, in which the Liberal John Simon replaced Arthur Henderson as foreign secretary. Simon, a perfectionist in background details, had very little time to prepare himself for the disarmament conference where many people looked to Britain as the principal moderating power.[55]

The long expected conference finally opened on 5 February 1932 in Geneva with dim prospects for a reconciliation of the various countries' different positions. The chances for its success could hardly have been less favourable. Essentially, as Bennett observes, not one but three conferences took place, the whole gathering being 'not so much a meeting on the subject of disarmament as an arena for conflicting subjects of debate'.[56] The Germans fought for their equality of rights while the French aimed at making the sessions a conference on security. And Britain was represented by a foreign secretary whose policies were vague and incoherent and who was unable to formulate a clear position between the two opposing sides. After five weeks of negotiations, Cadogan sarcastically wrote back to London: 'It is refreshing to find the French and the Germans agreeing on anything, even if it is only

---

[53] CID, disarmament sub-committee, meeting of 12 June 1931, ibid.
[54] Curtius memo (outlining the German attitude towards disarmament), 30 July 1931; Sargent minute, 18 Aug. 1931, PRO, FO 371/15705/W 8890.
[55] D. Dutton, *Simon: a political biography of Sir John Simon*, London 1992, 151–60.
[56] Bennett, *German rearmament*, 132; R. C. Richardson, 'The Geneva disarmament conference, 1932–34', in D. Richardson and G. A. Stone (eds), *Decisions and diplomacy: essays in international history*, London 1995, 60–81; R. C. Richardson and C. Kitching, 'Britain and the world disarmament conference', in C. Catterall and C. J. Morris (eds), *Britain and the threat to stability in Europe, 1918–1945*, Leicester 1993, 35–56.

to differ, and we may hope that things will pass off in a spirit of reasonable amiability.'[57]

The conference would have been doomed from the outset had it not been for the permanent British readiness to mediate without, however, assuming political leadership. During the first few months of 1932, British delegates at Geneva were still convinced of the genuineness of the German demands for equality and hence supported Berlin's claims against the French. However, during the summer of 1932, General von Schleicher's speeches as *Reichswehr* minister in the new Papen government made it increasingly plain that Germany was in fact rearming. This appeared to prove that the nationalist and militarist revival which had brought the general and his colleagues into power, had already begun to influence German foreign policy to rearm. Faced with this new situation, British sympathies shifted back to France. Tensions reached a peak when Germany left the disarmament conference on 16 September 1932 following an exchange of *aide-memoires*, in the course of which Britain expressed stronger sympathies with French rather than German arguments.[58]

Germany returned to Geneva in December 1932 as a result of British diplomacy. Because of the political crisis in Germany following the fall of the Papen government and take-over by General von Schleicher as *Reichskanzler* in December 1932, informal talks were held between Britain, Germany, France, Italy and the United States, and a five-power declaration was signed. However, by now it was clear even to the British that the German claim for equality of rights meant rearmament.

The previously held view that Germany might turn for support to the Soviet Union if her demands for equality were not met, did not materialise. Before the beginning of the disarmament conference in February 1932, Russian and German officials had renewed their agreement for consultations – this time at a German initiative[59] – but this resulted more in parallel than in co-operative work at Geneva. As will be shown, the German–Russian consent dwindled particularly during Papen's time in office, but to a lesser extent also during Schleicher's, and finally Hitler's tenure. Moscow was no longer informed about German strategy; Litvinov's complaint that the Italians were a lot more forthcoming than the Germans in exchanging views was fruitless. German answers would henceforth be evasive.

Throughout the period of the preparatory conferences German–Russian co-operation had been a nuisance to Britain, but had never seriously

---

57 Cadogan to Howard-Smith, 12 Mar. 1932, PRO, FO 371/16461/W 3192. See also J. Wheeler-Bennett, *The pipe dream of peace: the story of the collapse of disarmament*, 3rd edn, New York 1971.
58 Toynbee, *Survey, 1932*, 266–86; Bennett, *German rearmament*, 169–207.
59 Dirksen to AA, 23 Aug. 1931, PA-AA, R 32141; Aufzeichnung Bülow, 28 Jan. 1932, R 29451.

disturbed conference procedures. However, when Britain began to consider Russo-German co-operation in 1932, the political conditions in Berlin had changed so radically that there was no longer any question of prolonged intimacy with the Russian bear.

10

The Rapallo Relationship and Hitler's Rise to Power

The year 1930 marked a turning point in European, and also British politics after the First World War. Within a few months, the spirit which had been decisive for the post-Locarno era faded away, after two of the main guarantors of peace and of increasing conciliation between the former victors and vanquished had left the political stage. Austen Chamberlain was forced out of office when the Conservatives lost the general election on 30 May 1929. Gustav Stresemann, the German foreign minister, died on 3 October 1929. Only the French foreign minister, Aristide Briand, continued, in the new Tardieu government which was formed in October 1929, but he had far more difficult counterparts in Arthur Henderson, the new British Labour foreign secretary, and Julius Curtius, the German foreign minister in the government of *Reichskanzler* Heinrich Brüning.

Also the general political and economic outlook rapidly changed for the worse. The consequences of the Wall Street crash of October 1929 were soon felt in Europe, destroying all efforts made during the 1920s to restore the pre-war international and commercial system. After a successful first six months, Ramsay MacDonald's second Labour government got into severe political trouble following the economic crisis and was forced to form a national government in the summer of 1931.

On the foreign policy agenda of the Labour government, disarmament was one of the major issues, as was the search for a solution to Germany's loudly voiced request for equality. The Young plan, agreed upon at the first Hague conference, which ended Germany's reparation payments, was a further step in this direction. But The Hague had also revealed that Anglo-French relations would continue less smoothly under a Labour government than during the Briand–Chamberlain era. Labour had been a longstanding critic of the 'excessive' French security requirements, and was generally more inclined to concede further modifications of the Versailles treaty to Germany. Yet prime minister MacDonald and foreign secretary Henderson differed on this matter, and MacDonald defeated Henderson's efforts to satisfy French demands for military assistance. The two men's opinions on the role of the League of Nations also differed sharply. MacDonald's conviction that the League was no more than a world forum, was more in line with the traditions of British foreign policy than Henderson's faith in the Geneva body as an embryonic super-state. The prime minister's views eventually determined the shape of Labour's policy, but at the time MacDonald's and Henderson's diverging attitudes on important issues made British policy appear inconsistent.[1]

Labour was also critical of its predecessor's policy of ignoring the Soviet Union. One of its first actions was thus the re-establishment of diplomatic relations with Moscow, but the improvement in political and economic relations between the two countries remained slow. On the imperial front, Britain was much preoccupied with unrest in India and China and with the general problem that the principal imperial possessions refused continued subordination. With the Manchurian crisis following the Japanese attack on China in 1931–2, significant British economic interests in Shanghai were at stake and the Anglo-Japanese struggle for supremacy in the region forced Britain to reconsider its imperial policy in the Far East.

Against this background, it is hardly surprising that German–Soviet relations – with all their implications for German revisionism and European stability in general – received less attention in Britain than during the 1920s, when the Rapallo alliance was still used as a frequent bargaining chip by both Russia and Germany. Moreover, Russo-German relations noticeably cooled after 1928/29. Germany's *rapprochement* with the western powers in her pursuit of a renegotiated reparations settlement and the evacuation of the Rhineland, led to an inevitable neglect of Soviet Russia, much to Moscow's displeasure and anxiety. The Soviets, in turn, contributed to deteriorating relations by ridiculing German politicians and the German military during the 1 May 1929 parade in Moscow, by stepping up a communist propaganda campaign, and by fuelling Comintern initiated riots and violent clashes between the German communist party (KPD) and the Social Democrats (SPD) in Berlin. Sir Horace Rumbold, the British ambassador to Berlin, commented that 'if a graph were drawn of them [i.e. Russo-German relations], it would show a marked downward curve'. In conversations, however, German officials only admitted temporary economic difficulties.[2]

Trusting Rumbold's reports, the Foreign Office watched the deterioration of Russo-German relations calmly. From Moscow, Sir Esmond Ovey, the British ambassador, reported that the Soviets obviously felt encircled by capitalist powers.[3] As far as Germany was concerned, the Foreign Office had difficulty in judging how far the deterioration of Soviet–German relations was due to particular incidents and how far to the improvement of Germany's relations with the western powers. Either way, its advantages for Britain were obvious.

---

1   Carlton, *MacDonald versus Henderson*, 25–32.
2   Rumbold to Henderson, 31 Jan., 19 Feb. 1930, *DBFP*, 1A ser. vii, docs 59, 65; Rumbold to Henderson, 14 Feb. 1930, PRO, FO 371/14371/C 1386; Dyck, *Weimar Germany*, 154–6, 162–84; Weingartner, *Stalin*, 10–23. On KPD–SPD antagonism see H. A. Winkler, *Der Weg in die Katastrophe. Arbeiter und Arbeiterbewegung in der Weimarer Republik 1930–1933*, Berlin–Bonn 1987, 148–54.
3   Ovey to Henderson, 6 Feb. 1930, *DBFP*, 2nd ser. vii, doc. 62.

Germany's enthusiasm after the treaty of Rapallo, and the belief that amicable relations with Moscow were essential to counterbalance the Versailles powers, had indeed evaporated. Foreign minister Curtius, like Stresemann, gave priority to Germany's balancing role between east and west and sought to avoid a one-sided eastern commitment. Locarno and the treaty of Berlin, rather than Rapallo, were the basis of his policy. Closer co-operation with Moscow was only needed to serve Germany's revisionist intentions, and ideological differences were not allowed to exceed a certain level. Nevertheless, Curtius needed and supported the Russian connection for the sake of the revisionist goals that were implicit in the treaty of Rapallo – namely a revision of the German–Polish border. In this policy, Curtius was backed by Wilhelmstraße officials like Wilhelm von Bülow or Ernst von Weizsäcker, who held leading positions after 1930 and advocated a revisionist policy which sharply contrasted with the intentions of Stresemann and Carl von Schubert, the former secretary of state. While their policy challenged France, this group believed in the need for friendly bilateral relations with Great Britain and the Soviet Union as the best means to speed up revision.

By contrast, *Reichskanzler* Brüning, as a devoted Catholic, was reserved towards the Soviet Union and kept his support of bilateral contacts between Moscow and Berlin to a bare minimum.[4] He refused to renew the treaty of Berlin for more than two years out of consideration for French opinion.[5] Generally, however, the foreign policy of the Brüning government was conducted more with an eye to domestic needs than to its reception abroad. The number of confrontations and misunderstandings between the former Locarno partners, Britain, France and Germany, grew when Berlin bluntly demanded speedy revision, i.e. a solution to the issues of reparations, disarmament or the abortive customs union of 1932 all at once. In Britain, however, Brüning enjoyed respect because he seemed to continue Stresemann's political legacy and was therefore seen as the sole guarantor of the increasingly unstable German domestic political and economic situation.

With rapidly deteriorating Franco-German relations following Stresemann's death, British officials in London came to anticipate that German revisionism would replace the Locarno spirit and Stresemann's concept of conciliation. One of the key revisionist issues for the Wilhelmstraße would be the Polish border. By contrast, ambassador Rumbold believed an immediate change in Germany's political orientation to be less likely:

> The present parliamentary situation is too confused to enable an observer to predict what the outcome is likely to be. Obviously, if the Nationalists got control of the government, they might be expected to take up the Polish question at no distant date, and with considerable vigour . . . [German] relations

4 Rödder, *Stresemanns Erbe*, 158–64; Dirksen, *Moscow, Tokyo, London*, 112.
5 Weingartner, *Stalin*, 100 at n. 273.

with Russia at the time, would in my view, necessarily have a bearing on any attempt to open up the Polish question. If those relations were good, they might be encouraged to endeavour to obtain such a revision of the eastern frontier. If they were bad, such an attempt would have less prospect of success. In fact, the state of affairs in Russia must be postulated before a satisfactory answer could be given.[6]

Sargent's subsequent minute that 'there is little chance of Germany embarking on a policy of foreign adventures', reflects the Foreign Office's detailed knowledge of the uneasy state of Russo-German relations, given the fact that intimacy between the Rapallo partners was a prerequisite for joint action against Poland. Nevertheless, British officials kept a watchful eye on German revisionism although Berlin gave priority to disarmament and the evacuation of the Rhineland – at least for the moment. But Curtius had referred to the 'unsatisfactory state of the German–Polish border' during a conversation with Rumbold on 3 July 1930.[7] Moreover, the speech by Gottfried Treviranus, leader of the right-wing People's Conservative Party and minister of the occupied territories during the constitution day celebrations on 10 August 1930, in which he demanded the unification of all German people and complained about the 'unhealed wounds in the eastern flank',[8] created considerable unease in Poland. British officials, however, expressed little sympathy for the Poles. 'It is something worse than childish for the Poles to attempt to work up a storm in a teacup that any other grown up would, and is trying to, allow to cool. A little mild coolness on our side will not be amiss,' was Vansittart's laconic comment.[9]

Yet, as Rumbold wrote to Henderson, 'the snowball of "revision" continues to roll down the electoral slopes, and, as it rolls, it is gathering speed and size'.[10] At the German elections in September 1930, and against the background of the rapidly deteriorating economic situation, virtually all parties included revisionist demands in their election manifestos. The Polish frontier, the modification of the Young plan, and the alternatives of general disarmament or German rearmament, were all on the political agenda and were all interconnected. British officials were almost certain that the Polish question would come to the fore once the financial crisis was over. They expected Berlin to concentrate first on establishing military equality with Poland before seriously putting forward the Corridor claim, 'for then, for the first time, will the German government have some prospect of being able to enforce the attention of a reluctant Europe'. London dreaded the moment when Germany would press for military parity with Warsaw, especially in

---

6 Rumbold to Sargent, 28 Feb. 1930; Sargent minute, 4 Mar. 1930, PRO, FO 371/14365/C 1753.
7 Rumbold to Henderson, 3 July 1930, *DBFP*, 2nd ser. i, doc. 311.
8 Rumbold to Henderson, 12 Aug. 1930, 15 May 1930, ibid. docs 312, 315, 316.
9 Vansittart minute, 20 Aug. 1930, PRO, FO 371/14370/C 6483.
10 Rumbold to Henderson, 29 Aug. 1930, *DBFP*, 2nd ser. i, doc. 318.

view of its effect on the disarmament conference, and French reactions in particular, given that then Britain might be forced to take sides. Therefore, 'the maintenance of Herr Brüning in power . . . becomes a matter of European importance'.[11]

British officials felt increasingly compelled to pay serious attention to the German–Polish border question. Philip Nichols's view that 'the eastern frontier constitutes by far the most important *political* problem in Europe today',[12] summarised the dominant Foreign Office opinion in 1931. For years the issue had been awaiting a solution, making some Polish sacrifices necessary and justified. An early settlement seemed desirable not only for Germany. 'Among the infection spots in Europe capable under certain conditions of leading eventually to the disease of war the eastern frontier of Germany must be admitted as one of the most dangerous,' stated a Foreign Office memorandum of January 1931. 'The aims of British policy demand the peaceful settlement of this question, and the British interests in the matter are direct and unequivocal; nor should we, if we could, try and evade responsibility.'[13]

This Foreign Office statement sounds almost revolutionary. Ever since the days of the Paris peace conference, British officials had felt uncomfortable about the Polish Corridor settlement but had argued that no sphere of British influence or interests was touched. There was ample awareness that this open sore in German–Polish relations would have to be treated at some point in the future, but it was hoped that this moment would not come for some time. The Central department's view that Britain could not remain aloof in the case of a conflict in east central Europe, and that the preservation of peace depended on the British attitude, reflects the growing conviction that some form of appeasement *vis-à-vis* Germany had to be adopted in order to prevent uncontrollable nationalistic forces from coming to power. Britain worried about the possibility that Germany – under pressure from internal forces such as the National Socialists, and against the better judgement of her elder statesmen – would once again turn eastwards in the hope that with Russia as an ally or a vassal she might be able to force the issue against Poland.[14]

The key to German revisionism and the Polish border issue lay in Moscow. Hence, Germany could not afford to be on bad terms with Russia. But Germany also held the key to British commitment in east central Europe. The Foreign Office thus faced a dilemma. No conceivable solution of the eastern frontiers was in sight unless Russia's position *vis-à-vis* Europe became more clearly defined.

> The question now is whether we should leave things as they stand now, or try some preparatory approach . . . Central and western Europe may find

---

11 Sargent minute, 15 Oct. 1930, PRO, FO 371/14364/C 7653.
12 Nichols minute, 20 July 1931, PRO, FO 371/15222/C 5169 (original emphasis).
13 Annex C in FO memo, 13 July 1931, PRO, FO 371/15222/C 5171.
14 M. Gilbert, *The roots of appeasement*, London 1966, 159.

themselves in the thick of trouble before they are out of the fog, indeed we may not expect that this will stand still after Germany has begun rearming in earnest, as – on present showing – she will in 1932,

minuted Vansittart,[15] but other members of the Foreign Office were less pessimistic than the permanent under-secretary. As the financial crisis worsened, domestic problems like unemployment, strikes and political extremism grew and Russo-German relations turned ever more frosty, the Polish question temporarily retreated into the background of German politics. This relieved Britain from preparing a strategy for the day when the border question would be on the political agenda. It also postponed a British decision on new security guarantees for France, a question of prime importance for the British position at the disarmament conference.

Twelve months later, the Foreign Office's view of German ambitions towards the Corridor was entirely negative. The present German restraint seemed to be merely the 'lull before the storm' and the issues of German equality of status and rearmament would only serve to speed up the opening of the Corridor question.[16] Still, intimate German–Russian relations in this context were no longer a factor of consideration – one day Germany would go for Poland, with or without Russian support.

Russian assistance, however, remained vital for other parts of German revisionism. German rearmament, about which Allied intelligence services were well informed, was impossible without Soviet assistance. Through numerous reports, Whitehall was familiar with German violations of the treaty of Versailles. British officials, keen to appease Germany, found this development not worthy of any *démarche* in Berlin. They did not want to provoke French aggravation and thus endanger the disarmament conference by protesting against these 'minor infractions' of the treaty. Yet those 'minor infractions' would have made a formidable case against Germany. In fact, they provided the nucleus for Hitler's *Wehrmacht*.

Russo-German military co-operation reached its peak in the years between 1927 and 1932.[17] Whitehall had observed Russo-German military contacts ever since the conclusion of the treaty of Rapallo. The air ministry had known, since 1929, that the Lipeck flying school existed, that each year about fifty *Reichswehr* officers came for a two-year training programme on Junker and Albatros planes, and that the agreement between Moscow and Berlin for the use of the site had been renewed in April 1932 for another year. In September 1932, Rumbold reported the participation of high-ranking Soviet officers in German army manoeuvres, including General Tuchachevski, at this time chiefly responsible for weapons and ammunition

[15] Vansittart minute, 31 Jan. 1931, PRO, FO 371/15221/C 561.
[16] Hankey minute, 22 Sept. 1932, and Sargent minute, 4 Oct. 1932, quoted in Carsten, *Weimar Republic*, 245.
[17] Zeidler, 'Reichswehr und Rote Armee', 25–49.

within the Red Army. The results of Moscow's contract with the German steel plant Krupp for metallurgical aid for the production of special military steel was also registered in Britain: the Department for Overseas Trade noted an increasing import of ferro-alloys into the Soviet Union and concluded that Moscow was stockpiling this material, but only remarked that the Soviets paid cash and bought at unnecessarily high prices.[18]

The conclusions of British officials reveal an astonishing indifference. One reason for this attitude was the entirely misleading judgements of the military attaché in Berlin, Colonel Marshall-Cornwall, and air attaché, Wing Commander Herring. In a report to the Foreign Office, the latter reported that during the period 1928–32 the German defence ministry had loosened its ties with the Russian army for a variety of unspecified reasons. In fact, just the contrary was the case. Marshall-Cornwall gave powerful evidence of the exchange of military visits and Soviet officers in uniform attending *Reichswehr* manoeuvres, of German officers nominally retiring from the *Reichswehr* while undergoing training in Russia, as well as of a clique of generals around General von Schleicher who were plotting to gain control of the chief posts in the army. The military attaché reported that Schleicher – at this time in charge of the *Wehrmacht* department within the *Reichswehr* ministry but one year later first *Reichswehr* minister and then *Reichskanzler* – favoured a direct policy in co-operation with Soviet Russia against Poland. Nevertheless, he concluded that Russo-German co-operation remained on shaky ground. His future reports were no less illuminating. His general impression remained that while Germany's present army contained some of the best fighting material in the world, the restrictions and limitations imposed on her by the peace treaty had seriously held back her efforts to become a first-class fighting entity. Marshall-Cornwall had obviously fallen victim to the extraordinary lies used by German officers to distract British attention.[19]

The military attaché's reports certainly influenced Foreign Office opinion, which now also disregarded the danger posed by Russo-German military co-operation.[20] Although in early 1932, Marshall-Cornwall produced 'an exhaustive account . . . of the recent systematic flouting of the treaty', and the War Office compiled a memorandum on the extent and effects of the military violations of the treaty of Versailles, the cabinet still decided against an open protest. As the information in the memorandum was based on secret reports, no public use could be made of it without endangering the informants. More

---

18 Ibid. 39; *ADAP*, ser. B, xi, doc. 208; memo on the uses of ferro-alloys, 21 July 1930, PRO, FO 371/14878/N 5056; Miss Rosenberg to Henderson, 30 June 1931, FO 371/15621/N 4686; Rumbold to Henderson, 6 Sept. 1930, FO 371/14372/C 7031; Rumbold to Simon, 29 Sept. 1932, FO 371/15950/C 8233; Strang to Seymour, undated [July/Aug. 1931], FO 371/15614/N 6234; Carsten, *Weimar Republic*, 260–1.
19 Rumbold to Henderson, 12 Sept., 1 Oct. 1930, PRO, FO 371/14372/C 7017, C 7483; Rumbold to Henderson, 25, 27 Feb. 1931, FO 371/15224/C 1355, C 1357.
20 Rumbold to Henderson, 25 Feb. 1931, PRO, FO 371/15224/C 1355.

importantly, however, the Foreign Office's view had consistently been that the German military violations of the peace treaty were not severe enough to endanger the disarmament conference, and had therefore refrained from protesting officially.[21]

This was the Foreign Office's last word on the matter of German re-armament with Soviet assistance. Russo-German military co-operation was undesirable but unimportant. Hence it was to be ignored. British officials remained convinced that despite the importance of military, political and economic collaboration, Russo-German relations were going downhill. The political climate between the Rapallo partners visibly deteriorated after the Russophobe Franz von Papen had replaced Brüning as *Reichskanzler* in June 1932. Moreover, the British Foreign Office was unimpressed with the new chancellor. Sargent's characterisation reflected the views of his colleagues when he commented that Papen's appointment looked

> very much like the final bankruptcy of German politicians and the establish-ment of a semi-military dictatorship which, in a country like Germany, is the obvious alternative to a constitutional ministry [sic]. Whether or not von Papen is to be a mere stop-gap, his appointment will probably constitute an important landmark in Germany's political development.[22]

Britain's moderately sceptical attitude was not shared in Moscow, where Papen was regarded as 'rabidly anti-Bolshevik'.[23] Papen's attempt, during a gentlemen's club meeting in Berlin on 27 February 1931, to form a German–French–Polish economic *accord à trois* directed against the Soviet five-year plan,[24] had not been forgotten by the Kremlin. With even greater dismay, the Soviet government learnt of Papen's – eventually fruitless – attempt to form a Franco-German alliance during the Lausanne conference, the military provisions of which included an exchange of general staff officers.[25] MacDonald's reaction, when he learnt of Papen's endeavours, illus-trates the minimal British interest in a Russo-German rupture. For Britain, the danger of a clandestine Franco-German *rapprochement* excluding and

---

[21] WO memo, communicated to FO 2 Mar. 1932, PRO, FO 371/15938/C 1696; R. M. A. Hankey minute, 28 June 1932, FO 331/15948/C 5153; Carsten, *Weimar Republic*, 261.
[22] Sargent minute, 2 June 1932, PRO, FO 371/15944/C 4380.
[23] Dirksen, *Moscow, Tokyo, London*, 114.
[24] J. A. Bach, *Franz von Papen in der Weimarer Republik. Aktivitäten in Politik und Presse 1918–1932*, Düsseldorf 1977, 162. Bach clearly shows that Papen's religion-based fight against 'Bolshevik world danger' was the chief motive for his Francophile attitude and his constant attempt to bring about Franco-German reconciliation. See also Adams, *Rebel patriot*, 126, 128.
[25] Dirksen to Bülow, 13 Aug. 1932, PA-AA, R 29518; unsigned letter (probably Köster) to Meyer, 26 Aug. 1932, Deutsche Botschaft Paris 536b, vol. 2; F. von Papen, *Der Wahrheit eine Gasse*, Munich 1952, 202–7; H. Brüning, *Memoiren 1918–1934*, Stuttgart 1970, 616; E. Herriot, *Jadis*, II: *D'une guerre à l'autre 1914–1936*, Paris 1952, 322, 338; Vaïsse, *Sécurité*, 264–6.

isolating London was far greater than the benefits of less cordial Russo-German relations.

But there was a new, disturbing element in Russo-German relations. Increasingly the British embassy in Berlin reported back to London about National Socialist activities in which their hostile attitude towards communism figured prominently.[26] British officials only gradually understood the driving forces behind the Nazi–communist confrontations and attempted to draw conclusions for the future of the Rapallo relationship. Until Hitler's appointment as *Reichskanzler*, and even during his first year in office, Britain underestimated the National Socialist movement's strength and appeal to the people, its driving forces and its political objectives.[27] The importance of Hitler's personality was misjudged as much as the impact of National Socialist ideology on German domestic and foreign policy. In fact, until Rumbold's famous *Mein Kampf* despatch of 26 April 1933,[28] British officials had hardly realised that there was a National Socialist ideology and even then they did not really understand its implications for domestic and international affairs. When British officials were finally acquainted with Hitler's foreign political aims, particularly his anti-Bolshevism and concept of living space, they found it difficult to understand *Lebensraum* as an end in itself and as central to National Socialist ideology. Since, however, British officials underestimated the ideological impact of Hitler's anti-Bolshevism, they did not draw any conclusions for the future of Russo-German relations.

British officials had never expected Hitler to become *Reichskanzler*. Rumbold discounted this possibility until the German elections in November 1932, since he took the loss of two million votes after the July elections as a sign that the National Socialist party was in decline. Moreover, neither the British press nor diplomatic observers regarded Hitler as the leading force behind the Nazi movement. They were more impressed by the characters of Hermann Göring, Joseph Goebbels and Wilhelm Frick than by 'the stubby little Austrian . . . with a Charlie Chaplin moustache'.[29] The heterogeneous structure of the movement, particularly the strength of the Strasser wing, further complicated an assessment of the party's leading figures and goals. During 1932, many British began to regard Gregor Strasser as the only true politician among the Nazis.[30]

26 Rumbold to Simon, 16 July, 10, 23, 30 Aug. 1932, *DBFP*, 2nd ser. iv, docs 3, 10, 19, 22; C. Striefler, *Kampf um die Macht. Kommunisten und Nationalsozialisten am Ende der Weimarer Republik*, Berlin 1993.

27 There has been no monograph on the British reaction to the Nazi *Machtergreifung* to date. The following account is based on P. Mohr, 'Reaction to Hitler's seizure of power in Great Britain: the first year', unpubl. MPhil. diss. Cambridge 1991.

28 Rumbold to Simon, 26 Apr. 1933, *DBFP*, 2nd ser. v, doc. 36; J. J. Barnes and P. J. Barnes, *Hitler's* Mein Kampf *in Britain and America: a publishing history, 1930–1939*, Cambridge 1980, 21–4.

29 *Daily Herald*, 31 Jan. 1933, quoted in Mohr, 'Hitler's seizure of power', 10.

30 Ibid. 6; B. Granzow, *A mirror of Nazism: British opinion and the emergence of Hitler, 1929–1933*, London 1964, 167, 169.

The news of Hitler's appointment was received calmly in Britain. 'The Hitler experiment had to be made some time or other', was Rumbold's laconic comment.[31] To most British officials, a Hitler cabinet was preferable to a government led by either Papen or Hugenberg and their anti-democratic, militarist and nationalist Junkerdom. Alfred Hugenberg, the 'principal intriguer', had for a long time been regarded in the British press as the strong man and was the most feared person in the new German government.

Most British observers saw in Hitler the 'least dangerous solution' for German politics.[32] They were confident that the coalition would 'tame' the three Nazis in the cabinet, and could not imagine that Hitler would be able to overrule his 'guardians' and the traditional élites of his country. Neurath's remaining in office as foreign minister, and *Reichspräsident* Hindenburg's statement that he would not permit a change of foreign political direction, increased British confidence in the new government.

British officials approached the Hitler cabinet with the same wait-and-see attitude as any other legally appointed government. So far, they were unaware, firstly that Hitler was the personification of National Socialism and, secondly, that he was the author of *Mein Kampf*, the 'full-blown blood-and-thunder book', as Rumbold's successor Eric Phipps called it.[33] British diplomats underrated this correlation because they were not familiar with the content of *Mein Kampf*. With the exception of the Germanophobe Robert Vansittart, no one in the Foreign Office had read *Mein Kampf* before 1933, and even then it was ignored by most officials.[34]

The attitude of officials in London towards the new Germany was largely determined by the British ambassador in Berlin. Although Nazi activities had been widely covered in Rumbold's despatches since 1930, he had missed the ideological component. By always giving adequate descriptions of events in Germany, he had provided a profound analysis of Hitlerism as a new socio-political phenomenon,[35] but had not examined the motives behind Nazi actions. When, in October 1930, he transmitted the party's election programme, his description of the final aims, 'the consolidation of all

---

[31] Quoted from Mohr, 'Hitler's seizure of power', 13–14.

[32] Quoted from Granzow, *Mirror*, 182–9 at p. 184.

[33] Phipps to Simon, 21 Nov. 1933, *DBFP*, 2nd ser. vi, doc. 60. On Phipps see M. Jaroch, *'Too much wit and not enough warning?' Sir Eric Phipps als britischer Botschafter in Berlin von 1933–1937*, Frankfurt-am-Main 1999.

[34] Hankey, the secretary to the cabinet, undertook his own analysis of *Mein Kampf* as late as the end of October 1933, and afterwards was very sceptical as to the prospects for Germany's future: Hankey to Phipps, 30 Oct. 1933, Phipps papers, CCAC, PHPP 3/3. See also Barnes and Barnes, *Hitler's* Mein Kampf, 21–4, 26. The authorised British translation of the book was considerably shortened and purged of particularly outspoken paragraphs. In the whole of the Foreign Office there existed but one copy of the original version, which went missing, so that officials assumed it had gone to Beijing but eventually it turned up in Sargent's room. The British embassy in Berlin did not have a copy of the English translation and therefore did not know which parts had been excised: ibid. 30–1.

[35] Wächter, 'The British view', 78.

Germans into one great German State, equal rights for the German people with other nations, the abolition of the treaties of Versailles and Saint-Germain, and space and colonies to feed the nation and absorb the surplus population', was brief and gave no further explanation of how they might be achieved. Instead he dwelled extensively on the Nazis' antisemitism.[36]

Rumbold's attitude is typical of British officials' difficulty in understanding the impact of ideology on policy. As D. C. Watt argues, it was against British thinking and education to understand the nature of a state in which ideology was connected with a machinery of pressure, threat and the use of force.[37] It will be remembered that, after the Bolshevik revolution, British officials had a similar problem, and that it took the head of the British mission in Moscow, Sir Robert Hodgson, as well as the officials at the Northern desk of the Foreign Office, years to grasp fully the impact of communist ideology on Soviet foreign policy. Yet when Hodgson went to Moscow in 1921, Bolshevik ideology had already determined the direction of Soviet domestic and foreign policy for almost four years, whereas Rumbold, in Berlin since 1928, observed the rise of Nazism in Germany right from the start. There were also significant differences in perception arising from the 'novelty' value of the various ideologies: whereas in 1921 ideology was a completely new phenomenon, the Nazis were the third movement after the communists and the fascists to embark upon an ideology-driven foreign policy.

Rumbold had been aware of antisemitism as one key feature of National Socialism, yet he did not understand the second cornerstone of Hitler's programme, the concept of living space in the east as an end in itself, as the overall objective in which National Socialist policy, including antisemitism, culminated.[38] In his famous *Mein Kampf* despatch of 26 April 1933, on the subject of eastern colonialisation he was unsure 'how far Hitler is prepared to put his fantastic proposals into operation . . . but it is clear that he cannot abandon the cardinal points of his programme any more than Lenin or Mussolini could'.[39] Rumbold's judgement on this point was vague because, before 1933, the Nazis had made every effort to disguise their real intentions,

36 Rumbold to Henderson, 31 Oct. 1930, *DBFP*, 2nd ser. i, doc. 334. For the importance of *Mein Kampf* see H. R. Trevor-Roper, 'Hitlers Kriegsziele', in W. Michalka (ed.), *Nationalsozialistische Außenpolitik*, Darmstadt 1978, 31–48 at pp. 33–5 (first published in *VfZg* viii [1960], 212–33).
37 D. C. Watt, 'Zwischen Antipathie und Verständigung. Die Berichte der britischen Botschaft in Berlin', in *Das Parlament* iv/v, 29 Jan./5 Feb. 1983, 16.
38 On the connection between Hitler's antisemitism and his anti-Bolshevism see A. Hillgruber, 'Die "Endlösung" und das deutsche Ostimperium als Kernstück des rassenideologischen Programms des Nationalsozialismus', in A. Hillgruber, *Deutsche Großmacht- und Weltpolitik im 19. und 20. Jahrhundert*, Düsseldorf 1977, 252–75; E. Nolte, *Der europäische Bürgerkrieg 1917–1945. Nationalsozialismus und Bolschewismus*, 4th edn, Frankfurt-am-Main–Berlin 1989, 106–23; H.-A. Jacobsen, *Nationalsozialistische Außenpolitik 1933–1938*, Frankfurt-am-Main 1968, 445–60.
39 Rumbold to Simon, 26 Apr. 1933, *DBFP*, 2nd ser. v, doc. 36.

except for their aversion to communism.[40] Hitler's concept of *Lebensraum* sounded so fantastic that it was hard to take him seriously on this point. Antisemitism, by contrast, had been elaborated in *Mein Kampf*, antisemitic outrages were highly visible, and Rumbold was particularly appalled.[41] But for any British observer used to thinking in terms of traditional policies, it was inconceivable that already during the first year Hitler's actions, the consolidation of his domestic position, Germany's departure from the disarmament conference and the League of Nations, and the rearmament programme should all be directed towards the fulfilment of his *Lebensraum* 'dreams'.

By the beginning of 1933, therefore, the Foreign Office was still in the dark as to the implications of *Lebensraum* for Russo-German relations. British officials did not understand why Russo-German relations deteriorated sharply after Hitler's advent to power. Before and after Hitler's *Machtergreifung*, British officials regarded Nazis and communists as political rivals on the domestic scene and thought that their exceptionally bloody and brutal fighting was merely a struggle for power. Judging from Rumbold's despatches before 30 January 1933, the communists seemed to fight everyone, the Nazis and other right-wing groups like the *Stahlhelm*, as well as the Social Democrats on the left of the political spectrum. When London received news that Russia was providing financial support for Nazi activities during the 1930 elections, this was attributed to momentary 'mental deficits' on both sides.[42] Confusion increased when Nazis and communists co-operated for the first time on a conspicuous scale during the transport workers' strike in Berlin in October and November 1932.[43] The British embassy, however, did not draw any conclusions from this co-operation. For British officials a Nazi–communist *rapprochement* was not at all implausible, since Rumbold had reported back in January 1931 that the two party programmes coincided on several points.[44]

After 30 January 1933 the Foreign Office continued to believe in an ordinary struggle for power between the two groups. When, in mid-February, Rumbold reported sharply increasing political tensions in Germany, the *Reichstag* fire, which was blamed on an alleged communist, and the Nazis' admission that there would be no constructive work until communism had

---

[40] According to Jacobsen (*Nationalsozialistische Außenpolitik*, 445), Hitler pursued a 'Strategie grandioser Selbstverharmlosung'. A typical example of this strategy was Hitler's broadcast speech of 2 February 1933 in which he veiled so much of his programme that it was hardly recognisable, except, however, for its anti-communist component: G. Wollstein, *Vom Weimarer Revisionismus zu Hitler. Das Deutsche Reich und die europäischen Großmächte in der Anfangsphase der nationalsozialistischen Herrschaft in Deutschland*, Bonn 1973, 112–13.

[41] See the countless letters on the subject in the Rumbold papers, Bodleian Library, Oxford.

[42] Collier minute, 27 Sept. 1930, PRO, FO 371/14363/C 7156; Rumbold to Henderson, 18 Sept. 1930, DBFP, 2nd ser. i, doc. 323; Rumbold to Henderson, 11 Mar. 1931, FO 371/15213/C 1740.

[43] Newton to Simon, 19 Oct. 1932, PRO, FO 371/15936/C 8807; Newton to Simon, 9 Nov. 1932, DBFP, 2nd ser. iv, doc. 33; Striefler, *Kampf um die Macht*, 176–82.

[44] Rumbold to Henderson, 16 Jan. 1931, PRO, FO 371/15213/C 402.

been eradicated, Vansittart, the permanent under-secretary was full of sarcasm:

These wild-men and killers [i.e. the Nazis] are alienating the entire intelligentsia. The danger seems to me just this: either the wild-men will overcome the intelligentsia (*and* the communists). Then another European war will be within reasonable distance. Or else they will fail to grapple with the intelligentsia *and* the communists *and* the economic chaos. Then there will be worse political chaos, from which the communists are more likely to emerge in strength than the intelligentsia. These idiots are in fact almost bound to end by driving almost everyone either extreme right or extreme left – if they remain in power long enough.[45]

Vansittart's minute illustrates the bewilderment in the Foreign Office at the state of relations between Nazis and communists on the one hand, and Soviet Russia and Germany on the other. British officials regarded Hitler's fight against communism as a domestic German affair. They did not understand that the relationship between Moscow and Berlin now carried an ideological burden. In ideology terms, the principal enemies of the Nazis were the communists, whereas for the communists the opponents were not primarily the Nazis but the Social Democrats, in accordance with the Comintern decision of 1928. British confusion about the state of Russo-German relations resulted from the fact that the ideological differences between the two countries did not exclude a short-term interest on both sides to maintain reasonable relations.[46]

Russo-German relations played a subordinate role in British policy during the first months of 1933. Foreign Office attention was absorbed by the disarmament conference negotiations and the almost desperate British endeavours to prevent them breaking down.[47] Although British officials were seriously alarmed at the development of the German domestic situation, they hesitated to interfere in the country's internal affairs. They were reassured by foreign minister Neurath's reappointment and the apparent continuation of his policies. Even in Russo-German relations there seemed to be continuity, for the first foreign political action of Hitler's cabinet was the ratification of the extension of the treaty of Berlin with the Soviet Union, outstanding already since 1931.[48]

For Britain, Russo-German relations were of interest only in so far as they were observed from the German side. The factor of Soviet Russia had resumed its marginal role in British policy. Labour's initial optimism had not

45 Vansittart minute, 1 Mar. 1933, PRO, FO 371/16732/C 1699.
46 D. S. McMurry, *Deutschland und die Sowjetunion 1933–1936*, Cologne 1979, 4–5; Haslam, *The Soviet Union*, ch. ii.
47 Bennett, *German rearmament*, 356–405; Wollstein, *Weimarer Revisionismus*, 31–99; Nadolny, *Abrüstungsdiplomatie*, 264–309.
48 Strang to Simon, 6, 8 May 1933, PRO, FO 371/17250/N 3415, N 3645; Rumbold to Simon, 8 May 1933, FO 371/17250/N 3546.

lasted in the face of the day-to-day reality of Moscow politics. Accordingly, Simon remained sceptical when he took over at the Foreign Office. Most permanent officials in the Northern department had never shared Labour's enthusiasm for closer relations with Moscow and favoured a cautious approach, particularly given the continuing communist propaganda and Comintern activities in the empire. Officials believed the Soviet threat was not aimed only at Britain but at the entire empire and hence they viewed the Soviet Union as a permanent obstacle to international peace. British policy was not deliberately anti-Soviet, but contacts with Moscow remained at a minimum. The arrest and trial of the British Metropolitan-Vickers engineers in Russia caused a new Anglo-Russian crisis and resulted in a trade embargo.[49]

Russo-German tensions reached a first peak four weeks after Hitler's ascent to power. The Nazis alienated Moscow with their anti-communist outbursts, such as Hitler's *Sportpalast* speech on 2 March 1933, the persecution and arrests of German communists after the *Reichstag* fire, their election campaign under the motto 'Fight Marxism', and their actions against Soviet citizens living and working in Germany. Rumbold reported in March that Litvinov had complained bitterly to Neurath about the attacks on German communists but that the foreign minister had made it clear that Moscow should not interfere in German domestic issues.[50]

Neurath's firm words impressed both Litvinov and the Soviet ambassador in Berlin. The British ambassador in Moscow, Esmond Ovey, reported that in conversations and in the press the Soviets now held the view that recent events in Germany and the persecution of communists were matters of internal policy.[51] In Berlin, Rumbold was reassured by Hermann Göring – at that time still the president of the *Reichstag* – that the anti-communist campaign had nothing to do with general Russo-German relations which would remain as friendly as in past years.[52] Soviet authorities, however, did not swallow the Nazi actions without retaliation. According to British information, Moscow had countered Nazi raids on Derop, the Soviet oil organisation in Germany, and the ill-treatment of Soviet citizens with the decision to liquidate Drusag, the German agricultural concession in the

49 For Anglo-Soviet relations before 1933 see Haslam, *Impact of depression*, ch. x. For the Metro-Vickers incident see Strang, *Home and abroad*, 78–120; G. Niedhart, 'Zwischen Feindbild und Wunschbild: Die Sowjetunion in der britischen Urteilsbildung 1917–1945', in G. Niedhart (ed.), *Der Westen und die Sowjetunion. Einstellung und Politik gegenüber der UdSSR in Europa und den USA seit 1917*, Paderborn 1983, 105–18 at pp. 112–14.
50 Rumbold to Simon, 3 Mar. 1933, BDFA, II/A; *The Soviet Union*, xi, doc. 54. See also Aufzeichnungen Neurath, 1, 8 Mar. 1933, PA-AA, R 29507; K.-H. Niclauss, *Die Sowjetunion und Hitlers Machtergreifung. Eine Studie über die deutsch-russischen Beziehungen der Jahre 1929–1935*, Bonn 1966.
51 Ovey to Simon, 5 Mar. 1933, PRO, FO 371/17249/N 1432; McMurry, *Deutschland*, 68–73.
52 Rumbold to Simon, 22 Mar. 1933, PRO, FO 371/17249/N 2048.

Caucasus. Still, Hitler's decision to ratify the extension of the treaty of Berlin indicated to British observers that the Nazis remained interested in maintaining some sort of relationship with Moscow.[53]

The state of Russo-German relations appeared diffuse if not confused, given the peculiar mix of open hostilities and assurances of mutual friendship between Germany and Russia. Vansittart noted on 23 July that

> I have not seen much lately from Moscow on Germany. Ask the embassy for a report on the Russian view of the future. The two countries seem to be keeping rather surprisingly close at present. Do the Russians think this can last? Berlin probably means it to last. And is Berlin really closer to Moscow than Rome?[54]

The report of William Strang, the counsellor in Moscow, in reply to Vansittart's request, finally acquainted the Foreign Office with the relevant passages from Hitler's *Mein Kampf* on *Lebensraum* in the east.[55] Strang was in charge of the embassy after the ambassador, Ovey, had been recalled to London following the Metropolitan-Vickers trial. In its impact on the understanding of Nazi objectives in Britain his report is of similar importance to Rumbold's *Mein Kampf* despatch of 26 April 1933. Strang pointed to the uneasy state of relations which had come into being as a result of Hitler's concept of eastern colonisation and listed all the grievances and counter-grievances of the Rapallo partners since his advent to power. In order to elucidate Hitler's concept, the counsellor quoted some key sentences from Hitler's *Mein Kampf*: 'We have . . . finished with the pre-war policy of colonies and trade, and are going over to the land policy of the future. When we talk of new lands in Europe, we are bound to think first of Russia and her border states.'[56] Strang declared himself unable to make any forecast as to the future relationship of the two countries, except for the fact that the German attitude would be decisive. But Alfred Hugenberg, the leader of the German Nationalist People's Party (DNVP), which belonged to Hitler's 'Coalition government', had voiced similar ideas in a memorandum submitted to the world economic conference in London in June 1933.[57] And finally, Alfred Rosenberg, the chief Nazi ideologue, who – as the Foreign Office specifically noted – was himself a Balt from Estonia and a former Russian subject, was known to have a plan to give Poland the Ukraine in return for the Polish Corridor and a free hand for Germany in the Baltic states and northern Russia.[58]

---

[53] Strang to Simon, 10 Apr. 1933, BDFA, II/A, *The Soviet Union*, xi, doc. 71; Rumbold to Simon, 27 Apr. 1933, PRO, FO 371/17249/N 3328; Simon to Strang, 27 July 1933, *DBFP*, 2nd ser. vii, doc. 530.

[54] Vansittart minute, 23 July 1933, PRO, FO 371/17261/N 3646.

[55] Strang to Simon, 9 Aug. 1933, *DBFP*, 2nd ser. vii, doc. 532.

[56] Ibid.

[57] *Sevodina* newspaper (Riga), 26 June 1933, PRO, FO 371/17245/N 5026; *Daily Herald*, 4 July 1933, FO 371/17277/N 5202.

[58] Memo on German–Soviet relations 1922–33, BDFA, II/A: *The Soviet Union*, xi, doc. 229.

By early summer of 1933 it was evident to British officials that Russo-German relations were in severe crisis but until Strang's report of 9 August they could not locate its origins. Although Hitler now and again gave half-hearted guarantees about Russo-German relations,[59] Moscow had lost confidence. In May 1933, shortly after the renewal of the treaty of Berlin, *Pravda* still favoured a revision of the treaty of Versailles.[60] But Soviet attempts to normalise relations failed. Comintern member Karl Radek's article in the *Izvestiya* of 3 September 1933 entitled 'Brest–Versailles–Rapallo' showed the end of Soviet patience towards her former ally:

> Are we for Versailles or for Rapallo? We can reply precisely: We are for Rapallo, *i.e.* relations between Germany and the Soviet Union based on mutual profit and not directed against a third party. We are against Versailles, but not for a new Versailles, which in the past the Ludendorffs endeavoured to establish at Brest-Litovsk, and which is now being propagated by certain sections of a press subsidised by government money.[61]

Radek also threatened to conclude not only pacts of non-aggression but also defence alliances with other countries, should the Germans attempt to realise their colonisation ideas.[62] Moscow's endeavours to develop closer relations with France, Poland and the Little Entente were indeed met with open arms in Paris. After Radek's article and Strang's reports, British officials no longer doubted that 'the policy associated with the names of Chicherin and Brockdorff-Rantzau is now dead':

> Herr Hitler has lately been putting more and more water into his wine in the question of relations with the Soviet government; but evidently the latter are not yet convinced that he has really abandoned his 'anti-Rapallo' policy. If and when they are convinced of it (– and the Germans seem to be trying hard to convince them), they will no doubt make further advances to the Poles and the French (unless they see economic as well as political advantage in them).[63]

By the end of 1933 Britain was fairly sure that the German–Russian friendship signed at Rapallo was no longer in existence. British officials assumed that the initiative had come from Germany. Although the Foreign Office knew the reasons for the German move and Moscow's irritated response from

---

[59] Collier to Strang, 27 July 1933, PRO, FO 371/17261/N 3646.
[60] Strang to Simon (including Radek's article), 23 May 1933; Vyvyan memo, 23 May 1933, BDFA, II/A: *The Soviet Union*, xi, doc. 99. See also R. Ahmann, ' "Localisation of conflicts" or "indivisibility of peace": the German and the Soviet approaches towards collective security and east central Europe, 1925–1939', in Ahmann, Birke and Howard, *The quest for stability*, 201–47 at pp. 235–6.
[61] Coote to Simon, 12 Sept. 1933, PRO, FO 371/17261/N 6877.
[62] Strang to Simon, 11 Aug. 1933, PRO, FO 371/17261/N 6345.
[63] Collier minute, 20 Sept. 1933; Strang to Simon, 12 Aug. 1933, PRO, FO 371/17256/N 6266.

Strang's 'living space' despatch, officials failed to assess its connection with the German policy towards the Soviet Union. The furthest British officials expected Germany to go eastwards was into the Polish Corridor. Ambitions in this direction, moreover, were connected with the names of Rosenberg and Hugenberg rather than Hitler.[64] The importance of Hitler for National Socialism was still underestimated.

The future development of Russo-German relations was regarded as so important, however, that the Foreign Office compiled a detailed memorandum reviewing Russo-German relations in the last decade. Its conclusion was deeply pessimistic. The present Soviet attitude was considered to be determined merely by her current situation – her internal weakness on the one hand, and her feeling of being threatened by Germany and Japan on the other. While Moscow still adhered to its world-revolutionary desires, the British had little confidence in Russia's peaceful intentions.

Even more incalculable was the attitude of the German government:

> The signature of the treaty of Berlin has been confirmed by the Nazi government . . . it is not a treaty of non-aggression and therefore is not applicable to the question now under consideration, namely whether Germany is likely seriously to consider the conclusion of an agreement with Poland, to cover the 'Corridor' and the Silesian questions, at the expense of Russia and the Baltic states.

Yet British officials did not expect these plans to materialise at that time. 'Germany must first obtain the connivance of Poland in her alleged designs against Russia – which seems very unlikely, as Poland would have much to lose and little to gain by connivance in any such schemes, even in return for a settlement of her difficulties with Germany.'[65]

In December 1933 Germany's future in European affairs remained an open question. Foreign Office observers would not predict whether Germany would abandon the old Rapallo alliance completely or maintain a minimum working relationship with Moscow. The alternative considered by Hitler, a *rapprochement* with Poland, appeared utterly unrealistic as it would constitute a fundamental breach with Germany's foreign policy traditions. But Hitler was considered to be capable of almost any kind of surprise. Another surprise was Germany's exit from the League of Nations and her replacement by the Soviet Union.

In the overall context of European relations, the British had always hoped to stay out of continental conflicts. They had managed to do so, so far, but at the cost of making increasing concessions to Germany. Accommodating German demands at the disarmament conference to prevent Germany's uncontrolled rearmament had been fruitless, as she left the conference and

---

64 See ch. xi below.
65 FO memo on German–Soviet relations 1922–33, 5 Dec. 1933, *BDFA*, II/A: *The Soviet Union*, xi, doc. 229.

began to rearm. Concessions for other revisionist German goals had not been ruled out, such as on the issue of the Polish Corridor, which was considered to be one of the next points on the agenda. Underestimating the driving forces in Germany, John Simon was prepared to discuss the issue with Hitler.[66] But it was reassuring for the Foreign Office that the formerly most dangerous aspect of the Polish question, namely the intimate Rapallo relationship as associated with the names of Brockdorff-Rantzau and Chicherin in 1922, was now quite dead and would hardly be resurrected under the National Socialists. Yet Germany was good for surprises, as demonstrated by her next coup in foreign affairs – the German–Polish non-aggression pact.

66 Simon to Phipps, 27 Nov. 1933, PRO, FO 800/288.

11

The End of Rapallo:
The German–Polish Non-Aggression Treaty

The 'invitation to the waltz'[1] caused surprise. That it was even considered met with greater surprise, but to watch the two dancing off together was clearly the last thing anyone expected. Yet this was exactly what happened when Germany and Poland stole the show and signed a non-aggression treaty on 26 January 1934.

> The Germans had always looked down upon and detested the Poles, especially since Poland had formed an alliance with France . . . Moreover, the creation of the Corridor separating East Prussia from the body of Germany, and the granting to the city and territory of Danzig a status isolating them from the Reich, were considered by every German without exception as monstrous and unbearable.[2]

The bewilderment of the French ambassador in Berlin, André François-Poncet, was echoed in nearly every corner of western Europe. The German–Polish non-aggression pact was the move least expected from Hitler's ultra-right-wing nationalist Germany.

What irritated François-Poncet was not so much the German–Polish agreement as such, but the fact that he had dined with Joseph Lipski, the Polish ambassador, the evening before the treaty was signed, and Lipski had not mentioned a word. In contrast to François-Poncet's excitement, British officials gave the treaty a cautious welcome. The question of the Polish Corridor, Europe's most dangerous trouble-spot for fifteen years, had been put to rest and with it the danger of a war of revenge initiated by the revisionist powers. Moreover, the German–Polish agreement represented the end of yet another relict of the 'cold war' of the 1920s: the Rapallo relationship as synonym for Russo-German co-operation as well as German – and to a lesser extent Russian – revisionism. With the new German–Polish pact Rapallo had lost its 'right to exist'. It was not, however, the non-aggression pact that dealt Russo-German relations the final blow, but Hitler's advent to power.

Britain was not particularly excited about the German–Polish agreement, and similarly the French only grudgingly came to terms with their Polish

---

[1] Subheading of the chapter on the German–Polish non-aggression treaty in A. François-Poncet, *The fateful years: memoirs of a French ambassador in Berlin, 1931–1938*, London 1949, 109–10.
[2] Ibid.

155

ally's move towards Germany. Soviet Russia's subsequent *rapprochement* with the western powers and the League of Nations came to be regarded by Britain and France as a counterweight to an increasing German strength. Most importantly, however, the non-aggression treaty seemed to guarantee stability and to defuse the Polish Corridor problem, as the German–Soviet alliance no longer existed and Germany obviously could not immediately demand such far-reaching concessions from its new Polish partner as the abolition of the Corridor in Germany's favour.

It was the probability of German revisionism in the area of the Polish Corridor, which had been one of the more serious British concerns in 1933 when reflecting on German politics. After Stresemann's death in 1929, the question of the Polish Corridor had assumed a new importance in London. If no solution was found, the Corridor could well become a blood-soaked battleground in a struggle for what both Berlin and Warsaw considered to be legitimate claims. Robert Vansittart's statement in January 1931 that 'central and western Europe may find themselves in the thick of trouble before they are out of the fog',[3] appeared increasingly prophetic. It was an unintended but significant coincidence that on 1 February 1933, two days after Hitler had been appointed *Reichskanzler*, the British Foreign Office circulated a detailed 'Memorandum respecting Danzig and the Polish Corridor' dealing with the Corridor's origins, the working of the present settlement, political alternatives to the Corridor and, for the first time, offering specific suggestions for a solution of the Corridor controversy.[4] British officials had always favoured Germany more than Poland on the question of the Corridor. The abject Polish refusal to consider even the smallest concessions to Germany for the sake of a lasting settlement had caused considerable indignation amongst British diplomats and contributed to Britain's occasionally impatient attitude towards Warsaw.

Despite these preferences the British memorandum proposed a definitive solution to the Corridor issue without abandoning the middle course. Central to the plan were Danzig, the missing connection between East Prussia and the *Reich*, and Polish access to the sea. Danzig, militarily neutralised and under League governance, with a free area in the port and special transit facilities for Poland, should be returned to Germany since the Polish authorities had constructed the large Gdynia harbour just a few miles from Danzig to have their own access to the Baltic Sea. The connection of East Prussia with the Reich was to be achieved by giving Germany control of the main railway line from Berlin to Königsberg and by allowing the construction of a main road for trans-Corridor traffic. Special arrangements would have to be made where these lines went through mainly Polish inhabited areas. Borders, rivers and canals would be internationalised, and the whole solution was to be confirmed by a mutual guarantee modelled on Locarno.

---

3   Vansittart minute, 31 Mar. 1931, PRO, FO 371/15221/C 561.
4   R. M. A. Hankey memo, 1 Feb. 1933, PRO, FO 371/16715/C 943.

As British officials had recognised earlier, a solution of the Polish Corridor problem also involved consideration of Soviet Russia's attitude towards the matter.[5] The old German–Russian alliance had always been regarded as directed primarily against Poland. How far the Soviet Union would get involved in a settlement remained an open question for the Foreign Office. The uneasy state of relations between Moscow and Berlin did not facilitate any advance in this regard.

Hitler's advent to power had gradually changed the outlook of British diplomats on European affairs, especially on German–Soviet and German–Polish relations. London struggled to come to terms with the new blunt and aggressive tone in German domestic and also foreign politics. The prevailing view in Whitehall in 1933 was that Germany faced another battle between political 'moderates' and 'extremists' like the Nazis; thus the political aim became the strengthening of the moderates and isolation of the extremists. Hitler himself did his best to conceal his true intentions from Britain. While – in contrast to all his predecessors – being openly hostile towards Moscow and violently anti-communist, Hitler told everybody who would listen that he favoured reconciliation and friendly relations with Poland.[6] Warsaw, on the other hand, mistrusted Germany's intentions and continued to believe that Berlin would be content with nothing less than the return of what used to be German territory.[7] Since the Poles had strong doubts about the durability of their French alliance, prime minister Piłsudski and foreign minister Beck looked to Berlin. The Polish premier did not hesitate to spread rumours of a preventative war against Berlin and on 6 March 1933 ordered the increase of the Polish troop contingent on the Westerplatte, near Danzig.[8] In contrast to the Wilhelmstraße which was highly anti-Polish, Hitler – with an eye to the future – acted with unusual restraint and re-emphasised his preference for conciliation. Hitler's talk with the Polish ambassador Wysocki on 2 May 1933 and the publication of a joint communiqué expressing the mutual desire for good neighbourly relations is generally regarded as the turning point towards *détente* in German–Polish relations.

To British and other outside observers, German–Polish relations were full of surprises and confusion. The intentions of both sides remained mysterious. Were the two countries heading for real conciliation, or was this just a way for Germany to gain time for aggression? British diplomats soon realised that Germany was speaking with two voices. While Hitler was proclaiming peace

---

5 Rumbold to Sargent, 28 Feb. 1930, PRO, FO 371/14365/C 1753; Annex C in FO memo, 13 July 1931, FO 371/15522/C 5171.
6 Wollstein, *Weimarer Revisionismus*, 109–29, 134.
7 Simon to Erskine, 1 Feb. 1933, PRO, FO 371/16715/C 901.
8 For the Westerplatte incident see H. Roos, *Polen und Europa. Studien zur polnischen Außenpolitik 1931–1939*, Tübingen 1957, 61–71; Wandycz, *Twilight*, 269–73. For the debate on a preventive Polish war see H. Roos, 'Die "Präventivkriegspläne" Piłsudskis von 1933', *VfZg* iii (1955), 344–63; Phipps to Simon, 21 Nov. 1933, *DBFP*, 2nd ser. vi, doc. 59.

and friendship, the Foreign Office learned that vice-chancellor Franz von Papen had announced that Germany would not allow a settlement of the Corridor question to be delayed much longer. When asked what would be given to Poland in return for a restoration of the Corridor, Papen was reported to have bluntly replied 'Lithuania'.[9] Orme Sargent, the head of the Central department, commented that these remarks had been made at the height of the national hysteria during the election campaign, and therefore ought to be discounted. Vansittart minuted laconically: 'All the same it is ominous talk, even allowing for the limited intelligence of Herr von Papen.'[10] The Foreign Office, however, continued to believe in the necessity of a peaceful resolution of the Corridor question and predominantly welcomed a German–Polish *rapprochement*. When Mussolini included a passage for a possible settlement of the Corridor question in his proposals for the four-power pact, London was pleased although the Polish government was outraged.[11]

A German–Polish *rapprochement* would always inevitably have an impact on Russo-German relations. Hitler's attitude towards Moscow was visibly ambiguous. On the one hand, the German communists were violently perse-cuted, on the other hand Hitler made verbal statements stressing the need for good political relations with Moscow. Yet Hitler's flirtation with Poland seemed counterproductive to any *rapprochement* with Russia. During the spring of 1933 the Foreign Office therefore remained uncertain about the *Reichskanzler's* intentions. Statements made by Hitler's political entourage regarding political relations with both Poland and the Soviet Union enhanced these uncertainties. Particularly worrying were Alfred Hugenberg's utterances on living space in the east during the London world economic conference in June 1933. Hugenberg, leader of the DNVP, had long been considered as dangerously right wing and revisionist in Britain. Even more worrying was Nazi party ideologue Alfred Rosenberg's scheme for giving Poland the Ukraine in exchange for the Polish Corridor.

It is not clear when exactly the Foreign Office learnt of Rosenberg's views, but in his report of 4 June 1933, Strang, the counsellor, wrote from Moscow that

notwithstanding the recent renewal of the German–Soviet treaty of friendship and Herr Hitler's reconsecration of the Rapallo tradition, the Soviet government are not convinced that Germany can be counted upon not

---

[9] Conversation between Papen and Mr Sandys, Berlin, 7 Mar. 1933, PRO, FO 371/16719/C 2341.
[10] Sargent, Vansittart minutes, 16 Mar. 1933, ibid.
[11] Grahame to Simon, 4 Mar. 1933; note of a conversation between the prime minister, Sir John Simon, and Mr Benes, 17 Mar. 1933; Erskine to Simon, 29 Mar. 1933, *DBFP*, 2nd ser. v, docs 37, 43 enclosure, 58. On Poland and the four-power pact see J. Lipski, *Diplomat in Berlin, 1933–1939*, ed. W. Jedrzejewicz, New York–London 1968, 64–5; J. Laroche, *La Pologne de Piłsudski: souvenirs d'une ambassade, 1926–1935*, Paris 1953, 115–31.

to reverse what has come to be regarded as collaboration with the U.S.S.R.; and they have attached more importance than it merits to the fantastic scheme of Herr Rosenberg for the annexation of the Ukraine to Poland in return for the retrocession of West Prussia to Germany.[12]

The Corridor continued to trouble the Foreign Office, but now from a changed perspective. In previous years the danger spot had always been the possibility of a Russo-German attack on Poland. Now British officials began to worry about the Rosenberg scheme instead.

Moscow protested about Rosenberg's Ukrainian plans as early as 11 March 1933.[13] Rosenberg's hatred of Bolshevism, his ideas about an independent Ukraine and the break-up of the Soviet Union had figured in his publications both before and after 1933.[14] His main thesis was that Germany should seize the Ukraine in the event of a Japanese attack on Soviet Russia in the Far East. British assistance in this game should be secured by offering her a share in the oil reserves of the region. Rosenberg hated the Poles almost as much as he did the Russians. Yet he realised that a German advance towards Russia was impossible without Polish consent and that Warsaw had to be compensated for the loss of the Corridor. After the German–Polish *détente*, Rosenberg offered Warsaw parts of the Ukraine situated towards the Black Sea in exchange for the Polish Corridor.[15] Rosenberg's scheme was not as unrealistic as it might seem at first sight. Piłsudski had never fully abandoned his idea of splitting up the USSR into national states and he still believed in a comradeship of arms between Poland, the Ukraine and other minority nationalities in the Soviet Union against the Russian people. Soon, however, he realised that co-operation with Germany in this respect was by no means in Poland's interests, and he never responded to Rosenberg's overtures.

During the summer of 1933, the Foreign Office received so many reports referring either to Hugenberg's or Rosenberg's plans that the diplomats felt compelled to take them seriously. Most of this information came from the British embassy in Moscow and stressed the alarm that these plans had raised among the Soviet authorities. London also noted that Hitler's failure to reassure Moscow about these declarations was one of the primary reasons for the deterioration of relations. Strang's first report on Rosenberg's Ukrainian

---

[12] Strang to Simon, 4 June 1933, *BDFA*, II/A, *The Soviet Union*, xi, doc. 107.
[13] Dirksen to AA, 11 Mar. 1933, *ADAP*, ser. C, i, doc. 73.
[14] The best summary of Rosenberg's ideas and his position as Nazi chief ideologist and head of the Außenpolitisches Amt der NSDAP (APA) is given in Jacobsen, *Nationalsozialistische Außenpolitik*, 45–54, 85–90, 449–52. For the link with the Polish Corridor see Roos, *Polen und Europa*, 139–54.
[15] Ibid. 141–2, 147–55. Rosenberg's scheme won Hitler's support. The idea of an active Ukrainian policy was one important reason – among others – for Hitler's strategy towards Poland, although his motives were different from Piłsudski's in so far as he did not want primarily to weaken the USSR but to realise his concept of colonisation.

plans coincided with Hugenberg's controversial statement at the world economic conference about German eastern expansion for *Lebensraum*.[16]

Hugenberg's comments were all grist to the mill for those British diplomats
deeply suspicious of Nazi intentions. At the world economic conference
designed to remove barriers and bring about international co-operation, the
German economics minister combined a demand for 'economic nationalism'
and autarky with ideas of German ambitions for living space in the east. The
British did not know that Hugenberg's statement was a minority view, which
was not approved by the German cabinet, and that both foreign secretary
Neurath and Hitler opposed it. Hugenberg resigned over this speech, but the
bad international impression of German intentions remained.

British officials gradually came to share the Russian anxiety, which
prompted the Soviet Union to change diplomatic gear. Hitler's policy threatened the peace in Europe and hence Soviet security. But peace was a vital
precondition for the progress of Soviet industrialisation and the success of the
five-year plan. Collective security and dynamic support of the Versailles
status quo became Moscow's new concept for meeting Hitler's challenge.
Comintern delegate Karl Radek spoke openly of Moscow's strategy of
concluding non-aggression pacts with capitalist states in order to avoid
conflicts or to localise them where they occurred. As he told Strang, 'better
lose prestige, better perhaps even bargain away territory and keep the peace,
than be provoked into war and perhaps lose the revolution'.[17] The Soviet
government also desperately tried to improve relations with Poland and
sounded out the possibility of joint preparations against a German attack.
During his visit to Poland from 6 to 22 July 1933, Radek offered the Warsaw
government a Soviet guarantee for the German–Polish border.[18] At the same
time Moscow courted France, yet with little response until Paris was moved
into action by Germany's withdrawal from the League of Nations.

Warsaw resisted the Soviet courtship. Instead, and to its surprise, the
Foreign Office learnt of a serious German–Polish *rapprochement*. On
21 November, William Tyrrell, the British ambassador, wired from Paris that
definite negotiations between Berlin and Warsaw to settle outstanding questions could begin at any moment. According to Tyrrell, the ball had been put
in motion by Hitler's declaration that he was willing to give assurances to fill
the gap in Polish security caused by Germany's withdrawal from the disarmament conference. So far neither disarmament nor territorial questions, nor

[16] J. L. Heineman, 'Constantin von Neurath and German policy at the London economic
conference of 1933: backgrounds to the resignation of Alfred Hugenberg', *JMH* xli (1969),
160–88. For the Soviet attitude see, for example, K. Hildebrand, *Vom Reich zum Weltreich:
Hitler, NSDAP und koloniale Frage*, Munich 1969, 301–14.

[17] Strang to Simon, 4 June 1933, *BDFA*, II/A: *The Soviet Union*, xi, doc. 107; Strang to
Simon, 11 Aug. 1933, PRO, FO 371/17261/N 6345.

[18] Coote to Simon, 12 Sept. 1933, PRO, FO 371/17261/N 6877; *Sevodina* newspaper
(Riga), 20, 25 July 1933, FO 371/17245/N 5685/N 5814; Wojciechowski, *Die polnisch-
deutschen Beziehungen*, 51–3; Wandycz, *Twilight*, 294–5.

even a non-aggression pact had been raised but could be discussed at any time.[19]

For the next three weeks, however, there was silence as to the content and progress of German–Polish negotiations. During this time diplomats from the Little Entente and the Baltic states visited the Foreign Office in droves – all anxiously watching German–Polish relations and seeking British advice. British officials listened politely but refused to go beyond verbal sympathy and foreign secretary John Simon's general reassurance to the Latvian minister that France, Soviet Russia and also Britain would be opposed to any attempt by Hitler to embark on adventures and alter the *status quo*.[20]

New information on German–Polish talks arrived on 12 December 1933 from Britain's ambassador in Warsaw, Erskine, who had spoken to the Polish foreign minister, Colonel Beck.[21] Although he had 'made full use of his remarkable powers of circumlocution', Beck had discounted the possibility that Germany was seeking a temporary agreement in order to prepare for future aggression. He expressed the conviction that Berlin was serious in seeking friendly relations with Poland. In reply to the more pressing question concerning the future of the Polish Corridor, Beck answered that, given a period of normal relations during which there would be a cessation of mutual recriminations, he thought it quite possible that the Germans would become reconciled to the present frontiers. Erskine regarded this statement as fairly promising for future European stability. It was not clear from Erskine's despatch, however, whether or not Germany and Poland were negotiating a non-aggression treaty.

The Foreign Office in London remained sceptical both about the *volte-face* in Polish–German relations and the swift deterioration of the German–Soviet intimacy. Reports from Berlin by ambassador Phipps – the latest on 27 November – appeared to confirm the German government's ambitions in the Ukraine.[22] British officials, however, attributed the schemes of eastern colonialisation first and foremost to Hugenberg and Rosenberg rather than to Hitler. 'Hitler still hopes to revive the policy of Hugenberg and Rosenberg (who [i.e. Rosenberg] seems to have recovered the influence he was supposed to have lost some months ago)', commented Collier on 8 December.[23] His minute illustrates that the Foreign Office still believed German foreign

[19] Tyrrell to Simon, 21 Nov. 1933, and minute, PRO, FO 371/16716/C 10213. On the progress of the German–Polish negotiations see Lipski, *Diplomat in Berlin*, 100–29, and Ahmann, *Nichtangriffspakte*, 294–342.
[20] Eden memo on his conversation with Mr Benes, 23 Nov. 1933, PRO, FO 371/16711/C 10724; copy of a record of a conversation between Collier and the Latvian minister, Zarine, undated, in file of 5 Dec. 1933, FO 371/17262/N 8655; Simon to Knatchbull-Hugesson (Riga) on this conversation, 12 Dec. 1933, FO 371/17185/N 8707.
[21] Erskine to Simon, 5 Dec. 1933, PRO, FO 371/16716/C 10861.
[22] Memo on German–Soviet relations 1922–33, BDFA, II/A: *The Soviet Union*, xi, doc. 229.
[23] Collier minute, 8 Dec. 1933, PRO, FO 371/17250/N 8732.

policy to be formulated by various actors rather than solely by Hitler. No connection was made with the relevant passages of *Mein Kampf* which had been formulated well before the utterances of Rosenberg or Hugenberg.

Moscow's persisting apprehension with regard to the German plans to expand onto Soviet Russian territory and the severe consequences for European stability finally forced the British to act. Sargent sent a secret despatch to the heads of the missions in Berlin, Warsaw and Moscow, sounding out their views on this development.

To the Foreign Office's relief, the replies were reassuring. Erskine in Warsaw saw little likelihood of Germany and Poland advancing against Russia. It was extremely improbable that the Germans would trust the Poles with so dangerous a weapon as plans for a joint move against the Ukraine, at such an early state of the negotiations. If the talks failed, Poland would almost certainly inform the Russians of the German suggestions, with serious consequences for Russo-German relations. The idea of detaching the Ukraine from Russia seemed too fantastic to be taken seriously. The ambassador did not see how even Piłsudski could reconcile the country to surrendering the Corridor under any circumstances after the Polish failure to realise their ambitious territorial expansion plans at the expense of German eastern territories in 1919.[24]

As far as the Soviet attitude was concerned, the new ambassador in Moscow, Chilston, believed that even the Soviet authorities realised that the precise scheme for compensating Poland for the loss of the Corridor by means of the Soviet Ukraine, was less serious than was indicated by the indignant reactions of the Soviet press to the various Rosenberg and Hugenberg plans. To Chilston, the alarm over the 'Rosenberg plans' was raised mainly for the sake of internal and world propaganda against German National Socialism. It was also meant to be a reminder for the world that the Soviet Union might become the target of German aggression. However, the ambassador also believed that this Soviet propaganda reflected a genuine nervousness on the part of Russia, accentuated by the precarious nature of Soviet relations with Japan.[25]

British confusion about the regrouping of alliances on the continent reached its height at the beginning of 1934. The Versailles era, with its revisionist and anti-revisionist blocs, seemed to have come to an end, but the future direction of events was unclear. The British had no doubt, however,

---

[24] Erskine to Sargent, 19 Dec. 1933, PRO, FO 371/16716/C 11250. Polish ambitions, in their most extreme form, were directed towards taking Upper Silesia, including the city of Posnan, East and West Prussia, Pommerellia and Danzig from Germany: Krüger, *Außenpolitik*, 59–60.
[25] Chilston to Simon, 28 Dec. 1933, PRO, FO 371/18315/N 128. On Russo-Japanese relations see J. Haslam, *The Soviet Union and the threat from the east: Moscow, Tokyo and the prelude to the Pacific war*, Pittsburgh, PA 1992, 1–37.

that the old Russo-German Rapallo friendship was dead although the official 'funeral' would not take place until after the conclusion of the German–Polish non-aggression treaty. The Foreign Office watched these developments carefully. Various rumours circulated about different alliance alternatives: Paris seemed to court both Germany and Russia, but was cool towards her old Polish ally. Moscow made overtures to both France and Poland while pressing for a Russo-Polish security guarantee for the Baltic states, and seemed to contemplate a more favourable attitude towards the League of Nations. Warsaw appeared to be undecided whether to opt for the alliance with Germany or to take up the Russian offer, and was reluctant to alienate Paris completely. The conclusion of the German–Polish non-aggression pact on 26 January 1934 was observed with some relief at the Foreign Office, as it seemed to end this period of confusion.

In the meantime, however, the Soviet government had lost its patience with its former German ally. In various despatches the British ambassador, Chilston, dwelled on the Soviet government's nervousness about the aggressive intentions of both Japan and Germany. The Foreign Office learnt that foreign commissar Litvinov had even gone as far as to tell the German ambassador in Moscow, Nadolny, that he no longer had authority to accept a 'reaffirmation of the treaty of Berlin'.[26] This was a clear sign that the Soviet government, frightened by the *Lebensraum* ideas and acknowledging the shift in German policy, was no longer prepared to rely on the Rapallo friendship. Hence, Moscow sounded out the possibilities for a *rapprochement* with the western powers.

Litvinov's speech of 29 December 1933 showed the full extent of Moscow's anxiety. It revolutionised the outlook of Soviet foreign policy in three aspects:

1   It is far from being the case that all capitalist states are now striving for war or preparing for it.
2   The League of Nations as at present constituted is aiming at the maintenance of peace (or according to M. Molotov, it acts as a brake on forces making for war).
3   The Soviet government are not opposed to utilising any existing or future international organisations or combinations serving the cause of peace.[27]

According to Chilston, Litvinov's declaration was both an offer of general co-operation and the announcement that a *rapprochement* with France and her allies as the states most interested in maintaining the *status quo*, was imminent. Chilston also quoted Litvinov's cryptic offer of a mutual Russo-Polish guarantee:

---

26 Howe minute, 9 Jan. 1934, PRO, FO 371/183157/N 176.
27 Chilston to Simon, 2 Jan. 1934, PRO, FO 371/18297/N 140; Weingartner, *Stalin*, 255–6; Haslam, *The Soviet Union*, 30–1.

Political disturbances in Europe have created a community of interests and cares. If we and Poland were not aware of the common nature of these cares we would be reminded of them by those who caused them. Common cares and common danger are the best cement of friendship between States.

The Soviet government was indeed seriously perturbed by the shift in German policy towards Poland and made every effort to obstruct this relationship. The next Soviet step was an attempt to win a Polish guarantee of independence for the Baltic states.[28] However, the proposal was received unenthusiastically in Warsaw because it was so obviously aimed at preventing a further German–Polish *rapprochement*.[29] The Polish counsellor in London, Orlowski, told foreign secretary Simon on 12 January that his government did not wish to offend either Moscow or Germany and had therefore consented to a joint Russo-Polish démarche. At the same time, however, Warsaw proposed to first consult the Finnish and Baltic governments, knowing that the former at least would not agree to the plan. The result was exactly what Simon had hoped for and anticipated:

> The German government were angry but uneasy; European public opinion was aroused and was beginning to consider – and to condemn – the 'Rosenberg schemes'; Poland was shown as committed to the Soviet and not to the German side in Baltic questions, and the general prestige of the Soviet government was enhanced – no mean achievement.[30]

With regard to the Soviet pact of non-aggression with Italy, concluded in September 1933, Moscow had expected that Mussolini would have a moderating influence on Berlin and the German move towards the east. However, this hope proved to be in vain.[31] This continued regrouping of alliances filled British officials with unease. The political system as established at the Paris peace conference seemed to be in crisis. Soviet Russia, Germany and Poland were by no means the only factors of insecurity. From Tyrrell's report on the French reactions to the German–Polish *rapprochement* dated 8 January 1934, British diplomats concluded that Paris was also searching for a new political orientation.[32] The French left, in power since 1932, had increasingly loosened its ties with Poland and the Little Entente, in the hope of a French *rapprochement* either with Germany or Italy. The Laval government seriously questioned the effectiveness of the satellite system as a means of containing Germany and preferred a policy of direct *rapprochement* with Berlin. The only

[28] Chilston to Simon, 15 Jan. 1934, *BDFA*, II/A, *The Soviet Union*, xii, doc. 16.
[29] Erskine to Simon, 17 Jan. 1934, ibid. doc. 9.
[30] Simon to Erskine, 25 Jan. 1934, ibid. doc. 21. On the reactions of the Baltic states to the proposed guarantee see Sperling to Simon, 8 Jan. 1934; Hill to Knatchbull-Hugesson, 20 Jan. 1934; Chilston to Simon, 20 Jan. 1934 (misdated – 25/26 Jan. 1934?), ibid. docs 10, 27, 26.
[31] Chilston to Simon, 2 Jan. 1934, PRO, FO 371/18297/N 140; Weingartner, *Stalin*, 238.
[32] Tyrrell to Simon, 8 Jan. 1934, *DBFP*, 2nd ser. vi, doc. 167.

alternative was a turn towards Moscow. Not even Hitler's rise to power had changed this attitude. On the contrary it had, to some extent, revived the policy of containing Germany by means of Soviet Russia. Paul-Boncour's offer of a Franco-Russian pact of mutual guarantee on 31 October 1933 certainly pointed in this direction.[33]

The rift in Franco-Polish relations seemed to deepen in 1933, leading to intensified Franco-Russian contacts. Ambassador Tyrrell referred to French anger about the satellite allies doing everything to frustrate the four-power pact in which they were not included. He also mentioned the unsuccessful visit of the Polish foreign minister, Beck, to Paris in September 1933, after which Warsaw embarked on the conversations with Berlin. According to the British ambassador, Paris's first reaction to the Polish move was anger, though tinged with a sense of relief. A *détente* in German–Polish relations diminished the risk of a bilateral conflict and thus a potential European quarrel.[34]

France, however, needed to compensate for the loss of her Polish ally. As British officials noticed, French hopes were once more directed towards Soviet Russia. Despite Paul-Boncour's unsuccessful bid in October 1933 for the pact of mutual guarantee, minimal contacts between the two countries had been kept alive. Yet little information about these contacts reached London. When France and Russia finally concluded a commercial agreement in January 1934, British officials in Moscow were pessimistic as to the prospect of real success. Chilston did not believe that the agreement would stabilise Franco-Soviet commercial relations. Rather he believed that it was concluded as a largely political gesture.[35]

In mid-January 1934, the diplomatic tangle, in which the British were merely observers, began to unravel. Although there was still little information available about the progress of German–Polish negotiations, the Foreign Office expected an agreement. This alliance would have far-reaching consequences. It would ruin any Soviet–Polish accord, no matter whether bilateral or multilateral, including the Baltic states. It would further diminish the value of the Franco-Polish alliance. An accord between Warsaw and Berlin would also increase Soviet fears and therefore result in a further *rapprochement* between the Soviet Union and the western powers. British officials, however, continued to mistrust the Soviets. Past experience with Moscow had done little to encourage a rapid change in the British attitude. One of the most important results of all this diplomatic activity, however, was a German–Polish agreement as it would not only solve the Corridor problem but also satisfy Polish pride and hopefully contain her future political ambitions.

On 17 January, Erskine, the British minister in Warsaw, quoted foreign

---

[33] M. Alexander, *The republic in danger: General Maurice Gamelin and the politics of French defence, 1933–1940*, Cambridge 1993, 34–55; Wandycz, *Twilight*, 304.
[34] Tyrrell to Simon, 8 Jan. 1934, *DBFP*, 2nd ser. vi, doc. 167; Wandycz, *Twilight*, 309–15.
[35] Chilston to Simon, 13 Jan. 1934, *BDFA*, II/A: *The Soviet Union*, xii, doc. 17.

minister Beck as welcoming a non-aggression pact if one were offered. Erskine believed that feelings of insecurity after the German withdrawal from the League, the fear of a Franco-German alliance that might leave Poland isolated, and political vanity were the driving forces behind the Polish move. Warsaw's grievances over the international disregard of her enhanced status increased after Beck succeeded Zaleski as foreign minister. 'Inconvenient and unjustified as these aspirations may seem, they are likely to gain in strength in the future . . . Poles in general and M. Beck in particular are very amenable to flattery.'[36]

At the same time, neither the prospect of a German–Polish agreement nor the knowledge that Soviet Russia's paranoia about German *Lebensraum* ideas was responsible for her turn towards the west could alter the critical British attitude towards Moscow. In the past, the Soviet government had abused British policy too often to expect greater assistance from Britain. The Foreign Office was convinced that neither Rosenberg's remarks nor German–Polish co-operation posed any serious threat to Russia.[37] Nevertheless, it was divided as to whether or not to take the change in Russian policy seriously and whether or not this transformation would last.

The more conciliatory faction of British officials saw the logical development of the Soviet government's *volte-face* from a 'revisionist' to an 'anti-revisionist' power 'because they fear worse things from any settlement other than that made at Versailles', and emphasised the Soviet Union's desire to be accepted as an equal among the great powers.[38] If Moscow had not felt threatened by Germany and Japan, and had Mussolini – who refused to use his moderating influence on Hitler as Litvinov had hoped – not also rebuffed her, Russia would not have dreamt of wooing France, Poland and the Little Entente. Generally, however, these officials were not unsympathetic towards Moscow's political reorientation and were willing to welcome it.

Two senior officials, the parliamentary and permanent under-secretaries Launcelot Oliphant and Robert Vansittart, took the opposite view. Given Russia's policy in the past, both were highly sceptical of Moscow's new attitude. As Vansittart bluntly put it:

The Soviet Union is feeling frightened. Fear – genuine fear and not the shams it has for years served out about capitalistic attacks impending – is evidently a most healthy medicine in Russia. A little more will do no harm, and she will certainly get it. These changed sentiments are too new and sudden to be taken at their face value, or indeed of any great value at all . . . After the abuse which it has for years heaped on us and all those connected with the League it would be a tactical mistake to show too much appreciation of these manoeuvres or to appear in any way to run after it.

[36] Erskine to Simon, 17 Jan. 1934, ibid. doc. 9.
[37] Shone minute, 9 Jan. 1934, PRO, FO 371/18297/N 140.
[38] Howe, Collier minutes, 9 Jan. 1934, ibid.

Vansittart and Oliphant saw 'purely temporary tactics' in the Soviet move towards the League, particularly as Soviet–Japanese tensions remained unresolved. 'In my view it will not only be no advantage but a positive misfortune for the League if Russia joined before she has settled her differences with Japan. Such a contingency will only lead the League into further difficulty and discredit it.'[39]

The importance of Russia's political reorientation temporarily retreated into the background of British attention against the news of the German–Polish non-aggression pact of 27 January 1934.[40] British officials generally welcomed the pact since it offered the prospect of peace in eastern Europe for the next decade. The meaning of peace in this respect was twofold: the dangers connected with Rapallo and Poland's geographical situation were finally removed by German–Polish conciliation, although the danger from the former had diminished since Hitler's ascent to power. By confirming the territorial *status quo*, the non-aggression pact also diminished fears of a realisation of the 'Rosenberg scheme' and German plans for eastern colonialisation.

In their overall evaluation of the impact of the German–Polish agreement on international affairs, however, British officials paid comparatively little attention to its effect both on eastern Europe and on Russo-German relations. The treaty only confirmed in writing what had been known for a long time, namely that the Rapallo friendship no longer existed. London was relieved that French unease about the new agreement did not result in greater disquiet.[41] Britain saw the importance of the treaty less in its immediate effect on international policy, than in its impact on German domestic affairs. According to the Foreign Office, Hitler had been the overall winner of the game; only one year after rising to power he could safely dismiss the German political élite's staunch opposition to *rapprochement* with Poland, without facing opposition. The fact that he imposed what looked like an eastern Locarno on the German people – the avoidance of which had been the core of Stresemann's policy – illustrated how unchallenged his position was. This achievement was of even greater importance against the background of German–Prussian militarism and the *Reichswehr*'s continuing hostility towards Poland. 'Most of the Reichswehr officers dream of nothing so much as the invasion of Poland – while last year there was reason to believe that the

39 Vansittart minute, 13 Jan. 1934, ibid. See also memo on the pacts of non-aggression and the conventions for the definition of aggression negotiated by the USSR during 1933, 14 Feb. 1934, BDFA, II/A: *The Soviet Union*, xii, doc. 29.
40 Phipps to Simon, 27 Jan. 1934, *DBFP*, 2nd ser. vi, doc. 219; Ahmann, *Nichtangriffspakte*, 449–529.
41 Simon to Campbell, 28 Jan. 1934, *DBFP*, 2nd ser. vi, doc. 226. See also Campbell to Simon no. 29, 28 Jan. 1934, ibid. doc. 227; Campbell to Simon no. 30, 28 Jan. 1934, PRO, FO 371/17744/C 11671; Erskine to Simon, 30 Jan. 1934, *DBFP*, 2nd ser. vi, doc. 237.

SA and SS were being told that the lessons (military) which they were being taught, would be put into practice for the first time against the Poles.'[42]

Judging the situation astonishingly accurately, British officials had no doubts that Hitler's conciliation with Poland was only the first step in a series of wider ambitions. The Austrian *Anschluss* and the Saar question were believed to be definitely on the agenda, and even the Corridor question was thought to be postponed rather than solved. Yet some uneasiness about future German–Polish co-operation remained in the Foreign Office.

> Looking further ahead, we may I think assume that Hitler would like to see this first move develop into a joint German–Polish policy directed against Russia, so as to be ready to exploit the situation in the event of a break-up of the Soviet government. Whether Poland would consent to play so dangerous a game with so dangerous a partner is of course quite another matter, but she may, as time goes on, find it increasingly difficult to resist Teutonic pressure and blandishments.[43]

Moscow gave the German–Polish non-aggression treaty a cool reception by intensifying her efforts for conciliation with France and concluding a non-aggression treaty with the Baltic states. Furthermore, it now seriously considered joining the League.[44] Warsaw, careful not to rebuff her eastern neighbour too harshly, sent foreign minister Beck on an official visit to Moscow barely two weeks after the agreement with Berlin had been made.[45] Only Hitler continued to display open hostility towards the Soviet Union.

This was the moment when the Versailles era was actively replaced by a new system of alliances. 'Victors' and 'vanquished' no longer existed. All states seemed to negotiate on equal footing with each other. Britain was the only country not directly involved in the regrouping of alliances, although Moscow began to display a more friendly attitude towards London. But the Foreign Office remained sceptical about Russia's *volte-face*.[46] The British role was largely confined to being – once again – the referee in European affairs. Germany would remain a source of unrest on the continent given her

---

[42] Perowne minutes, 29 Jan. 1934, PRO, FO 371/17744/C 676. On the *Reichswehr* and the attitude of the German élite towards Poland see K. Burk, 'Planungen und Maßnahmen der Reichswehr zur Sicherung der deutschen Ostgrenzen', in MGM ii (1990), 41–64.

[43] Perowne minutes, 29 Jan. 1934; Sargent minutes, 31 Jan. 1934, PRO, FO 371/17744/C 676.

[44] Charles to Simon, 6 Apr. 1932, BDFA, II/A: *The Soviet Union*, xii, docs 60, 61; memo on the pacts of non-aggression and the conventions for the definition of aggression, negotiated by the USSR during 1933, ibid. doc. 29; conversation between Eden and Massigli, 11 April 1934, ibid. doc. 62. For the reactions of the Baltic states to the German–Polish pact see Knatchbull-Hugesson to Simon, 3 Feb. 1934, PRO, FO 371/17744/C 1075.

[45] Erskine to Simon, 8 Feb. 1934, and minute, PRO, FO 371/18325/N 873; Erskine to Simon, 14 Feb. 1934, BDFA, II/A: *The Soviet Union*, xii, doc. 70; Chilston to Simon, 17 Feb. 1934, FO 371/18325/N 1188.

[46] Niedhart, 'Zwischen Feindbild und Wunschbild', 114; R. Manne, 'The Foreign Office and the failure of Anglo-Soviet rapprochement', *JCH* xvi (1981), 725–55.

excessive foreign policy aims. Her future revisionist policy would, however, surely be conducted without resorting to what used to be known as the Rapallo friendship during the Versailles era.

To British officials a Russo-German alliance seemed a 'very remote possibility' in January 1934.[47] A revival was extremely unlikely unless Hitlerism collapsed and the country's political orientation shifted to the left, or unless Hitler completely changed his attitude towards Russia. The Foreign Office, however, saw Hitler as too well established in power to believe in such a development. British officials did not even give a Russo-German revival a chance if 'Nazidom' were to be replaced by a political alternative emerging from the *Reichswehr* and the military class in Germany. If, however, not even the *Reichswehr*, Moscow's intimate friend for more than a decade, could revive the old Rapallo alliance, who else in Germany could?

Rapallo, the ghost and bargaining chip for almost twelve years, had faded away. There was no funeral, no grief, no sorrow. A 'threat' of Rapallo had never really existed, because Rapallo had never been a realistic political alternative for either Germany or Russia. It had not even succeeded in speeding up the revision of the treaty of Versailles. Both Berlin and Moscow lacked the military strength necessary for success. Both also lacked the political will when one side counted on the other's assistance. Revision could only be achieved by peaceful means and in accordance with the western powers. Rapallo did not even have the desired effect of constantly reminding the western powers that there was a political alternative for both Moscow and Berlin. Britain never seriously believed in this political alternative. Therefore the existence of Rapallo did not significantly influence any major decision although it was always an underlying political consideration. Nevertheless, British officials were relieved to see that the German–Russian intimacy had finally vanished. Separately, Russia and Germany could be kept in check. Together, however, this was virtually impossible and would, in any event, involve too much British commitment in Europe; and this, as always, was the last thing Britain desired.

---

[47] Sargent to Drummond, 30 Jan. 1934, *BDFA*, ii, 2nd ser., vii, doc. 569; memo respecting Soviet–German relations, Jan.–Nov. 1934, PRO, FO 371/18315/N 6668.

Conclusion

The treaty of Rapallo which Germany and the Soviet Russia signed on Easter Sunday 1922 during the Genoa conference, was the first serious challenge to the post-Versailles political system. Despite repeated German–Soviet denials, other states at once suspected second thoughts behind the agreement. From the outset, this caused the treaty to become a byword for potentially dangerous secret co-operation between the two revisionist European pariahs after the First World War. The burning question was whether – and to what degree – it would shatter the fragile new Europe and influence the policies of individual countries. A 'myth' of Rapallo had emerged.

The German–Soviet *coup de surprise* briefly disturbed the evolutionary process of re-establishing a stable European order after the great war, but never caused it lasting damage. Above all Rapallo challenged Britain and France, who had emerged as the leading powers in Europe's post-war political system. Neither country had yet recovered from the four years of war. Peace, stability and a gradual reintegration of the vanquished powers into European affairs, on terms which they would define, were therefore at the top of both countries' foreign policy agenda. The war had left France traumatised by Germany's strength and suffering from a severe inferiority complex. The goal driving French negotiations at the Paris peace conference had therefore been to weaken Germany as far as possible and limit her scope for political, economic and military recovery. Britain, by contrast, believed in the necessity of maintaining a certain balance of power on the continent. With the dissolution of tsarist Russia and its replacement by a communist authoritarian regime, as well as the disappearance of Austria–Hungary and the emergence of a number of small successor states trying to find their own position in the international system, Germany was needed to counterbalance France, the only remaining continental great power, to some extent. Britain therefore had an interest in preventing France from imposing excessively crushing peace terms on Germany but refused to give Paris any far-reaching security guarantees against the Teutonic neighbour. Consequently, the French demanded additional security guarantees before they would even consider agreeing to any modifications of the Versailles treaty in Germany's favour. Britain, however, was neither willing nor in a position to grant France the desired guarantees. Being an imperial power with worldwide responsibilities, Britain had stretched her capabilities to the limit and could not assume further assignments. Moreover, the great war had profoundly shattered the British economy, and a number of trouble-spots had emerged within the empire. Given that Britain's priorities remained imperial rather than continental, re-establishing Britain's global position was more important than commitments across the Channel.

The British desire to reduce her role in Europe to one of an impartial mediator was thwarted by the German–Soviet treaty of Rapallo. France, for one, was now even less likely to consider modifications of the peace treaty unless she received additional British guarantees. Britain, by contrast, had never regarded the Versailles settlement as definitive and sought its renegotiation in favour of Germany. In order to reconcile the two opposing positions, and avoid further Franco-German disturbances, Britain had no alternative but to remain involved in continental affairs, at least in the short term.

Secondly, the treaty of Rapallo was the first official agreement to recognise the Bolsheviks as the new Kremlin rulers. The Rapallo agreement thus helped to install a political system which fundamentally challenged the established international order. By being based on an ideology rather than on traditional diplomacy and power politics, the Bolshevik government in Russia defied rational calculation both in foreign and economic policy. Since communist activities posed the main outside threat to the British empire, London was forced to keep a watchful eye on Moscow's policy. Combined with German strength, Russia's activities could become really dangerous.

Soon after the Rapallo treaty, however, British policy-makers became convinced that they did not need to take the risk of German–Soviet co-operation very seriously. This attitude prevailed – with slight variations – throughout the period under discussion, i.e. between 1922 and the German–Polish non-aggression treaty of January 1934, which marked the visible end of the Rapallo friendship. The British conviction was the result of realistic assessments of Germany's and Russia's actual political strength – or rather weakness – but also of reactions to the tactics of German governments as well as misperceptions of the ideological basis of Soviet communism.

In the 1920s and early 1930s neither Germany nor the Soviet Union were strong enough to embark on an aggressive policy against their European neighbours, or to come to each other's assistance. Germany needed the support of the western powers for any revision of the treaty of Versailles. The Weimar Republic was a democratic, but politically highly unstable entity with repeatedly changing coalition governments. Germany's weakness was not only political. She was militarily disarmed, the *Reichswehr* was reduced to 100,000 soldiers, the production and use of certain military equipment were forbidden. Economically, Germany faced large reparation payments both financially and in kind. High unemployment and inflation twice brought the country to the brink of collapse. French and British troops occupied the Rhineland and, in 1923, France and Belgium marched into the Ruhr. The areas where Soviet Russia could significantly assist Germany in her recovery were limited. In military matters the two countries co-operated to each other's benefit by jointly developing and testing weapons and military equipment, as well as training officers and pursuing joint army manoeuvres on

Russian soil. With a view to Germany's speedy rearmament in the 1930s, military co-operation was indeed the most dangerous and far-reaching achievement. Economic benefits were limited, due to Moscow's state-planned economy, the abolition of private property which restricted German industry investments and German bankers' and the government's initial reluctance to grant large credits for German exports into Russia. The benefits of political co-operation were even less visible. Although German governments repeatedly used the bargaining card of closer Russo-German relations as a means of blackmailing Britain and France into further concessions regarding the peace treaty, they knew that Moscow was not reliable. Hence, British policy-makers did not really feel threatened. And on no occasion did Moscow ever come to assist its Rapallo partner politically.

The Soviet government, by contrast, was largely preoccupied with establishing its domestic power base. All political, economic and military issues were subordinated to the overall objective of establishing communist world revolution. To pursue this objective was even more important than occasional frictions with the Rapallo partner. More than once the Soviet government readily accepted that Comintern activities and communist propaganda in Germany threatened German domestic stability or endangered trade and financial relations. Only military relations were never called into question and survived even the most serious diplomatic tensions between Germany and the Soviet Union. On the international scene, Russia was ideologically – and thus diplomatically – isolated, but communist propaganda continued to worry Britain in the empire.

The British observed Russo-German co-operation with varying vigour. Yet repeated Foreign Office reviews found relations between Germany and the Soviet Union to be mostly inconspicuous, and discounted the likelihood of serious Russo-German co-operation. Whilst British officials did not like the German–Soviet friendship, they felt strong enough to treat it with disdain. However, given that both Germany and Russia were natural great powers, perceptions were bound to be inspired by anticipation of the future role of the two Rapallo partners as well as Britain's own long-term political objectives. For instance, the potential danger of a German–Soviet block was used several times by the British as a forceful argument in negotiations with the French to push them towards a limited revision of the Versailles treaty. Particularly during the run-up to Locarno, Austen Chamberlain, the foreign secretary, frequently used the clearly visible Soviet attempts to keep Germany out of the western orbit to impress on his French counterpart the need for certain concessions to Germany. This argument was also repeatedly used in later years. Whenever Franco-German relations reached a stalemate due to the uncompromising attitude of either side, thus endangering the spirit of Locarno, Chamberlain used the notion of the 'battle with Russia for the soul of Germany' to convince Aristide Briand of the need for concessions. In this context, the British foreign secretary obviously had a very personal reason to use the Rapallo bargaining card himself. As he considered Locarno as 'his baby', he was prepared to blackmail anybody with whatever argument in order to maintain the Locarno spirit. Moreover, a Franco-German *rapprochement* on the basis of Locarno was the first step towards a reduced British commitment in Europe.

The British, however, were never entirely sure how far Germany used the Rapallo connection merely as a bargaining chip and how strong Russo-German ties actually were. After the fierce western contest with Russia for the German soul during the months preceding Locarno – albeit followed by the German–Soviet treaty of Berlin – Britain knew that the Berlin government was determined to keep both options open. The deterioration of Anglo-Soviet relations in 1927 was hence a cause of great concern for Chamberlain, who worried about the impact this development might have on Germany and her Locarno orientation. At the same time, he came to appreciate the German role as mediator in restraining the Soviet Union. As such the Rapallo connection was, for once, even useful for Britain.

Thus the Rapallo alliance never posed a serious political or revisionist threat to the post-1919 *status quo*, as Germany and the Soviet Union were both too weak. This was clearly and correctly analysed by the Foreign Office and British policy was adjusted accordingly. However, there were two areas in which Britain seriously underestimated the impact of the Rapallo alliance. One was the threat to British economic interests caused by Russo-German economic co-operation during the great depression following the Wall Street crash. The other was a threat – though indirect – to the overall objective of disarmament.

An 'economic Rapallo' endangered British economic and financial interests in 1930/31 during the world economic crisis. Germany's endeavours in the late 1920s to increase trade with the Soviet Union had resulted in large credits to Moscow. With the depression also affecting the Soviet economy, Moscow's difficulties in paying back credits made them demand further long-term credits from Germany to prevent the Russian economy from collapse. At the same time, Moscow also approached Britain with a request for long-term credits. This caused Germany to review its economic policy towards Russia. The result was the German attempt to get out of the Rapallo trap and co-ordinate her own and British credit policies, in order to prevent Moscow from playing London and Berlin off against each other. Yet Britain failed to reply to this German request. This is even more astonishing, since it was not the German credit guarantees to Russia, but the consequences of a Russian default on Germany's ability to repay British short-term loans and reparations that were central to British fears. A German failure to honour its financial obligations in Britain would have had disastrous effects on the British economy.

Berlin received no response, as the Foreign Office's scope of action was paralysed by the division of competencies within Whitehall and negligence by the officials in charge of the issue. When the department responsible finally saw the need to act, it was too late. Economically, the two Rapallo partners had become a community of fate from which there was no escape without severe damage to the economies of both.

At the moment when Rapallo could have severely harmed Britain, British policy failed. It failed because London still preferred to keep its distance from Russia, misinterpreted certain reports and ignored inconvenient despatches concerning Russo-German co-operation. Fortunately for Britain, the evaluation of one Foreign Office official turned out to be correct, namely that the Soviets would rather see the Russian population starve than fail on credit repayment and thereby risk the complete stoppage of the international loans on which they depended. With the world economy recovering, the danger of an economic Rapallo diminished.

The other issue on which Britain seriously underestimated the impact of Rapallo was disarmament. It was not so much Russo-German co-operation during the preparatory disarmament conferences at Geneva itself which perturbed the British, but rather the effect of Russo-German military co-operation. The extent of intimacy of the Rapallo partners at Geneva was minimal, the result of increasingly strained political relations between the two countries. Yet despite these tensions, Russo-German military relations reached their peak between 1928 and 1932 and provided the nucleus for speedy German rearmament after 1933. The Foreign Office was very well acquainted with the state of Russo-German military contacts, as the information officials received from Berlin, Moscow and from intelligence sources was mostly accurate. Still, officials chose to turn a blind eye to these reports. London feared that if its knowledge became known, the disarmament negotiations would be complicated. The French would stiffen their resolve to refuse any move towards German equality before their own security needs had been met. Britain, in turn, was not prepared to follow the French interpretation of security as this implied further British guarantees to France, and possibly east central Europe, which were out of the question. To get out of this vicious circle Britain did the worst of all. Short-term interests gained the upper hand against long-term European security considerations. Rapallo seemed even further away since news of Russo-German tensions increased. With Hitler coming to power in Germany there was even less likelihood of dangerous Russo-German co-operation. But Rapallo had laid the basis for German rearmament and German revisionism. Britain could have prevented this by some open manifestation of disapproval. But she did not, as it seemed incompatible with overall British interests of not committing herself in European affairs.

The British response to the Rapallo friendship concentrated largely on the benefits which Germany would enjoy as a result of the agreement. Britain centred her attention on Germany which she realistically considered as the more important power with regard to British interests and other continental states. With Moscow's assistance, Germany could theoretically speed up revision, whereas Soviet Russia's acceptance by the rest of the world depended more on her diplomatic 'good behaviour' than on German support. The over-

riding principle of British foreign policy in the inter-war period was the maintenance of peace and stability. Collective security and disarmament, the
attempt to strengthen the League of Nations and integrate both Germany
and Soviet Russia into this body were all part of a policy to maintain peace – a
policy which continued until 1939. Yet at the same time Britain found herself
in what historians later described as the 'age of ideology' (K. D. Bracher),
which introduced new dimensions into international politics.

The parallels between British misinterpretations of the Soviet conduct of
affairs during the 1920s, and Hitler's aims in the 1930s are striking. Despite
the altered parameters of the post-Versailles world order, British diplomacy,
its assumptions and judgements remained unchanged, continuing the
pre-1914 line. Against this background, the British policy of appeasement
towards Germany in the 1930s can be regarded as a direct continuation of a
policy that had its origins in the political constellations shaped by the First
World War and the Bolshevik revolution in Russia. The political principles
that were applied to the Soviet Union in the 1920s would be used again in
the treatment of Nazi Germany in the 1930s.

It took Britain several years to really understand the new driving forces
behind the communist regime. Since ideology was a new phenomenon in
international relations after 1917, Britain faced great difficulties in bridging
the gap between a theoretical awareness of a communist ideology which
guided the Kremlin rulers, and the transfer of this knowledge into practical
daily politics. Although ideology played a role at the political level of Conservative administrations in the early 1920s, this was a primarily academic exer-
cise with little impact on actual diplomacy. Throughout his time in office, Sir
Robert Hodgson, British *chargé d'affaires* in Moscow from 1921 to 1927,
analysed Soviet policy by applying the criteria of pre-war traditional diplomacy. Hodgson thus inevitably reached wrong conclusions whenever he
attempted to evaluate circumstances or predict future Soviet intentions. He
neither naturally possessed nor ever developed a feeling for the importance of
ideology in Soviet policy since he did not understand the ideological dimension. The Foreign Office decision-makers had similar problems in coming to
terms with the new era in Russia. Despite a theoretical awareness of the ideological dimension, they continued to apply their own rational values to their
analyses of Moscow's policy. Foreign Office reactions therefore often varied
between mystification and alarm. In British political strategy, however,
specific attempts were never made to deduce any likely Soviet political
actions from the ideological concept of communism and to prepare British
countermeasures. Whenever Moscow ignored British protests against propaganda or interference in the empire, British officials responded by using traditional means of diplomacy. 'Killing Bolshevism with kindness' (Lloyd
George) or diplomatic isolation was considered the best – but ineffective –
means to bring Moscow to its senses.

With regard to Nazi Germany, Britain had the same difficulty in understanding the impact of ideology on domestic and foreign policy. As in the

case of the Soviet Union a few years earlier, Britain sought to deal with National Socialism on a basis of power politics, leaving the ideological component aside. The consequence was a fundamental underestimation of National Socialism, caused partly by the failure of the British ambassador to Berlin to acquaint the Foreign Office officially with parts of the Nazi ideology. Foreign Office officials were often unable to put certain statements or actions of the Nazis into the appropriate context. Even in 1933 Rumbold missed a major part of Hitler's programme – that of 'living space' in the east – and left it to his colleagues in Moscow to acquaint London with the full picture of Nazi ideology – but not before August 1933. These omissions did not facilitate an appropriate reaction to Nazi policy.

Maintaining peace and stability in post-1919 Europe substantially depended on the political actors in the respective countries. The British response to the treaty of Rapallo between 1922 and 1934 was therefore largely determined by the leading personalities in the cabinet and the Foreign Office. There are interesting variations in their perception of a Russo-German threat, both immediately after the conclusion of the Rapallo agreement and in later years.

In the government, the principal actor was David Lloyd George, the Liberal prime minister in 1922. It was he who was responsible for Britain's restrained reaction to Rapallo during the Genoa conference. Lloyd George had personal reasons for not criticising the Rapallo treaty too openly, as he himself felt a personal mission to reintegrate Bolshevik Russia into the post-war community of states. He had carefully hidden this objective from his foreign secretary, Lord Curzon, and from the Foreign Office where his plans met with stiff resistance. The prime minister was little concerned by the ideological creed of the new regime in Moscow, as he thought that in time Soviet ideology would be diluted and gradually adapted to the standards of western civilisation. Rapallo obviously disturbed his ambition of achieving an accord with Soviet Russia in his own right, but he quickly changed direction and sought to achieve his goal by other means, namely via Germany and by using the Rapallo connection.

Lloyd George's pragmatic approach to the Rapallo relationship contrasted markedly with that of the Foreign Office. Curzon saw a considerable danger to the empire in Bolshevism and this absorbed most of his attention. Leading officials like Eyre Crowe, William Tyrrell, John D. Gregory and Miles Lampson also feared the reactions of France, Poland and the Little Entente to signs of Germany's political resurrection as a result of Rapallo. The Foreign Office under Curzon largely reflected the views of Conservative circles in Britain who believed in a policy of 'taming Russia by ignoring her' throughout the 1920s. By contrast, Conservative vision saw Germany gradually reassuming its place in the European balance of power system. Germany's constant friction with the French forced London to maintain its presence in Europe at a time when imperial problems should have received greater attention. But British mediation in Franco-German conflicts was particularly necessary as Germany repeatedly played the Rapallo card to speed up revision of the peace treaty.

The inauguration of the first Labour government under prime minister and foreign secretary Ramsay MacDonald in 1924 brought both continuity and elements of change into British foreign policy. In foreign affairs MacDonald was increasingly supported by his parliamentary under-secretary, Arthur Ponsonby, who came to carry much of the daily burden which MacDonald in his dual function could not carry. Labour and the Conservatives were united in their desire to reduce Britain's role as worldwide mediator and allow her to concentrate on essentially British interests. Idealism combined with pragmatism determined the Labour party attitude towards both Germany and the Soviet Union. The two countries were no longer regarded as the Rapallo block, but treated as individual countries. MacDonald to some extent continued Lloyd George's policy of 'killing Bolshevism with kindness' and hoped that patience and the search for common values would result in a gradual change in the Soviet system. His policy towards Germany was also more conciliatory. Critical from the outset of the Versailles treaty, the Labour party took an interest in improving Germany's international situation and reducing her grievances. The treaty of Rapallo was never of great concern. Rapallo would lose much of its threat once the two countries were reintegrated into the European community of nations. MacDonald was therefore eager to bring both Germany and Russia into the League of Nations. His idealism failed largely for two reasons. Labour's approach to Soviet Russia did not pass the test of practical politics as Moscow did not respond to Labour's 'carrot and stick' approach. Germany, moreover, had no intention of leaving a political position for what she considered to be an insufficient return. The Rapallo alliance was still manifest, for instance in the joint Russo-German refusal to join the League of Nations. Rapallo could have severely disturbed Labour's long-term objectives had not Moscow's ideology-driven policy eventually alienated even her Rapallo partner, thereby driving Berlin into western arms. MacDonald came to realise that the best strategy to defuse Rapallo was to concentrate on Germany's reintegration into the western orbit. But it was left to the Conservatives to continue along this path which Labour had paved.

What has come to be called the 'Locarno era' also marked the height of the Rapallo alliance. When the Conservatives returned to power in November 1924, prime minister Stanley Baldwin left the area of foreign policy entirely to his foreign secretary Austen Chamberlain. Deeply suspicious of the Soviet system and after Labour's unsuccessful initiatives towards *rapprochement*, Chamberlain and his advisers at the Foreign Office sought to keep Russia at a safe distance. At the same time, they worked on a step-by-step reintegration of Germany into the west. With Chamberlain himself playing the role of constant mediator between German and French security interests, the western powers were increasingly engaged in a battle with Russia for the soul of Germany, as Chamberlain put it. This battle began before Locarno and continued well into the late 1920s. The Soviet Union faced diplomatic isolation if the Rapallo partner joined the western camp and thus tried to undermine such a German step by all means at her disposal. The western powers, by contrast, sought to remove the threats posed to French security by an excessively strong Germany, and to east central European stability by Russo-German co-operation, by separating the two Rapallo partners. Germany's principal interest was in the revision of the treaty of Versailles and the re-establishment of her great power status. For this, she needed the Soviet alliance, both as a constant reminder to the west of her political 'alternative' and as a bargaining card in the east and the west to meet her revisionist demands. Gustav Stresemann, Chamberlain's German counterpart, was a master in using this argument to forward German revisionism. Chamberlain, by contrast, was equally brilliant in balancing French and German demands, thereby maintaining European peace but at the price of constant British involvement and mediation in European affairs. Chamberlain, who was an outspoken Francophile with a considerable dislike for Germany, possibly owed his success as mediator between Berlin and Paris to the ever-present Rapallo cloud on the horizon. Its dark shadow constantly reminded him that German and French needs had to be met equally. This required concessions from both sides which only Chamberlain could extract from them.

On one occasion, Rapallo even became useful to Britain. In 1927, when the cabinet decided to break off diplomatic relations with Moscow following severe Soviet interference in British imperial policy, Germany adopted the awkward position of mediator between the Rapallo and Locarno sides, thus acting as the bridge between Moscow and London until the two countries resumed diplomatic relations later in 1929.

As no foreign secretary before or after him, Chamberlain took a personal and active involvement in German–Soviet relations and the impact of Rapallo on European affairs. When Chamberlain left the political stage after the Baldwin government lost the 1929 elections to the Labour party, Rapallo receded into the background of later foreign secretaries' attention. Neither Arthur Henderson, nor John Simon in the National government after 1931, ever got directly involved in Russo-German relations or referred to the Rapallo alliance. This question was now left to officials in the Foreign Office who dealt with it on a passing basis without giving much attention to it. Henderson and Simon were involved in the really pressing problems on the international stage: disarmament, reparations, the great depression of the early 1930s, and Germany's increasingly outspoken revisionism. Neither Henderson nor Simon managed to mediate between French and German interests in the same way as Chamberlain had done. British involvement became less necessary as relations between Moscow and Berlin were increasingly and visibly strained and the Rapallo cloud receded into the distance.

Rapallo continued to receive some attention only in the wider context of disarmament and revisionist military co-operation. The latter aspect had troubled Britain since 1922, but so far no serious danger had been caused by it. Officials therefore turned a blind eye to the increasing number of reports on the grounds that an official protest would harm the overall objective of disarmament. With hindsight, this was a serious and far-reaching omission. At the time, however, and given the general context of British policy, there was no alternative if Britain did not want to risk major international disquiet with unforeseeable consequences for herself and for European affairs.

The other aspect in which the Rapallo alliance played a role as late as the 1930s, was the Polish Corridor which remained one of the major targets of German revisionism. Foreign Office officials were initially convinced that Germany would require Soviet assistance to speed up the revision of the Corridor arrangement. With deteriorating German–Soviet relations, particularly after Hitler's rise to power, the importance of Rapallo in this context diminished. Germany would seek revision in this area with or without Russian support. The German–Polish non-aggression treaty was therefore a surprising, but not unwelcome event. For the time being, it seemed to take away an object of friction which Britain had not yet been able to remove, by providing a solution that was acceptable to both the German and the Polish side. The end of the Rapallo friendship itself was also welcome, as it removed an additional trouble-spot.

Rapallo immediately retreated into the background of British attention. Between 1922 and 1934, the German–Soviet treaty had never posed a serious threat to British policy. As Rapallo turned out to be a myth rather than reality, the fears of contemporaries were unfounded. Still, Rapallo had an impact on British policy, albeit subtle. Without Rapallo, there would have been less need for mediation and conciliation in the 1920s and early 1930s. Without Rapallo, Anglo-Soviet relations or the situation in east central Europe might have looked different. The importance of Rapallo for British policy lies in the anticipation of the roles played by Germany and the Soviet Union in the future world order. Within the framework of overall British policy and the desire to reduce Britain's commitments outside the empire, the only appropriate policy was a form of appeasement in order to restrain the two only temporarily weakened great powers. While this policy failed with regard to the Soviet Union, it was successful with the Germany of the Weimar Republic. It failed with the Soviet Union because Britain did not find an adequate response to the new dimension of ideology in Soviet Russia's policy. It was successful in Germany, because Britain and the government in Berlin still spoke the same political language, i.e. they found a more or less common understanding on the basis of democratic principles. This changed once the National Socialists came to power and Britain faced difficulties similar to those she had experienced in her dealings with Moscow.

During the period under consideration, between 1922 and 1934, Rapallo remained a myth. It was left to two ideology-driven, unscrupulous, authoritarian regimes to turn into reality what people in the 1920s had always associated with Rapallo: the upsetting of the European *status quo* by force with an attack on Poland. This is precisely what Hitler and Stalin did in 1939.

Bibliography

Unpublished primary sources

FRANCE

Paris, Ministère des affaires étrangères
Série Z, Europe, Russie–URSS, 1919–29

GERMANY

Berlin, Politisches Archiv des Auswärtigen Amtes
Abteilung II F – Abrüstung
Abteilung II F–M (Militär und Marine)
Abteilung III England
Abteilung III Wirtschaft
Abteilung IV Wirtschaft
Büro Reichsminister
Büro Staatssekretär
Delegationen, Bevollmächtigte, Kommissionen
Deutsche Botschaft London
Deutsche Botschaft Moskau
Deutsche Botschaft Paris
Direktoren/Handakten
    A. v. Bernstorff
    H. v. Dirksen,
    H. Hauschild
    G. Köpke
    K. Ritter
    M. Schlesinger
    C. v. Schubert
    O. Trautmann
    W. T. E. Wallroth,
Geheimakten, 1920–36
Länder III England
Länder IV Randstaaten
Länder IV Rußland
Nachlässe
    U. v. Brockdorff-Rantzau
    A. Dufour-Feronce
    E. Kordt
    G. Stresemann
Parlamentarischer Untersuchungsausschuß

Politische Abteilung IV Rußland
Wirtschaft Reparationen
Wirtschaft Sonderreferat

Koblenz, Bundesarchiv
R 43 Reichskanzlei
H. Luther papers
H. Pünder papers
J. Wirth papers

Marburg, Peter Krüger (Marburg University), private collection
C. v. Schubert papers

Munich, Institut für Zeitgeschichte
E. Kordt papers
H. Schäffer papers

Potsdam, Bundesarchiv (documents have been transferred to the Bundesarchiv, Berlin)
Deutsche Botschaft Moskau
H. v. Dirksen papers
Präsidialkanzlei

UNITED KINGDOM

Birmingham, University Library
A. Chamberlain papers

Cambridge, Churchill College Archives Centre
A. Cadogan papers
M. Christie papers
A. Duff Cooper papers
M. Hankey papers
B. Newton papers
P. Noel-Baker papers
E. Phipps papers
W. Strang papers
Lord Swinton papers
R. Vansittart papers

Cambridge, University Library
S. Baldwin papers
Lord Crewe papers
Lord Templewood (Sir S. Hoare) papers

London, British Library
A. J. Balfour papers
Lord R. Cecil papers
Lord D'Abernon papers

London, British Library of Political and Economic Science (LSE)
H. Dalton papers

London, House of Lords Record Office
A. Bonar Law papers
D. Lloyd George papers

London, India Office Library
Lord Curzon papers

London, Public Record Office
FO 371 Foreign Office, general correspondence, 1922–34
FO 408 Germany, confidential prints
FO 418 Russia, confidential prints
FO 800
    A. J. Balfour papers
    Lord R. Cecil/E. Drummond papers
    A. Chamberlain papers
    Lord Curzon papers
    A. Henderson papers
    G. Locker-Lampson/Ponsonby papers
    L. Oliphant papers
    O. Sargent papers
PRO 30/69 R. MacDonald papers
CAB 23
CAB 26

Oxford, Bodleian Library
E. Grigg papers
G. Murray papers
A. Ponsonby papers
H. Rumbold papers
J. Simon papers

Published primary sources

Akten der Reichskanzlei: die Kabinette Wirth I und II, ed. I. Schulze-Bidlingmaier, Boppard 1973
Akten der Reichskanzlei: die Kabinette Luther I und II, ed. K.-H. Minuth, Boppard 1977

Akten zur deutschen auswärtigen Politik, A: *1918–25*, Göttingen 1982–95

Akten zur deutschen auswärtigen Politik, B: *1925–33*, Göttingen 1966–83

British documents on foreign affairs, II/A: *The Soviet Union*, University Publications of America 1984–

British documents on foreign affairs, II/J: *The League of Nations*, University Publications of America 1992–

Degas, J., *Soviet documents on foreign policy*, i, Oxford 1951

Deutsch-sowjetische Beziehungen von den Verhandlungen in Brest-Litowsk bis zum Abschluß des Rapallo-Vertrages, ed. Ministerium für Auswärtige Angelegenheiten der DDR and Ministerium für Auswärtige Angelegenheiten der UdSSR, Berlin (East) 1971

Deutsch-sowjetische Beziehungen 1922–1925. Vom Rapallovertrag bis zu den Verträgen vom 12. Oktober 1925, ed. Ministerium für Auswärtige Angelegenheiten der DDR and Ministerium für Auswärtige Angelegenheiten der UdSSR, Berlin (East) 1978

Documents on British foreign policy, 1918–1939, 1st ser., London 1947–84

Documents on British foreign policy, 1918–1939, 1A ser., London 1966–75

Documents on British foreign policy, 1918–1939, 2nd ser., London 1947–50

Parliamentary debates (official report), House of Commons, 5th ser., London 1922–34

Soviet treaties series: a collection of bilateral treaties, agreements and conventions concluded between the Soviet Union and foreign powers, ed. L. Shapiro, Washington 1950–5

Secondary sources

Adams, H. M. and R. K. Adams, *Rebel patriot: a biography of Franz von Papen*, Santa Barbara, CA 1987

Ahmann, R., *Nichtangriffspakte. Entwicklung und operative Nutzung in Europa 1922–1939*, Baden-Baden 1986

———— ' "Localisation of conflicts" or "indivisibility of peace": the German and the Soviet approaches towards collective security and east central Europe, 1925–1939', in Ahmann, Birke and Howard, *The quest for stability*, 201–47

———— A. M. Birke and M. Howard (eds), *The quest for stability: problems of west European security, 1918–1957*, Oxford 1993

Alexander, M., *The republic in danger: General Maurice Gamelin and the policy of French defence, 1933–1940*, Cambridge 1993

Allard, S., *Stalin und Hitler. Die sowjetrussische Außenpolitik 1930–1941*, Munich–Bern 1974

Anderle, A., *Die deutsche Rapallo-Politik. Deutsch-sowjetische Beziehungen 1922–29*, Berlin (East) 1962

———— 'Der Vertrag von Rapallo – eine nationale Chance', ZfG x (1962), 336–70

———— *Rapallo und die friedliche Koexistenz*, Berlin (East) 1963

Andrew, C., 'The British secret service and Anglo-Soviet relations in the 1920s: from the trade negotiations to the Zinoviev letter', *HJ* xx (1977), 673–706

—— 'British intelligence and the breach with Russia in 1927', *HJ* xxv (1982), 957–64

—— *Secret service: the making of the British intelligence community*, London 1985

Angress, W. T., *Stillborn revolution: the communist bid for power in Germany, 1921–1923*, Princeton, NJ 1963

Arnot, R. P., *The impact of the Russian revolution in Britain*, London 1967

Artaud, D., 'Die Hintergründe der Ruhrbesetzung 1923. Das Problem der interalliierten Schulden', *VfZg* xxvii (1979), 241–59

Bach, J. A., *Franz von Papen in der Weimarer Republik. Aktivitäten in Politik und Presse 1918–1932*, Düsseldorf 1977

Baechler, C., *Gustave Stresemann: de l'impérialisme à la sécurité collective*, Strasbourg 1996

Bariéty, J., *Les Relations franco-allemandes après la première guerre mondiale: 10 novembre 1918–10 janvier 1925: de l'exécution à la négociation*, Paris 1977

—— 'Die französische Politik in der Ruhrkrise', in Schwabe, *Die Ruhrkrise 1923*, 11–28

Barnes, J. J. and P. J. Barnes, *Hitler's Mein Kampf in Britain and America: a publishing history, 1930–1939*, Cambridge 1980

Baumgart, C., *Stresemann und England*, Cologne 1996

Becker, J. and K. Hildebrand (eds), *Internationale Beziehungen in der Weltwirtschaftskrise*, Munich 1980

Beitel, W. and J. Nötzold, *Deutsch-sowjetische Wirtschaftsbeziehungen in der Zeit der Weimarer Republik. Eine Bilanz im Hinblick auf gegenwärtige Probleme*, Baden-Baden 1979

Bennett, E. W., *Germany and the diplomacy of the financial crisis, 1931*, Cambridge, MA 1962

Bennett, G. H., *German rearmament and the west, 1932–1933*, Princeton, NJ 1979

—— *British foreign policy during the Curzon period, 1919–1924*, London 1995

Berghan, V. and M. Kitchen (eds), *Germany in the age of total war*, London–Totowa, NJ 1981

Bernstorff, J., *The memoirs of Count Bernstorff*, London–Toronto 1936

Bertram-Libal, G., *Aspekte der britischen Deutschlandpolitik 1919–1922*, Göppingen 1972

Boadle, D. G., 'The formation of the Foreign Office economic relations section, 1930–1937', *HJ* xx (1977), 919–36

Bournazel, R., *Rapallo: naissance d'un mythe*, Paris 1974

Boveri, M., 'Rapallo. Geheimnis – Wunschtraum – Gespenst', *Merkur* vi (1952), 872–88

Boyce, R. W. D., 'Britain's first "no" to Europe: Britain and the Briand plan, 1929–1930', *ESR* x (1980), 17–45

Brüning, H., *Memoiren 1918–1934*, Stuttgart 1970

Bryant, F. R., 'Lord D'Abernon, the Anglo-French mission and the battle of Warsaw, 1920', *JbfGO* xxxviii (1990), 526–47

Burk, K., 'Planungen und Maßnahmen der Reichswehr zur Sicherung der deutschen Ostgrenzen', MGM ii (1990), 41–64

Carlton, D., 'Great Britain and the League council crisis of 1926', HJ xi (1968), 354–64

———— 'The Anglo-French compromise on arms limitation, 1928', JBS viii (1969), 141–62

———— MacDonald versus Henderson: the policy of the second Labour government, London 1970

Carr, E. H., German–Soviet relations between the two world wars, 1919–1939, Baltimore, MD 1951

———— The Bolshevik revolution, 1917–1923, iii, London 1961

———— Socialism in one country, 1924–1926, London 1964

———— The interregnum, 1923–1924, London 1969

———— Foundations of a planned economy, 1926–1929, London 1970–2

———— The twilight of Comintern, 1930–35, London 1972

Carsten, F. L., The Reichswehr and politics, 1918–1933, Oxford 1966

———— Britain and the Weimar Republic: the British documents, London 1984

Catterall, C. and C. J. Morris (eds), Britain and the threat to stability in Europe, 1918–1945, Leicester 1993

Cecil, R., A great experiment, London 1941

Chaizman, W. M., Die UdSSR und die Abrüstung zwischen den beiden Weltkriegen, Berlin (East) 1963

Conte, F., 'Lloyd George et le traité de Rapallo', RHMC xxiii (1976), 44–67

Cowling, M., The impact of Labour, 1920–1924, London 1971

Craig, G. A. and F. Gilbert (eds), The diplomats, Princeton, NJ 1953

Crowe, S., Our ablest public servant: Sir Eyre Crowe, 1864–1925, Braunton 1993

D'Abernon, E. V., An ambassador of peace, London 1929–30

Dalton, H., Call back yesterday: memoirs, 1887–1931, London 1953

Debo, R. K., 'Lloyd George and the Copenhagen conference of 1919–1920: the initiation of Anglo-Soviet negotiations', HJ xxiv (1981), 419–41

Dirksen, H. von, Moscow, Tokyo, London: twenty years of German foreign policy, London 1951

Dockrill, M. L. and D. Goold, Peace without promise: Britain and the peace conferences, 1919–1923, London 1981

Dohrmann, B., Die englische Europapolitik in der Wirtschaftskrise 1921–23. Zur Interdependenz von Wirtschaftsinteressen und Außenpolitik, Munich 1980

Dutton, D., Austen Chamberlain: gentleman in politics, Bolton 1985

———— 'John Simon and the post-war National Liberal party: a historical postscript', HJ xxxii (1989), 357–67

———— 'Lloyd George, John Simon and the politics of the Liberal party', in Loades, Lloyd George, 71–86

———— Simon: a political biography of Sir John Simon, London 1992

Dyck, H. L., 'German–Soviet relations and the Anglo-Soviet break, 1927', Slavic Review xxv (1966), 67–83

———— Weimar Germany and Soviet Russia, 1926–33, London 1966

Eichengreen, B., 'The origins and nature of the great slump revisited', *EcHR* xxxv (1992), 213–39

Ender, W., *Konservative und rechtsliberale Deuter des Nationalsozialismus 1930–1945. Eine historisch-politische Kritik*, Frankfurt-am-Main 1984

Erdmann, K. D., 'Der Europaplan Briands im Lichte der englischen Akten', in *GWU* i (1950), 16–32

——— 'Deutschland, Rapallo und der Westen', *VfZg* xi (1963), 105–65

Fink, C., *The Genoa conference*, Chapel Hill, NC 1984

——— A. Frohn and J. Heideking (eds), *Genoa, Rapallo and European reconstruction in 1922*, Cambridge 1992

François-Poncet, A., *The fateful years: memoirs of a French ambassador in Berlin, 1931–1938*, London 1949

Geyer, M., *Aufrüstung oder Sicherheit. Die Reichswehr in der Krise der Machtpolitik 1924–1936*, Wiesbaden 1980

——— 'Die Konferenz für die Herabsetzung und Beschränkung der Rüstungen und das Problem der Abrüstung', in Becker and Hildebrand, *Internationale Beziehungen*, 155–202

Gilbert, M., *The roots of appeasement*, London 1966

——— *Sir Horace Rumbold: portrait of a diplomat, 1869–1941*, London 1973

——— (ed.), *Winston S. Churchill, 1874–1965*, and companion vols, London 1979

Gilmour, D., *Curzon*, London 1994

Goldbach, M. L., *Karl Radek und die deutsch-sowjetischen Beziehungen 1918–1923*, Bonn–Bad Godesberg 1973

Gorodetsky, G., 'The Soviet Union and Britain's general strike of May 1926', *Cahiers du monde russe et soviétique* xvii (1976), 287–310

——— *The precarious truce: Anglo-Soviet relations, 1924–1927*, Cambridge 1977

Gosmann, W., 'Die Stellung der Reparationsfrage in der Außenpolitik der Kabinette Brüning', in Becker and Hildebrand, *Internationale Beziehungen*, 237–63

Graml, H., 'Die Rapallo-Politik im Urteil der westdeutschen Forschung', *VfZg* xviii (1970), 366–91

Granzow, B., *A mirror of Nazism: British opinion and the emergence of Hitler, 1929–1933*, London 1964

Grathwol, R. P., *Stresemann and the DNVP: reconciliation or revenge in German foreign policy, 1924–1928*, Lawrence, KS 1980

Grayson, R., *Austen Chamberlain and the commitment to Europe, 1924–1929*, London 1997

Gregory, J. D., *On the edge of diplomacy*, London 1929

Haslam, J., *Soviet foreign policy, 1930–1933: the impact of the depression*, London 1983

——— *The Soviet Union and the struggle for collective security in Europe, 1933–1939*, New York 1984

——— *The Soviet Union and the threat from the east: Moscow, Tokyo and the prelude to the Pacific war*, Pittsburgh, PA 1992

Heideking, J., 'Vom Versailler Vertrag zur Genfer Abrüstungskonferenz. Das Scheitern der alliierten Militärkontrollpolitik gegenüber Deutschland nach dem Ersten Weltkrieg', MGM ii (1980), 45–68

Heineman, J. L., 'Constantin von Neurath and German policy at the London economic conference of 1933: backgrounds to the resignation of Alfred Hugenberg', JMH xli (1969), 160–88

——— Hitler's first foreign minister: Constantin Freiherr von Neurath, diplomat and statesman, Berkeley, CA 1979

Helbig, H., Die Träger der Rapallo-Politik, Göttingen 1958

Herriot, E., Jadis, II: D'une guerre à l'autre, 1914–1936, Paris 1952

Hiden, J. W., 'The "Baltic problem" in Weimar's Ostpolitik, 1923–33', in Berghan and Kitchen, Germany in the age of total war, 147–70

——— The Baltic states and Weimar Ostpolitik, Cambridge 1987

——— and P. Salomon, The Baltic nations and Europe: Estonia, Latvia and Lithuania in the twentieth century, London–New York, 1991

Hildebrand, K., Vom Reich zum Weltreich. Hitler, NSDAP und koloniale Frage, Munich 1969

——— (ed.), Das Deutsche Reich und die Sowjetunion im internationalen System 1918–1933, Wiesbaden 1977

Hilger, G. and A. Mayer, The incompatible allies: a memoir history of German–Soviet relations, 1918–1941, New York 1953

Hill, L. (ed.), Die Weizsäcker-Tagebücher 1900–1932, Berlin 1982

Hillgruber, A., 'Die "Endlösung" und das deutsche Ostimperium als Kernstück des rassenideologischen Programms des Nationalsozialismus', in A. Hillgruber, Deutsche Großmacht- und Weltpolitik im 19. und 20. Jahrhundert, Düsseldorf 1977, 252–75

——— ' "Revisionismus" – Kontinuität und Wandel in der Außenpolitik der Weimarer Republik', HZ ccxxxvii (1983), 597–621

Hinkkanen-Lievonen, M.-L., British trade and enterprise in the Baltic states, 1919–1925, Helsinki 1984

Hodgson, R., 'Memoirs of an official agent', World Today viii (1954), 522–8, 613–17

Holland, R. F., Britain and the Commonwealth alliance, 1918–1939, London 1981

——— The pursuit of greatness: Britain and the world role, 1900–1970, London 1991

Jacobsen, H.-A., Nationalsozialistische Außenpolitik 1933–1938, Frankfurt-am-Main 1968

Jacobson, J., Locarno diplomacy: Germany and the west, 1925–29, Princeton, NJ 1972

——— When the Soviet Union entered world politics, Berkeley, CA 1994

Jaitner, K., 'Deutschland, Brüning und die Formulierung der britischen Außenpolitik von Mai 1930 bis Juni 1932', VfZg xxviii (1980), 440–86

James, H., 'The causes of the German banking crisis of 1931', EcHR xxxvii (1984), 68–87

—— The Reichsbank and public finance in Germany, 1924–1933: a study of the politics of economics during the great depression, Frankfurt-am-Main 1985

—— The German slump: politics and economics, 1924–1936, Oxford 1986

Jaroch, M., 'Too much wit and not enough warning'? Sir Eric Phipps als britischer Botschafter in Berlin von 1933–1937, Frankfurt-am-Main 1999

Jones, B., The Russia complex: the British Labour party and the Soviet Union, Manchester 1977

Kaiser, A., Lord D'Abernon und die britische Deutschlandpolitik 1920–1926, Frankfurt-am-Main 1989

Keeton, E. D., Briand's Locarno policy: French economics, politics and diplomacy, 1925–1929, New York–London 1987

Kessler, H. Graf, Tagebücher 1918–1937, ed. W. Pfeiffer-Belli, Frankfurt-am-Main 1996

Kimmich, C., Germany and the League of Nations, Chicago 1976

Kissinger, H., Diplomacy, New York 1994

Kluke, P., 'Deutschland und Rußland zwischen den Weltkriegen', HZ clxxi (1951), 519–52

Korbel, J., Poland between east and west: Soviet and German diplomacy towards Poland, 1919–1933, Princeton, NJ 1963

Krieger, W., Labour Party und Weimarer Republik. Ein Beitrag zur Außenpolitik der britischen Arbeiterbewegung zwischen Programmatik und Parteitaktik 1918–1924, Bonn 1978

Kruedener, J. von, Economic crisis and political collapse: the Weimar Republic, 1924–1933, New York–Oxford–Munich 1990

Krüger, P., 'Der deutsch-polnische Schiedsvertrag im Rahmen der deutschen Sicherheitsinitiative von 1925', HZ ccxxx (1980), 577–612

—— Die Außenpolitik der Republik von Weimar, Darmstadt 1985

—— ' "A rainy day", April 16, 1922: the Rapallo treaty and the cloudy perspective for German foreign policy', in Fink, Frohn and Heideking, Genoa, 49–64

Laroche, J., La Pologne de Piłsudski: souvenirs d'une ambassade, 1926–1935, Paris 1953

Laubach, E., Die Politik der Kabinette Wirth 1921/22, Lübeck–Hamburg 1968

—— 'Maltzan's Aufzeichnungen über die letzten Vorgänge vor dem Abschluß des Rapallo-Vertrages', JbfGO xxii (1974), 556–79

Leventhal, F. M., Arthur Henderson, Manchester 1989

Link, W., Die amerikanische Stabilisierungspolitik in Deutschland 1921–1932. Die Vereinigten Staaten von Amerika und der Wiederaufstieg Deutschlands nach dem Ersten Weltkrieg, Düsseldorf 1970

Linke, H.-G., Deutsch-sowjetische Beziehungen bis Rapallo, 2nd edn, Cologne 1972

Lipgens, W., 'Europäische Einigungsidee 1923–1930 und Briands Europaplan im Urteil der deutschen Akten', HZ cciii (1966), 46–89, 316–63

Lipski, J., Diplomat in Berlin, 1933–1939, ed. W. Jedrzejewicz, New York–London 1968

Loades, J. (ed.), The life and times of David Lloyd George, Ipswich 1991

Lyman, R., *The first Labour government, 1924*, London 1957

McDougall, W. A., *France's Rhineland diplomacy, 1914–1924: the last bid for a balance of power in Europe*, Princeton, NJ 1978

McKercher, B. J. C., 'Austen Chamberlain's control of British foreign policy, 1924–1929', *IHR* vi (1984), 570–91

McMurry, D. S., *Deutschland und die Sowjetunion 1933–1936*, Cologne 1979

Maisel, E., *The Foreign Office and foreign policy, 1919–1926*, Brighton 1994

Manne, R., 'The Foreign Office and the failure of Anglo-Soviet rapprochement', *JCH* xvi (1981), 725–55

Marquand, D., *Ramsay MacDonald*, London 1977

Martin, T. S., 'The Urquhart concession and Anglo-Soviet relations, 1921–22', *JbfGO* xx (1972), 551–70

Maxelon, M. O., *Stresemann und Frankreich 1914–1929. Deutsche Politik in der Ost–West Balance*, Düsseldorf 1972

Michalka, W. (ed.), *Nationalsozialistische Außenpolitik*, Darmstadt 1978

———— *Die nationalsozialistische Machtergreifung*, Paderborn–Munich 1984

———— and M. Lee (eds), *Gustav Stresemann*, Darmstadt 1982

Morgan, K. O., *The age of Lloyd George*, London 1971

———— *Consensus and disunity: the Lloyd George coalition government, 1918–1922*, Oxford 1979

Müller, R.-D., *Das Tor zur Weltmacht. Die Bedeutung der Sowjetunion für die Wirtschafts- und Rüstungspolitik zwischen den Weltkriegen*, Boppard 1984

Nadolny, S., *Abrüstungsdiplomatie 1932/33. Deutschland auf der Genfer Konferenz im Übergang von Weimar zu Hitler*, Munich 1978

Niclauss, K.-H., *Die Sowjetunion und Hitlers Machtergreifung. Eine Studie über die deutsch-russischen Beziehungen der Jahre 1929–1935*, Bonn 1966

Nicolson, H., *Curzon: the last phase*, London 1934

Niedhart, G., 'Zwischen Feindbild und Wunschbild: Die Sowjetunion in der britischen Urteilsbildung 1917–1945', in G. Niedhart (ed.), *Der Westen und die Sowjetunion. Einstellungen und Politik gegenüber der UdSSR in Europa und den USA seit 1917*, Paderborn 1983

———— 'Zwischen negativem Deutschlandbild und Primat des Friedens: Großbritannien und der Beginn der nationalsozialistischen Herrschaft in Deutschland', in Michalka, *Die nationalsozialistische Machtergreifung*, 274–87

Niemann, H.-W., 'Die Russengeschäfte in der Ära Brüning', *VSWG* lxxii (1985), 153–74

Nolte, E., *Der europäische Bürgerkrieg 1917–1945. Nationalsozialismus und Bolschewismus*, 4th edn, Frankfurt-am-Main–Berlin 1989

Northedge, F. S., *The troubled giant: Britain among the great powers, 1916–1939*, London 1966

———— *The foreign policy of the powers*, London 1974

———— *The League of Nations: its life and times, 1920–1946*, 2nd edn, Leicester 1988

———— and A. Wells, *Britain and Soviet communism: the impact of a revolution*, London 1982

Orde, A., *Great Britain and international security, 1920–1926*, London 1978
———— *British policy and European reconstruction after the First World War*, Cambridge 1990
Papen, F. von, *Der Wahrheit eine Gasse*, Munich 1952
Pitts, V. J., *France and the German problem: politics and economics in the Locarno period, 1924–1929*, New York–London 1987
Pogge von Strandmann, H., 'Großindustrie und Rapallopolitik. Deutsch-sowjetische Handelsbeziehungen in der Weimarer Republik', *HZ* ccxxii (1976), 265–341
———— 'Rapallo – strategy in preventive diplomacy: new sources and new interpretations', in Berghan and Kitchen, *Germany in the age of total war*, 123–46
Rathenau, W., *Tagebuch 1907–1922*, ed. H. Pogge von Strandmann, Düsseldorf 1967
Rauch, G. von, *Geschichte der baltischen Staaten*, 3rd edn, Munich 1990
Rheinbaben, W. von, *Viermal Deutschland*, Berlin 1954
Richardson, R. C., *The evolution of British disarmament policy in the 1920s*, London 1989
———— 'The Geneva disarmament conference, 1932–34', in R. C. Richardson and G. A. Stone (eds), *Decisions and diplomacy: essays in international history*, London 1995, 60–81
———— and C. Kitching, 'Britain and the world disarmament conference', in Catterall and Morris, *Britain and the threat to stability*, 35–56
Rödder, A., *Stresemanns Erbe. Julius Curtius und die deutsche Außenpolitik 1929–1931*, Paderborn 1996
Ronaldshay, earl of, *The life of Lord Curzon, being the authorised biography of George Nathaniel, Marquess Curzon of Kedleston, K.G.*, iii, London 1928
Roos, H., 'Die "Präventivkriegspläne" Piłsudskis von 1933', *VfZg* iii (1955), 344–63
———— *Polen und Europa. Studien zur polnischen Außenpolitik 1931–1939*, Tübingen 1957
Rosen, F., *Aus einem diplomatischen Wanderleben*, ed. H. Müller-Werth, iii/4, Wiesbaden 1959
Rosenbaum, K., 'The German involvement in the Shakhty trial', *The Russian Review* xxi (1962), 238–60
Röskau-Rydel, I., 'Polnisch-litauische Beziehungen zwischen 1918 und 1939', *JbfGO* xxxv (1987), 556–81
Roskill, S., *Hankey: man of secrets*, ii, London 1971
Ruge, W., *Die Stellung der Sowjetunion gegen die Besetzung des Ruhrgebiets. Zur Geschichte der deutsch-sowjetischen Beziehungen von Januar–September 1923*, Berlin (East) 1962
Salewski, M., 'Zur deutschen Sicherheitspolitik in der Spätzeit der Weimarer Republik', *VfZg* xxii (1974), 121–47
Schattkowski, R., *Locarno und Osteuropa*, Marburg 1994
Schieder, T., *Die Probleme des Rapallo-Vertrages*, Cologne 1956

———— 'Die Entstehungsgeschichte des Rapallo-Vertrages', *HZ* cciv (1967), 545–609

Schlesinger, M., *Erinnerungen eines Außenseiters im auswärtigen Dienst*, Cologne 1977

Schmidt, G., 'Außenpolitik und Kriegsziele Englands 1905–1922', *Neue Politische Literatur* xviii (1973), 359–72

———— *England in der Krise. Grundzüge und Grundlagen der britischen Appeasement-Politik 1930–1937*, Opladen 1981

Schramm, G., 'Grundmuster deutscher Ostpolitik 1918–1939', in B. Wegner (ed.), *Zwei Wege nach Moskau. Vom Hitler-Stalin-Pakt zum Unternehmen Barbarossa*, Munich 1991, 3–18

Schuker, S. A., *The end of French predominance in Europe: the financial crisis of 1924 and the adoption of the Dawes plan*, Chapel Hill, NC 1976

Schulin, E., 'Noch etwas zur Entstehung des Rapallo-Vertrages', in H. v. Hentig and A. Nitschke (eds), *Was die Wirklichkeit lehrt. Golo Mann zum 70. Geburtstag*, Frankfurt-am-Main 1979, 179–202

———— *Walther Rathenau. Repräsentant, Kritiker und Opfer seiner Zeit*, Göttingen 1979

Schulz, G., *Von Brüning zu Hitler*, Berlin 1992

Schwabe, K. (ed.), *Die Ruhrkrise 1923. Wendepunkt der internationalen Beziehungen nach dem Ersten Weltkrieg*, Paderborn 1985

Senn, A. E., 'The Polish–Lithuanian war scare, 1927', *CEA* xxi (1961), 267–84

———— *The great powers, Lithuania and the Vilna question, 1920–1928*, Leiden 1966

———— 'The Soviet Union's road to Geneva, 1924–1927', *JbfGO* xxvii (1979), 69–84

Sharp, A. J., 'The Foreign Office in eclipse, 1919–1922', *History* lxi (1976), 198–218

———— 'Lloyd George and foreign policy, 1918–1922: the "and yet" factor', in Loades, *Lloyd George*, 139–52

Stambrook, F. G., ' "Das Kind" – Lord D'Abernon and the origins of the Locarno pact', *CEH* i (1968), 233–63

Stamm, C., *Lloyd George zwischen Innen- und Außenpolitik. Die britische Deutschlandpolitik 1921/22*, Cologne 1977

Stein, L., *Aus dem Leben eines Optimisten*, Berlin 1930

Steiner, Z. S., *The Foreign Office and foreign policy, 1898–1914*, 2nd edn, Cambridge 1986

———— 'The League of Nations and the quest for security', in Ahmann, Birke and Howard, *The quest for stability*, 35–70

Strang, W., *Home and abroad*, London 1956

Stresemann, G., *Vermächtnis*, ed. H. Bernhard, Berlin 1932–3

Striefler, C., *Kampf um die Macht. Kommunisten und Nationalsozialisten am Ende der Weimarer Republik*, Berlin 1993

Sturm, P., 'Die Sowjetunion und ihre asiatischen Nachbarn in der

Zwischenkriegszeit – das Problem "Großbritannien" ', *JbfGO* xxxix (1991), 1–32

Sundbäck, E., 'Finland, Scandinavia and the Baltic states viewed within the framework of the border state policy of Great Britain from the autumn of 1918 to the spring of 1919', *Scandinavian Journal of History* xvi (1991), 313–34

Temperley, A. C., *The whispering gallery of Europe*, London 1939

Thompson, J. M., *Russia, Bolshevism and the Versailles peace*, Princeton, NJ 1966

Thorpe, A., 'Arthur Henderson and the British political crisis of 1931', *HJ* xxxi (1988), 117–39

Towle, P., 'British security and disarmament policy in Europe in the 1920s', in Ahmann, Birke and Howard, *The quest for stability*, 127–53

Toynbee, A. J. (ed.), *Survey of international affairs, 1927–34*, 8 vols, Oxford–London 1929–36

Trevor-Roper, H. R., 'Hitlers Kriegsziele', in Michalka, *Nationalsozialistische Außenpolitik*, 31–48

Turner, J., *Lloyd George's secretariat*, Cambridge 1980

Ullman, R. H., *Anglo-Soviet relations, 1917–1921*, Princeton, NJ 1961–72

Vaïsse, M., *Sécurité d'abord: la politique française en matière de désarmement: 9 décembre 1930 à 17 avril 1934*, Paris 1981

Wächter, D., *Von Stresemann zu Hitler. Deutschland 1928–1933 im Spiegel der Berichte des britischen Botschafters Sir Horace Rumbold*, Frankfurt-am-Main 1997

Walder, D., *The Chanak affair*, London 1969

Walsdorff, M., *Westorientierung und Ostpolitik. Stresemanns Rußlandpolitik in der Locarno-Ära*, Bremen 1971

Wandycz, P. S., *France and her eastern alliances: French–Czechoslovak–Polish relations from the Paris peace conference to Locarno*, Minneapolis 1962

────── *The twilight of French eastern alliances, 1926–36: French–Czechoslovak–Polish relations from Locarno to the remilitarisation of the Rhineland*, Princeton, NJ 1988

Watt, D. C., 'Zwischen Antipathie und Verständigung. Die Berichte der britischen Botschaft in Berlin', *Das Parlament* iv/4, 29 Jan./5 Feb. 1983, 16

Weidenfeld, W., *Die Englandpolitik Gustav Stresemanns. Theoretische und praktische Aspekte der Außenpolitik*, Mainz 1972

Weingartner, T., *Stalin und der Aufstieg Hitlers. Die Deutschlandpolitik der Sowjetunion und der kommunistischen Internationale 1929–1934*, Berlin 1970

Wendt, B. J. (ed.), *Das britische Deutschlandbild im Wandel des 19. und 20. Jahrhunderts*, Bochum 1984

Wheeler-Bennett, J. W., *Disarmament and security since Locarno, 1925–1931*, rev. edn, London [1st edn 1932]

────── *The disarmament deadlock*, London 1934

────── *The pipe dream of peace: the story of the collapse of disarmament*, 3rd edn, New York 1971

White, S, *Britain and the Bolshevik revolution: a study in the politics of diplomacy, 1920–1924*, London 1979

—— The origins of detente: the Genoa conference and Soviet–Western relations, 1921–22, Cambridge 1985

Williams, A., The Labour Party's attitude to the Soviet Union, 1927–1935: an overview with specific reference to unemployment politics and peace', JCH xxii (1987), 71–90

—— Labour and Russia: the attitude of the Labour Party to the USSR, 1924–1934, Manchester 1989

—— Trading with the Bolsheviks: the politics of east–west trade, 1920–1939, Manchester 1992

Williamson, D. G., Great Britain and the Ruhr crisis, 1923–1924', BJIS iii (1977), 70–91

Williamson, P., National crisis and national government: British politics, the economy and the empire, 1926–1932, Cambridge 1992

Winkler, H. A., Der Weg in die Katastrophe. Arbeiter und Arbeiterbewegung in der Weimarer Republik 1930–1933, Berlin–Bonn 1987

Wojciechowski, M., Die polnisch-deutschen Beziehungen 1933–1938, Leiden 1971

Wollstein, G., Vom Weimarer Revisionismus zu Hitler. Das Deutsche Reich und die europäischen Großmächte in der Anfangsphase der nationalsozialistischen Herrschaft in Deutschland, Bonn 1973

Wrigley, C., Arthur Henderson, Cardiff 1990

Wurm, C. A., Die französische Sicherheitspolitik in der Phase der Umorientierung 1924–1926, Frankfurt-am-Main 1979

Zeidler, M., 'Reichswehr und Rote Armee 1920–1933', in Deutschland und das bolschewistische Rußland von Brest-Litowsk bis 1941, ed. Göttinger Arbeitskreis, Berlin 1991

—— Reichswehr und Rote Armee 1920–1933. Wege und Stationen einer ungewöhnlichen Zusammenarbeit, Munich 1993

Unpublished sources

Haslam, J., 'Soviet foreign policy, 1924–1927', MLitt. diss. Cambridge 1978

Krüger, P., 'Schubert, Maltzan und die Neugestaltung der auswärtigen Politik in den 20er Jahren', Vortrag anläßlich einer Gedenkfeier des Auswärtigen Amtes für die Staatssekretäre Ago Freiherr von Maltzan und Dr Carl von Schubert, unpubl. typescript, Bonn, 18 Sept. 1987

Mohr, P., 'Reaction to Hitler's seizure of power in Great Britain – the first year', MPhil. diss. Cambridge 1991

Schwarte, C., 'Le Plan Briand d'Union Européenne: sa genèse au Quai d'Orsay et la tentative de sa réalisation à la commission d'étude pour l'union européenne', mémoire de D.E.A. (Institut des Etudes Politiques), Paris 1992

Wächter, D., 'The British view on Germany, 1928–1933: Sir Horace Rumbold and the Foreign Office', MPhil. diss. Cambridge 1991

White, R. T., 'Cordial caution: British policy towards the French proposal for the European Federal Union', PhD diss. Salford 1981

Index